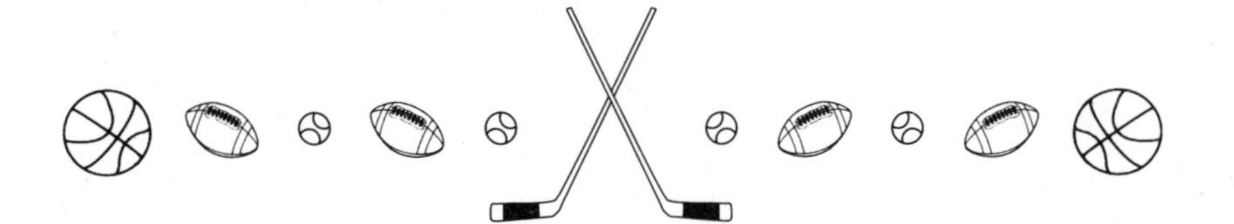

The Name of the Game

Also from Ernst & Young

The Ernst & Young Business Plan Guide, Second Edition
The Ernst & Young Guide to Financing for Growth
The Ernst & Young Almanac and Guide to U.S. Business Cities: 65 Leading Places to Do Business
The Ernst & Young Guide to Total Cost Management
The Complete Guide to Special Event Management
Managing Information Strategically
Development Effectiveness: Strategies for IS Organizational Transition
Understanding and Using Financial Data: An Ernst & Young Guide for Attorneys
Mergers and Acquisitions, Second Edition
Privatization: Investing in Infrastructures Around the World

The Name of the Game

The Business of Sports

Jerry Gorman
Kirk Calhoun
with Skip Rozin

John Wiley & Sons, Inc.

New York ♦ Chichester ♦ Brisbane ♦ Toronto ♦ Singapore

This text is printed on acid-free paper.

Published by John Wiley & Sons, Inc.

Library of Congress Cataloging in Publication Data:

Gorman, Jerry.
The name of the game : the business of sports / Jerry Gorman, Kirk Calhoun : with Skip Rozin.
p. cm.
Includes bibliographical references (p.).
ISBN 0-471-59423-7
1. Sports—Economic aspects—United States. 2. Professionalism in sports. I. Calhoun, Kirk. II. Rozin, Skip. III. Title.
GV716.G67 1994
338.4'3—dc20 93-6046

Printed in the United States of America

10 9 8 7 6 5 4 3 2

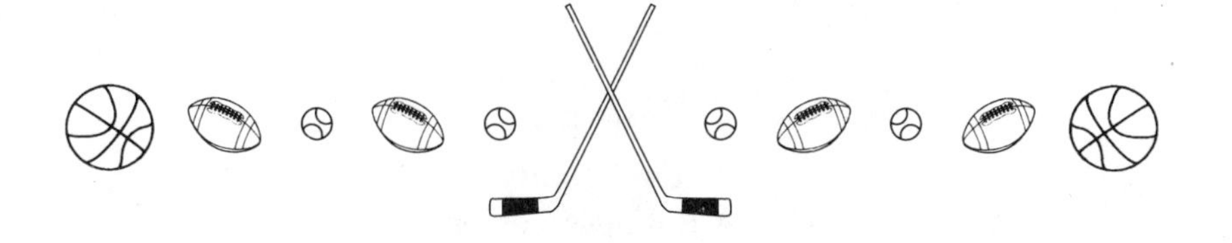

Contents

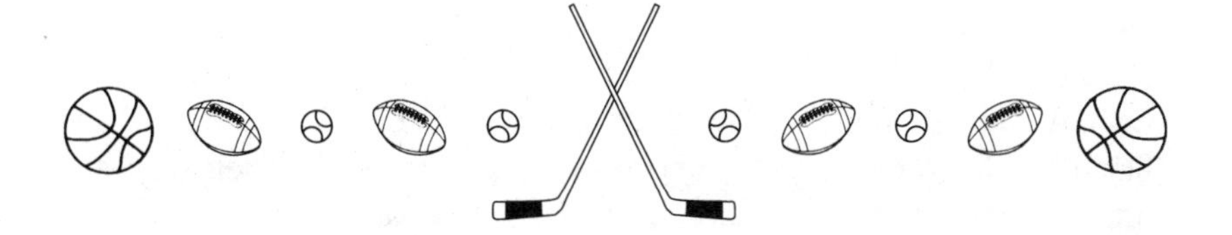

Acknowledgments

This book is based on Ernst & Young's professional work as consultants, accountants, tax advisors, and auditors for organizations in all areas of professional sports. The authors would like to acknowledge the leaders of the firm's sports practice and the assistance they gave in writing this book:

Michael Breit
Don Erickson
Fred Kuntzman
Mark Manoff
Lester Marks
Russ Rudish
Pat Schaefer
Todd Sloan

The authors would also like to thank the many outstanding consulting, tax, and audit professionals who serve our sports clients throughout the United States and Canada and whose combined expertise and experience in sports made this book possible. These include:

Yves Anidjar
Robert Ballweg
Carl Baucum
Philip Bass
George Berry
Richard Birk
Dave Brown
Mike Brown
John Buckley
Scott Campbell
Tim Cash
Danny Caswell
Joe Chianese
Ron Cooper
Michael DiLecce
Jim Docks
Tom Guilfoile
Don Gutman
Brent Hirokawa
Bob Johnson
Ginger Johnson
Brent Jones
Doug King
Brian Lane
Michele Lanteigne
Bob Lynch
Tom Maurer
Don McEntee
Tom Mitchell
Michael Parma
Larry Pollard
Ron Price
Bill Ruddy
Joe Scott
Steve Seneca
Howard Shearson
Rich Stein
Dick Wood
Major Wright

In addition, we are grateful to Mort Meyerson, our National Director of Public Communications, who first conceptualized—and then managed—the project. We are also especially grateful for the help offered by Suzanne

Bish, Al Meyers, Ruth Kaplan, and Pat Agard. Among these people, Todd Sloan and Ruth Kaplan were uncommonly generous with their time and professional expertise. We are particularly indebted to them.

In collecting information on any subject, it is necessary to rely on the research of the expert news gatherers in the field. The news gatherers here are the journalists and writers covering sports and the business of sports. You will find many of their works listed in the Bibliography, but we wish to single out, in gratitude for the work they have produced, Paul Attner, Ira Berkow, Murray Chass, Jack Craig, Peter Gammons, William Oscar Johnson, Richard Justice, Peter King, Frank Litsky, James E. Miller, Benjamin Rader, Bob Ryan, Richard Sandomir, Dave Sell, Dan Shaughnessy, Larry Wigge, and Andrew Zimbalist. Their acute observations and fine reporting were invaluable in the writing of this book.

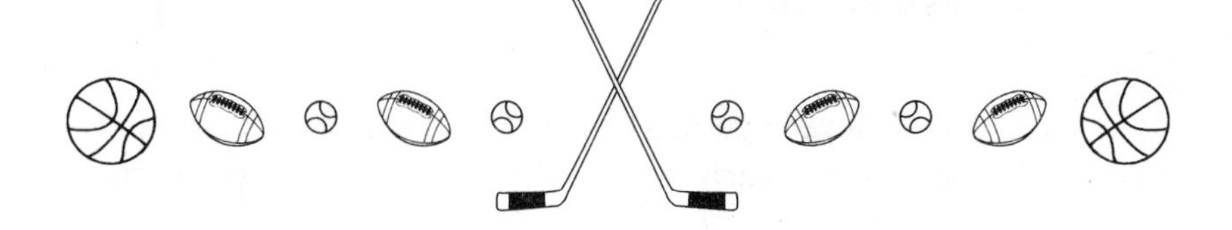

Preface

Baltimore attorney Peter G. Angelos assembled a group of fellow Marylanders early in 1993 to purchase the hometown baseball team, the Orioles. The 64-year-old Angelos, who amassed his personal fortune litigating workers' asbestos damage suits, numbered among his partners writer Tom Clancy, tennis star Pam Shriver, sportscaster Jim McKay, and movie director Barry Levinson. In the following pages, he addresses the reasons why any group would spend $173 million—a record price—to buy a baseball team when players' salaries are at an all-time high and climbing, and future profits have been thrown into uncertainty by shrinking television revenues.

A lot of people in Baltimore were deeply affected by the spiriting away of the Colts in 1984. I was saddened by the loss of our NFL team, too, but for a lot of my friends it was even more painful. It was a kind of spiritual death, not so much for them personally, but for all of us as citizens of Baltimore and as Marylanders.

People have asked if this had anything to do with my wanting to lead the effort to return the ownership of the Orioles to Maryland. Well, it did and it didn't.

I never felt that Baltimore was in danger of losing the Orioles. This is far too successful a franchise; the financial health of the club was an accepted fact, and in the short term losing the team was not a realistic possibility. But it was the long term that concerned me, and I knew this could be put to rest if Marylanders once again owned the Orioles.

This does not mean I was offended by the Edward Bennett Williams ownership [1979–1988], or for that matter the Eli Jacobs ownership [1988–1993]. Both men made contributions to the Orioles that will benefit that organization for many years to come. But since this community was fortunate enough to have a major league baseball club, I believed there were enough Marylanders—and Baltimoreans particularly—to come together and bring back local ownership and local control.

I have always believed that hometown control brings the team closer to the public and more clearly demonstrates that a major league franchise is a key community asset.

When I was growing up in East Baltimore, the ball clubs were a part of our everyday life. These were not just teams, owned and run as businesses. They were part of the community. And that's how I see baseball today, even in this economic environment. Baseball is not a business through which one expects to derive great profits, or maybe any profits at all. Baseball is America's traditional game, and the Baltimore Orioles are a Maryland institution.

Where you have a major league baseball franchise in a city that claims to be a major city, and you don't have local ownership, it rightfully raises a question about the city's local business and professional community and their willingness to put themselves and their money on the line.

I am not questioning the devotion of the fans. I am questioning the commitment of the commercial interests, the power centers, the movers and shakers.

Ultimately, it comes down to a question of pride in your city. Do we care enough—are we proud enough—to get involved? It would be inconsistent to claim major city status and permit people from out of town to own a community asset such as our baseball team.

I never looked at buying the Orioles as an investment. There was always much more to it. It was intensely more than a business transaction, and I knew in the beginning that the eventual price paid might be more than economics alone could justify. And it happened; it was how we got to $173 million. But in light of the greater goal—to accomplish Maryland ownership—paying that premium, however momentarily painful, was justified.

That said, the actual running of a baseball club must be done in a business-like manner. The operation must be financially viable to be a success and a continued source of community pride. How to accomplish this is the challenge.

Even as a new owner, I can see that baseball must improve as a business operation. The entire methodology of compensating players is obviously an imperfect one. While many ball players get too little money, some get the lion's share. The current system serves neither the players nor the owners effectively. Together, we must find another way. I have no answers, and I'm sure owners and players have been searching for one for years. Finding the solution will take luck and more than a little ingenuity.

It will also take cooperation, more than we have seen exhibited in the past by either side.

As owners, we must look at the overall health of the game, not only at the success of our own individual franchises. I do see this coming. All the owners—those who are making money and those who are not—realize baseball has to be looked at in its totality. The day is long past when we can afford that old attitude of self-interest, ignoring what happens to anyone else.

Players, too, are going to have to separate themselves from that narrow, personal perspective and look at the greater good. They fought the good fight, gained free agency, and now it's time to make some concessions to ensure that the game remains healthy.

I may be new to the inner workings of baseball, but I am not new to the necessity for compromise. I believe my years of experience representing steelworkers and construction unions will help me see the other side of an argument. It's never a one-sided argument; the validity is never with only one party. Both sides have requirements; both sides also have good ideas and should be listened to. The key is to get the good and workable positions from each side and put them together so that both prosper. Not just survive, but prosper.

Our goal must be to make sure the fan, our customer, gets a first-class product from management and labor. In the last 30 years we have seen management and labor wage full-scale war—especially in the automobile industry—and we've ended up creating products inferior to those produced abroad. As a consequence, both labor and management suffered greatly.

While we in baseball do not have foreign competition, there certainly are many things competing for our fans' time and money.

It is important that all of us recognize that if we don't get our house in order, the public will become disenchanted. More wrangling and more acrimony will only lead to fans determining that the great American pastime has deteriorated into nothing more than a money-making operation, with management and labor fighting over the spoils.

I also believe we must devise a workable system that permits a strong commissioner, one able to act "in the best interest of baseball." In the days when we had a strong commissioner, baseball was a thriving sport that had the deep respect of the public and the fans. We cannot survive without that respect—without the fans' confidence that we are all working toward the betterment of the game.

This does imply some sacrifice, or at least measured expectations; we are capable of finding a way.

Those of us involved with the Orioles know exactly what is needed. We must assess what revenues we can expect, what savings we can effect, and from that decide how much money we can commit to improve the ball club. We are not concerned with how many dollars might be returned for investors—that is at the bottom of the priority list. This is a very special kind of business, and profit should not be the primary goal for owners.

What is a primary goal for this franchise is the providing of long-term stability and community pride. We see that pride as an active force and feel a responsibility to nurture it. Love of baseball begins at a very young age, and if our youngsters are not exposed to the excitement of our sport, they will never know the joy that the game has been giving for generations. We intend to enter into partnerships with schools and local communities to see that more of our young people have the opportunity to enjoy Orioles baseball. They are the future and we are committed to them.

The perspective is local; insuring that perspective is why we bought the Orioles. Local owners tend to be right-thinking owners. We are part of the community; our fans are our neighbors. Regular contact with the fans who support the ball club reminds an owner who the fans really are and what the relationship should be between the fans and the ball club.

We on the Orioles know we are privileged to own this ball team. But we are not unique in that regard. What owner could feel otherwise? We all hold our teams in trust for our communities, for our fans and our neighbors.

Peter Angelos

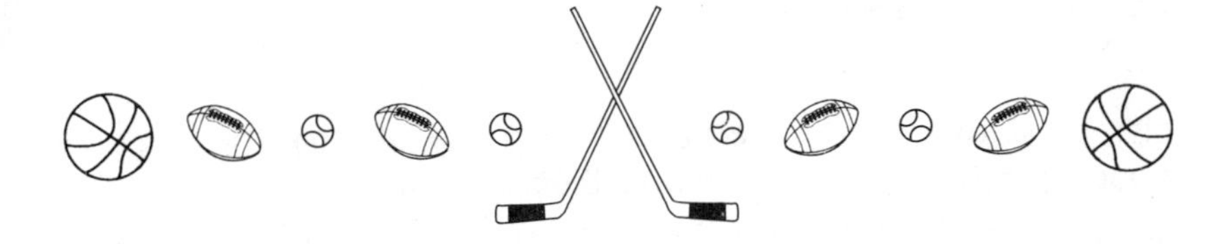

INTRODUCTION

Games and Money

The classic images of sports have traditionally been conjured up by the mind automatically, as each year progresses through its seasons:

Springtime and summer are baseball: the collision of bat striking ball; the hitter charging out of the batter's box, legs churning toward first bases; the flight of the fielder, pursuing the ball across the rich, green outfield grass.

Fall is football: that tense instant at the line before the ball is snapped; the crashing together of giant men clad in plastic armor; the receiver streaking down the sideline, lunging through the air to catch the brown, oblong projectile, fired by the quarterback.

Winter has basketball: elongated bodies, suspended high in midair while slamming the ball through the basket. And hockey: the explosion of a puck, rocketed by the mere flick of a wrist from the blueline, skipping at 100 miles an hour over the ice.

That's what sport is. Or, more accurately, that's what sport was until recently.

Welcome to the modern world of sports. Those scenes remain; the games themselves have not changed so much. But we the fans are barraged by other images, fed to us daily by our morning paper and evening sports report on television.

That baseball player is attending the winter meetings with his agent, fielding not fly balls but the highest offers for his services. That football player is in court, forcing his league to grant him the freedom to bargain as a free agent, doing his best to join the baseball player in the millionaire's club. The basketball player is trying to get his league to give up some percentage of what comes from luxury seating in the stadiums; the hockey player wants a little of that revenue generated by trading cards.

How did this happen? When did the world of our favorite games become the world of big business? The pace may have sped up in recent years, and the stakes increased, but sports was always business, right from the start.

The Business of Baseball

To understand this pattern, we look at baseball. Because it is the oldest professional team sport in this country, it has the most history.

Most of what we have come to know as characteristics of major league baseball has evolved because of the pressure of business, from something so basic as the number of leagues to the complexity of multimillion-dollar salaries. The starting time of games, who plays on a team, even the existence of a big-league team in your hometown—all, in one way or another, were driven by decisions of commerce.

Sports on the field, but business at the helm.

Baseball began on the eve of the Civil War, then flourished in the years that followed, moving rapidly from a recreational activity to become its own industry. Part of the popularity was the times: America was in a period of transition, a nation of farms becoming a nation of cities. Baseball aided that conversion. Played outdoors on grass in the sunshine, it incorporated the rural past with the speed and excitement of the new age to come.

The sport struggled with its professionalism—who gets paid and who doesn't—until the Cincinnati Red Stockings fielded the first openly all-salaried team in 1869. Charging money to watch paid players proved to be so successful that the National League was formed in 1876. Moving into the new century, it held the keys to what was essentially a locked house.

Several attempts were made to start other leagues, but the National League was too well entrenched. It threatened, bullied, and sued challengers out of existence, while insisting it was keeping the game pure for America. If one of the new leagues had a team that showed particular promise, the National League absorbed it.

It exhibited that same control over its athletes. Players were blocked from changing teams by the reserve rule, and the league established a salary cap. No player could earn more than $2,400 a season, including such future Hall of Famers as Honus Wagner, Wee Willie Keeler, and Cy Young.

But holding down players and competition took energy, and the game suffered. Instances of drunkenness and rowdiness in the stands kept more and more people from the games; baseball was becoming an event nice people avoided. Teams started losing money; four were disbanded.

Suddenly the once powerful National League was vulnerable. A new rival, the Western League, was headed by a man with a keen sense of how to subvert the competition.

The man was Ban Johnson. He realized that the country, while fascinated with baseball, was uncomfortable with the crude exhibition the National League was delivering. Not only were there hooligan conditions at parks but also a lack of order on the field. Catchers would tip the bat as the hitter began his swing to disrupt his timing; infielders threw blocks into base runners. When umpires tried to bring order, they were booed and baited. All this contributed to the game's sinking image and falling attendance.

Johnson had nothing personal against the roughness, but he saw an angle. Pursuing a more genteel game and a better class of clientele, he banned the sale of liquor, discouraged the use of rowdyism, and made games played in his Western League a more civil experience. He also gave umpires complete control over the game, with fines and suspensions at their disposal to maintain order.

In 1900, Johnson renamed his alliance the American League and went after the National League. What followed were the great baseball "wars," with the American League raiding National League teams of some of their top players, paying as much as $20,000 a season for the stars.

It looked like baseball but it was business, pure and simple. And good business. In 1902 the new league boasted an attendance of $2.20 million, while the National League dropped to $1.68 million. By 1903 there was a merger, with two leagues and a World Series to decide the champion.

The Die Was Cast

Baseball arrived early on the American scene, and became a model. For the most part, the others—first football, then hockey and basketball—would follow its lead, growing as it grew, through the challenges of rival leagues, through expansion and clashes with labor. That pattern exists to this day.

And in all these sports, as their histories evolved, it was business that shaped them. The sizes of playing surfaces differed, as did the means of scoring and rules for each game, but profit controlled decisions and policies in every sport.

Basketball got its start as a professional sport because the owners of arenas needed another attraction for the long winter. Baseball's All-Star Game was originally a promotion to announce the beginning of the season and stimulate attendance during the game's troubled 1930s. Sunday became pro football day because early in the sport's history the more popular college games played on Saturday and drew all the fans.

Business is what made the Boston Red Sox sell Babe Ruth to the Yankees, what made the New York Nets sell Julius Erving to the Philadelphia 76ers, what made the Edmonton Oilers trade Wayne Gretzky to the Los Angeles Kings. Business moved the Dodgers out of Brooklyn and the Colts out of Baltimore.

Sports is an elite business, its dealings conducted by powerful individuals behind closed doors, all in sharp contrast to the bright lights and intense press coverage of games.

Business is the inner game of sports, the game of the really big players—the owners. This is a book about the forces that make them do what they do.

PART ONE

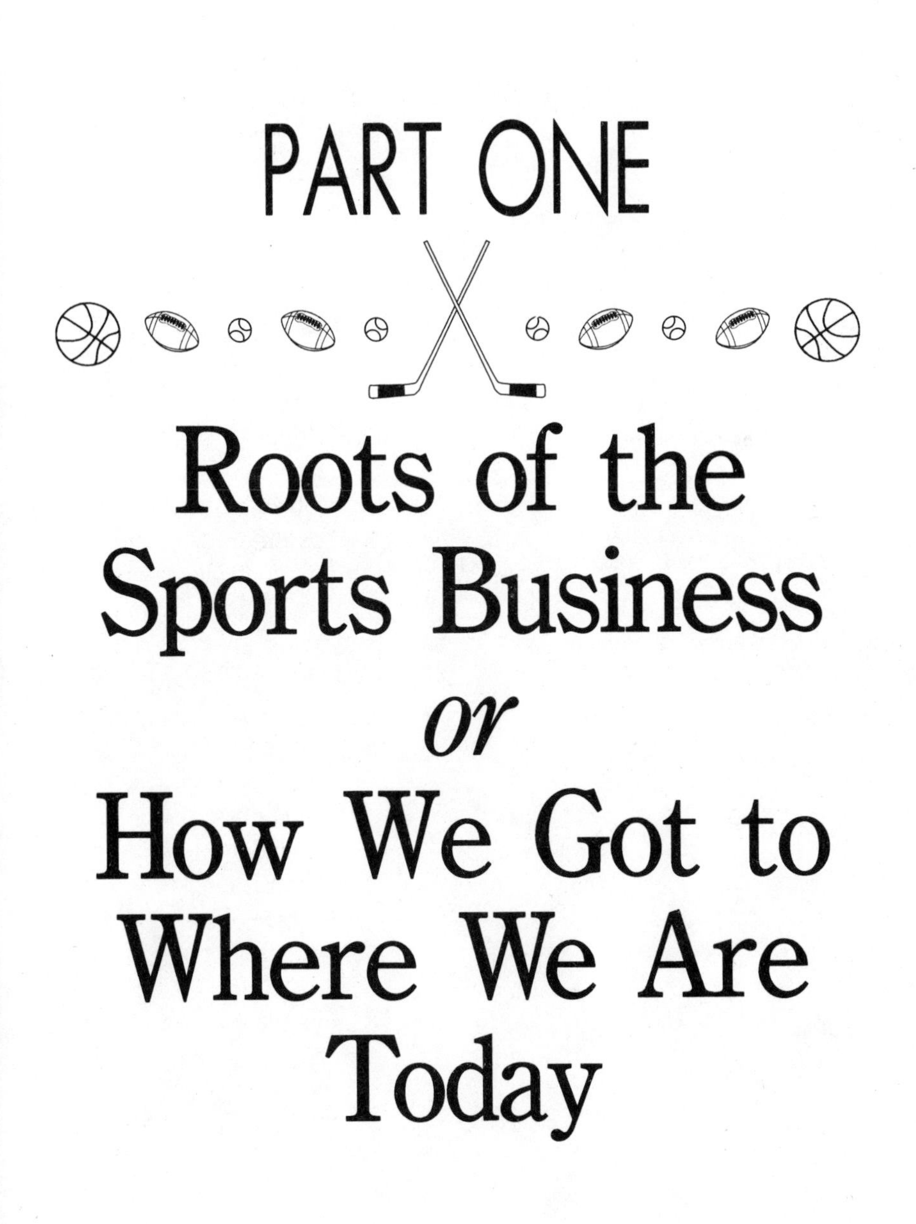

Roots of the Sports Business *or* How We Got to Where We Are Today

1

Baseball

To the average fan, the Chicago White Sox did not appear to be such a bad baseball team through the 1960s and 1970s.

True, they lost a lot of ball games: 95 in 1968, 104 in 1970, and 97 in 1976. But just across town during those two decades, the National League Cubs suffered through equally hard times: two seasons in which they lost 103 games, and seven with 90 or more defeats.

In those same 20 years, ten expansion teams joined the major leagues, every one of them a loser at the start. The New York Mets redefined bad*; in four of their first five seasons they finished last and lost more than 100 games. But those Mets got good fast. They won the World Series in 1969, took the National League pennant in '73, and would go on to win their second Series in 1986. Four other new teams—the San Diego Padres, Kansas City Royals, the Milwaukee Brewers, and Toronto Blue Jays—made it to the Series within 20 years of their creation.*

No such claims could be made on the South Side of Chicago for those 20 years. While the White Sox showed signs of life during the '60s and '70s, four times winning 90 or more games and four times finishing second *in the American League, they were mostly a study in frustration. One pennant—in 1959—was a tease; they lost the Series to the Dodgers in six games. The last time the team was world champ was way back in 1917. Sox fans considered it the fate of the city. After all, the Cubs had not won a World Series since 1908.*

But it was not fate or tradition that kept the White Sox down during this period. It was a lack of money. Especially in the 1970s, when free agency changed the face of baseball, the Sox were badly underfinanced. Management tried all kinds of gimmicks to draw fans into the park: picnic areas under the stands, an exploding scoreboard, broadcasting games from the outfield seats, even a cool shower in the bleachers for those hot summer days on the South Side.

The gimmicks rarely worked. In only one season during the decade did the Sox outdraw their crosstown rivals, who played in smaller Wrigley Field. As a result, there was little money to buy players, pay coaches or scouts, or maintain an effective farm system. The owners couldn't even keep up with needed repairs in the old ballpark; instead of addressing structural problems, white paint covered the decay. Paint did not help the cracked wooden seats, or keep chunks of cement from falling from the walkways. And in an era where modern stadiums offered athletes luxurious clubhouses, old, cramped facilities were cursed by visiting players and White Sox alike.

"It was a hard time for White Sox baseball," recalls Glen Rosenbaum, who, as batting practice pitcher and later traveling secretary, has been with the organization for 22 years. "Everybody did double duty—his own job and at least one other person's. Getting players and keeping players was a problem. We'd have a guy for the last years of his contract, and the next year he was gone.

"It was serious. We didn't know from one day to the next how we stood; the most basic essentials were a problem. You've heard the old story about the general manager who traded a pitcher for a used bus—it was like that.

"Things were so tough that one year we even sold a player just to make the payroll. Honest. Buddy Bradford. No question who was the Sox most valuable player that June."

The force behind the Chicago White Sox through a large part of those lean years was Bill Veeck. At two different times he owned the team—from 1959–1961 and 1975–1981—and in between it was owned by his friends and partners, the Allyn brothers. Regardless of his legal status with the club, Veeck was never far from the center of power.

Veeck was a baseball original, a man who understood every element of the game. He came by it naturally. His father, William Veeck, Sr., was president of the Chicago Cubs while young Bill was growing up. Instead of hearing bedtime stories as a small boy, he listened at his father's knee to conversations involving some of the most knowledgeable and powerful men in baseball.

Bill remembered what he heard, and very soon began compiling information on the practical side of the game. He worked at Wrigley Field from the time he was eight, starting out as a vendor in the stands. After his father died in 1933, he became the Cubs' jack-of-all-trades. He ran the commissary and worked with the ushers; he manned ticket windows, ran the tryout camp for high school players and was in charge of park maintenance. It was Bill Veeck's idea to string bittersweet from the top of the outfield wall to the bottom, and to plant the famous ivy at the base; he ordered design of a manually operated scoreboard, another feature of Wrigley to this day. Veeck ended his 12-year apprenticeship as the team's treasurer and assistant secretary.

Veeck took that knowledge and, with hardly a dime of his own, seriously entered the baseball business in 1941. He pulled together a small but trusting group to purchase a nearly bankrupt Double A team in Milwaukee—an early version of today's Brewers—for $25,000. Veeck so improved the team he was named Minor League Executive of the Year by *The Sporting News* in 1942, and the club went on to win pennants in 1943, 1944, and 1945. When he sold the Brewers in '45, he cleared enough to walk away with $250,000 after taxes.

What he wanted more than anything else was to own the White Sox, but he could not wrest control from the Comiskey family. Instead, he formed a syndicate in 1946 to buy the Cleveland Indians, a mediocre team that he built into the World Series winner in 1948. He did it with pure Veeck magic: getting the acrobatic Joe Gordon from the Yankees to help anchor his infield; adding a kid named Gene Bearden, who was 20–7 in his only winning season; signing the American League's first black player, Larry Doby, then the legendary Satchel Paige.

Veeck sold the Indians after the 1949 season, and later bought the St. Louis Browns before wending his way back to Chicago, finally managing to install himself as owner of the White Sox in 1959.

Most of this, again, was with other people's money. Veeck was never a money man; just a man who understood and loved the game. People liked to joke that if Bill Veeck could, he would never leave the ballpark. That was no joke to Veeck. When he owned the Browns, he turned a set of offices in their home field of Sportsman's Park into an eight-room, three-bedroom apartment, and moved in. That passion lasted until his death in 1984. During his last summer, every afternoon that the Cubs were at home, Veeck could be found sitting in the bleachers at Wrigley Field, his shirt off, drinking beer and talking baseball with the fans.

At his very core, Veeck was a fan—and, when he owned the White Sox for the last time, an anachronism. Baseball by then had moved to a different place, a place where owning a team required more money than Bill Veeck had, more even than he could borrow from his many friends. His old magic did not work in the new era, and he could no longer produce consistent winners.

Baseball, a business since it fielded its first professional team, was by then big business. The process, begun with the first payment from owner to player, shifted into overdrive in the 1970s.

That jump to ultra-high finance took so long because of the game's relationship with the law. Ever since its beginning—either by action of the U.S. Congress and the courts, or by their inaction—baseball was exempt from the laws that govern most big business, leaving the owners to rule their own house. While this meant many things in many areas, it had great impact upon players.

By the mutual agreement of the two leagues and with the blessing of Congress, the lower courts, and eventually the Supreme Court, players were the property of the teams that signed them, bound by something called the reserve rule.

Major league teams were always expensive to operate; stadiums had to be maintained, players obtained, and, in modern times, farm systems financed. But the largest single item for any team—the annual payment to athletes—was a controllable figure. If a player did not like the amount of money his team was offering, his only option was to leave baseball. That was the law, and it applied to everyone.

Mickey Mantle in 1956 won the triple crown; his .353 batting average led the American League, as did his 52 home runs and 130 runs batted in. That earned him a raise to $65,000 the next season. But when his 1957 was slightly less productive—he raised his batting average to .365, but hit only 34 home runs and knocked in 94 runs—the Yankees tried to cut his salary by $5,000. Mantle balked, and, after sitting out part of the spring, settled for a $10,000 raise. "I had no choice," says the man who was arguably the game's best hitter at the time. "It was that or stay home."

Mantle's options were limited; the reserve rule bound him to the Yankees until the team decided otherwise. That changed when the rule was successfully challenged in court; we will see exactly how and why later. But for now, it is enough to understand that today a baseball player is bound to the first team that signs him for six years—presumably long enough for that team to recoup its initial investment in finding and developing that player. Thereafter, he is free to offer his services on the open market.

As a result, the market for players has shot up, and with it, the operating expenses of ball teams. In 1976, before the impact of free agency could take effect, the average major league salary was $51,500. By 1992, the figure had soared to nearly $1,087,000. And that is average for *all* of baseball. For the New York Mets, with the biggest payroll in the game in 1992, the average was more than $1.7 million per player.

New Players in a New Game

The trend affected all teams—even those newly created, still without a single ticket sold, much less a foundation of years of fan support and a well-developed market to rely on. The National League expansion price for the two new teams to begin play in 1993 was a whopping $95 million, just for the privilege of each to join the league. Negotiating for a place to play and paying players was extra.

The obvious question is, at these prices, who wants to get into this very expensive game? The quick answer is people with lots of money, or at least access to it. Look at some of the individuals who bid in 1991 for the two new National League franchises that began play in 1993:

H. Wayne Huizenga of Miami, 53 at the time, chairman of Blockbuster Entertainment Corporation, with a reported net worth of $350 million (up to $600 million in 1993).

Richard M. DeVos of Orlando, then 64, co-founder and president of Amway Corporation, with a reported net worth of $315 million (estimated in 1993 at $3 billion).

Bob Rich, Jr., of Buffalo, then 49-year-old president of Rich Products Corporation, the nation's leading privately held frozen foods manufacturer, with a reported net worth of $440 million.

Wealthy as these men were, they were not willing to proceed alone. All were enough aware of the serious business responsibilities in owning a baseball team to line up a number of partners to share the financial load.

And these men had something else in common: None had been born or grown up in baseball, as was the case with so many of the early owners. Charlie Comiskey, who started and owned the White Sox until he died, had been a player; Connie Mack, also a player, went on to own and manage the Philadelphia Athletics for 50 years. And while Bill Veeck was never a player, his life was immersed in baseball from the start.

This new breed is different. Many of them appear to have no deeper involvement with the game than as a fan. Something other than a lifelong personal commitment to baseball—or sports in general—drove them to pursue ownership of a major league team.

But what? And why now, a time when storm flags wave throughout the sports world? Newspapers and magazines are full of the bleakness that lies ahead, especially for baseball. Expenses are up, and profits down; 13 of the 26 big-league teams reportedly lost money in 1992. The owners say if baseball does not make some dramatic changes—even introduce revenue sharing, so the richer teams in big markets help out the poorer teams in smaller markets—the game could be permanently damaged.

In such a hostile environment, what is the attraction? What makes so many people so eager to enter this complex business in which they have so little expertise?

The question is not easily answered. Let us try by looking at one of the more fluid baseball properties of recent times—the Seattle Mariners. In 1992, this American League team, located in the northwestern corner of the country, was only 16 years old and on its fourth set of owners.

In 1989, the team was still struggling with its second owner, and it was clear that this was a franchise with problems. Some observers suggested all along the main problem was very basic, that major league baseball did not belong in the state of Washington. While this possibility is not being suggested here, it is worth noting the sport took a long time to discover the Northwest. Until 1959, no major league team was based west of the Mississippi River; St. Louis marked the frontier.

The Giants and Dodgers, who moved from upper Manhattan and Brooklyn to California after the 1958 season, were the pioneers. Then came 1961 and the major league's first expansion in modern times. In addition to replacing the Washington Senators, which fled D.C. for Minnesota and became the Twins the same year, the American League added a second team to Los Angeles, the Angels; they later moved to the suburb of Anaheim.

The National League expanded in 1962, replacing the two teams that fled New York with the Mets, and putting a team in Houston. The next expansion came eight years later, in 1969. Four cities received teams: Montreal and San Diego in the National League; Kansas City and Seattle in the American. That Seattle team, called the Pilots, lost 98 games and drew only 677,944 people. The owners went bankrupt, and by opening day of 1970 the team had been renamed the Brewers and was playing in Milwaukee. (Yes, Milwaukee had a team before; actually two. An American League team played there for one season, then moved to St. Louis in 1902 and on to Baltimore in 1954. In the National League, the Boston Braves moved to Milwaukee in 1953, but then left for Atlanta in 1966.)

As randomly as teams seemed to move from one part of the country to another, the placing in 1977 of a second American League expansion team in Seattle again raised skeptics' voices. Why Seattle again, they cried, just eight years after the first failure?

Their protest seemed vague, based in history and sociology: The Northwest surely loved its football, and had shown flashes of passion for hockey, but had no prior experience with major league baseball. In the world of sports, a valid force is being questioned here. This force is the natural attraction for an event or activity; not simply an interest, but a hunger. It is a vital ingredient in something that we call "fan equity," or the public's personal investment in a sport and the athletes who play it. Fan equity is explored later in this book; no franchise can survive without it. And it concerned those who questioned baseball's chances for success in Seattle.

What skeptics did not know was that logic had no part in the Seattle decisions of 1977. It was all preordained. When major league owners allowed the Pilots to move to Milwaukee, the state of Washington sued to reclaim its team. That suit ultimately resulted in the creation of the Mariners.

But law does not win ball games or fill stadiums. And right from the start, the new franchise showed little stability on the field or off. The Mariners had only one winning season up through 1992, and they never finished higher than fourth place. With the exception of their one winning season, attendance constantly lagged behind the major league average. In addition to four owners in their first 16 years, the team had ten different managers.

The original owners, among them actor Danny Kaye, lasted five years. They sold the team in 1981 to George Argyros, an Orange County Californian who had made his money in real estate. The price was reported to be $13.1 million.

Argyros had many detractors in both Seattle and major league baseball. Fans were angered by his refusal to keep with the rising pay scale in baseball; he let top pitchers Floyd Bannister and Mike Moore go to free agency, and traded Mark Langston for three low-marquee players. In the words of the local press, he "bled the team and its landlord of cash while destroying the team's looks, and talent." The league felt he was handling his team as if it were just one more piece of business property; their criticism was fueled when he attempted in 1987 to sell the Mariners and purchase the San Diego Padres, a deal, he said, that would permit him to keep a closer eye on his real estate interests while remaining in baseball. The deal collapsed early, at least partly because National League owners did not want Argyros in their club. Midway through the 1989 season, Argyros sold to Indianapolis businessmen Jeffrey Smulyan and Michael Browning for $76 million.

A Man with a Dream

Smulyan was the main man. He had made a name for himself by purchasing troubled radio stations cheap and turning them into successes.

His company, Emmis, began its expansion in 1980 by purchasing WENS-FM in Indianapolis, a deal pulled off mostly with borrowed money. Within ten years, Emmis grew to 11 stations, each acquisition following a similar pattern. Smulyan looked for a station doing poorly, got it at a reduced price and then reformatted its programming to improve the ratings. And it worked. Times were good, and Smulyan knew his business.

One of his greatest successes came with KPWR in Los Angeles, bought for $12 million in 1984, reformatted, and built into the top station in the market. By 1988 its estimated worth was $100 million.

In the process, Smulyan was getting a reputation for turnarounds. His record so impressed the New York investment banking firm of Morgan Stanley that in 1986 it purchased 20 percent of Emmis.

Most of Smulyan's professional experience was with FM music stations. But he also had a feel for sports, and an idea he longed to test. In 1986 he took the first step.

That was the year Emmis bought three radio stations with the help of Morgan Stanley from Doubleday Broadcasting: WHN-AM and WAPP-FM, both in New York, and WAVA-FM in Washington, D.C. WHN was a moderately successful station that played country-and-western music, and carried the Mets baseball games. Sixteen months later Smulyan turned WHN into WFAN, the first successful all-sports radio station in America.

Smulyan was ambitious from the start. "We'll probably be a serious bidder for one of the two pro football teams when they're available," he was quoted as saying in 1987. "We might bid for the Knicks."

Everyone assumed he was talking about purchasing the broadcast rights. Probably he was, at one level. But Jeffery Smulyan was then and continues to be a man who enjoys a challenge. And even in 1987, he was thinking about getting into baseball.

"Emmis took off beyond our wildest dreams," recalls Smulyan, "and in the mid-1980s I began talking with a group trying to get a team for Indianapolis. That never happened, but it was a beginning.

"I began talking with another group about the possibility of buying another team, but nothing happened there, either. Then I heard from a friend in Seattle that George Argyros wanted out."

That information could not have been more correct. As the 1980s came to an end, the relationship between owner Argyros and Seattle had disintegrated badly. And no longer were the complaints about his dealings with his team only local; his critics were everywhere. Peter Gammons, writing in *Sports Illustrated* in 1989, called Argyros' trade of star pitcher Mark Langston "bungled and shortsighted." He went on to quote an American League executive as saying "Argyros doesn't view himself in terms of winning, only in terms of profit."

It was a sad picture, but one that fit Smulyan's old profile of a worthwhile project: a struggling entertainment franchise, under-performing in a market in which every one else was succeeding.

And he knew what he was getting into. Following the rules of due diligence, he had his people pore over the books and investigate every aspect of the market. Due diligence is the process of closely examining the financial statements, projections, operations, and contractual arrangements of an organization prior to making an investment. It is particularly important in sports, because the results of operations reported in financial statements are often muddied by related party transactions, indirect municipal subsidies, differences in accounting policies and, in certain cases, effects of previous acquisitions.

All this can present a prospective buyer with a confusing network of financial arrangements, making the true value of a franchise difficult to determine. Every case is different.

If someone were interested in purchasing the St. Louis Cardinals from the Busch family, it would be difficult to carve out the true profitability of the club because certain of its in-stadium operations are conducted by an affiliated company. The concessions in Busch Stadium are conducted not by the Cardinals Baseball Club but by another affiliate of Anheuser-Busch.

If someone wanted to buy the Atlanta Braves from Ted Turner, he would have to wonder what would happen to the local broadcasting revenue line, because it now receives its money from its sister company, TBS, also owned by Turner. A similar situation exists with the Chicago Cubs, whose games are televised by a station owned by their owner, the Chicago Tribune Company.

These "related party" contractual arrangements are common within the sports industry. The individual reviewing the financial statements of franchises involved in such arrangements must question whether they were entered into on an arms-length basis and, therefore, whether the financial statements of these franchises are truly reflective of ongoing operations.

Furthermore, the contract of each player must be carefully examined; they are often tailored to a specific player's or team's financial objectives. In dealing with bonuses, most teams capitalize bonuses and amortize them over the contract term, although certain franchises have "expensed" bonuses when paid. And some players ask that parts of their salaries be deferred; that money is included in the team's salary expense for the season it is earned, but remains on the books as a future liability of the team (though at a discounted value, reflecting the "time-value" of money).

A prospective buyer must know how a team has handled each and every situation. If, for example, a player has been signed for a $1 million bonus, has the team "expensed" that bonus, listing the $1 million as an expense in the year the contract was signed, or have they "capitalized and amortized" the bonus, spreading the million over the term of the contract? And that player with a deferred payment—has it been reflected in the financial statement and the footnotes at its discounted value and face value, respectively?

Prospective buyers need beware. Accounting practices differ. Arrangements previously agreed upon must be understood in advance, and the exact manner in which contracts are to be settled must be thoroughly dissected in order to determine the actual profitability of the club.

Solid Preparation

The many complexities of buying a team may have been new to Jeff Smulyan, but the rules of making such a purchase intelligently were not. Smulyan approached the transaction with the same high energy that had resulted in his previous success. The process included analyzing the spending and recreation habits of the population, and even studying the attendance figures of the old Seattle Rainiers minor league baseball team in the 1950s.

"The market size was indicative that revenues should grow remarkably," says Smulyan, looking back. "The community is not really small. It's the 13th largest TV market [now the 14th], eighth in most cabled households. The size of its corporate community, its tourism and conventions–it had all the things that should generate revenues in baseball." Smulyan was not alone in his enthusiasm. Morgan Stanley got involved, putting up a percentage of the money estimated to be a third.

To the city of Seattle and the Mariners organization, Smulyan appeared as a knight on a white horse. His agenda was impressive, and he spelled it out. He promised help for players and support systems alike: an increase in the players' salaries, which at $8.5 million in 1989 was among the league's lowest; more scouts to seek out good young players; new cars to ease the burden of their travel and multiyear contracts for job security; a $1 million advertising budget; new ticket packages; and other incentives intended to turn the franchise around.

This atmosphere of early bliss was disrupted even before Smulyan and the Mariners were able to start their first full season. The culprit was a sport-wide "lockout." Baseball's first labor-related interruption of play since 1985 lasted through all of the exhibition season and even pushed back the start of the regular 1990 season.

The lockout was no surprise. That too showed up in Smulyan's homework. The possibility of labor problems was a factor in their negotiations, and a "significant amount" of money was set aside in the event games were canceled. The Mariners also had access to the strike fund to which all major league franchises contribute. Still, it was a lost spring, and not the kind of beginning that the new owner had wanted.

Smulyan shrugged it off and worked hard to make that season a success. From a 1990 article in *The Seattle Times:*

> Smulyan . . . has tried to heal the wounds, lowering ticket and concession prices, worked quietly with county officials, showing concern for fans, employees, players and sponsors. He has passed raises and paid Christmas vacations. He had settled with all his arbitration players, adding more than $5 million to the payroll. He has added nearly $1 million to his front-office payroll. He convinced free-agent Pete O'Brien to turn down at least two other offers in order to play here. He will fly his team on more expensive charters for all trips. He has set up financial post-career counseling. Every draft choice will be given a Mariner package that includes a glove, jacket and shoes. Smulyan wants to demonstrate that Seattle is a first-class organization.

In praising Smulyan's efforts to promote the team "from Anchorage to Walla," the feature quoted some of his attitudes toward the game and his understanding that turning the team around was harder than reformatting radio stations.

> It's baseball. It's definitely mesmerizing. It's more complex. You have to attack it from the farm system, the drafting process, the scouting system, balancing the rosters, and all those issues that face the game, marketing the club, pricing the ads, radio/TV rights, season tickets, regionalization of the franchise, changing the approach to the Kingdome. It's a very complex project and there's no guarantee we won't screw up royally. But there are things we understand.

One was marketing, and he launched into a program of family sections and child-care centers, indoor fireworks, and rock concerts.

"We can't expect people to come to the ballpark and only be satisfied with a win," Smulyan said then. "They've got to feel good about that evening, win or lose. That's the challenge."

His efforts stimulated early signs of life in the franchise. Attendance jumped from 15,000 per game in 1989 to more than 18,000 in 1990. In 1991 the Mariners managed their first winning season, and a franchise record attendance of more than 25,000 per game.

But even as all this was going on, Smulyan's dream of owning a successful baseball team was eroding. The problem was money.

Smulyan started his Seattle adventure with less financial support than he planned, partly because of timing. Buying the team came after Emmis' purchase of the three radio stations. In his own words, "We were clearly over-leveraged, and we knew it." The answer was to sell radio stations for capital.

"But almost immediately after we made the commitment to buy the team," recalls Smulyan, "the radio industry dropped pretty dramatically. Instead of using the proceeds of the sale to take in the baseball investment, it went to an out-of-corporate debt."

Emmis ended up selling four stations—in Houston, San Francisco, Minneapolis, and Washington. But instead of realizing the $120 million Smulyan hoped, the total came to $80 million.

Meantime, the financial situation in the world of baseball was proving to be more difficult than he anticipated. That difficulty was composed of many parts. One was escalating player salaries, something that affected every team. The average player salary was $400,000 in 1987, about the time Smulyan was thinking of buying a team. It more than doubled to $825,000 in 1991, and by opening day of 1992, it was more than $1 million per player.

Another expense affecting all teams was the collusion payment assessed late in 1990 by an arbitrator. The ruling—which cost each team $11 million—came after it was decided that baseball owners jointly colluded to hold down salaries for players who were free agents. For a team such as the Mariners, already strapped for funds, the payout was crippling.

But it was still a one-time expense. More painful was the on-going burden of the team's low local television revenues. While some baseball games are carried on network and cable, most are on local television. And local television decides what it will pay for local programming. For some reason, Seattle television was not high on baseball. Local TV revenue was as low as $1.5 million in 1990, giving Seattle the lowest TV revenue in the American League. The New York Yankees, by comparison, had a reported $45 million cable television contract in that same year.

These numbers were wrecking Jeff Smulyan, but he did not give up easily. In an effort to keep things afloat, he sold WFAN in December of 1991 to the Infinity Broadcasting Corporation of New York.

It was a painful move. Smulyan had proved his idea a success, and he had hoped to bring it to other markets. Now others were doing that; all-sports stations soon appeared in Boston and Los Angeles. But WFAN was the first, and had grown into a superstar. According to *The New York Times,* Smulyan's selling price for the station was $70 million, about $55 million more than WFAN's value four years before.

"It was an offer that we found was hard to refuse, and we also felt we would like to stay in baseball," Smulyan told *The Times.*

The day-to-day expenses continued to add up, while at the same time, the additional pressures were mounting. One of the biggest was applied by the Security Pacific Bank of Seattle. According to an article in the *Indianapolis Business Journal,* Smulyan had borrowed $35 million from the bank originally to purchase the Mariners, a loan not due until March of 1996. But when he came back to Security Pacific for the additional $4.5 million to help meet the arbiter's collusion payment, the bank advanced the clock on his loan.

The *Business Journal* reported that to get the additional money, Smulyan agreed to line up alternative financing to pay back the debt by February of 1992. If he failed, he had to sell the team. At that point the Mariners had a long history of losing money, and Smulyan himself predicted a $10 million loss for 1992. The burden was too great; the Smulyan era in Seattle was as good as over. And in 1992 the team was in fact sold.

The question remains: Why did this successful radio man, head of the broadcasting corporation reputed to be the largest privately owned in the United States, want to buy a baseball team in the first place? And once he did, why couldn't he make it work?

The answer to the first question begins with fan equity . . . this time at a very personal level. Jeffrey Smulyan grew up as a fan of baseball and radio. He was taken to ball games throughout the Midwest by his father and grabbed whatever he could over his radio.

"Baseball and radio—I developed a love of both as a kid, growing up in Indianapolis," recalls Smulyan. "I used to lie in bed at night, scanning the dial for games. The Pirates over KDKA in Pittsburgh; the Braves over WTMJ in Milwaukee; the Reds over WLW in Cincinnati. It was the same with the top 40 stations around the country." As an adult, Smulyan brought an unusual attitude to his pursuit of a profession.

"I've always had this feeling that if you get into a business you love, you'll work harder at it and it really won't be work. That made us fairly successful in radio; we knew we loved it and worked at it 24 hours a day. We felt we could bring some of that energy to baseball."

But having researched the Mariners' situation—all those years of failure—would even such an effort be enough?

"I'm a nut about challenges," says the man who "only lost a little money" in Seattle. "That's more intense with baseball than something like widgets. Kids don't grow up dreaming about the widget business—they grow up dreaming about baseball. I did. And when you grow up loving something, when working in it is a dream, if you get the chance you take it."

A Magical Appeal

There is something about owning a sports team that is unlike any other business operation. It appeals to individuals as widely divergent as Gene Autry, the former movie idol who owns the California Angels; ship builder and Yankee owner George Steinbrenner; and real estate tycoon Donald Trump, who tried to buy the New England Patriots and did own the Jersey Generals in the short-lived World Football League.

These people are successful in their own areas; some, like Trump, are even stars. Still, something about the world of sports offers an extra measure of satisfaction.

For some, clearly, that appeal is celebrity. George Steinbrenner said it to *The New York Times* in 1991, while still on suspension for his dealings with a known gambler: "When you're a shipbuilder nobody pays attention to you. But when you own the New York Yankees, they do, and I loved it."

For others, owning a team is perfect for airing one's unique personal style. Sports embraces all styles, so long as they don't get in the way of good business. Few cases illustrate this better than the one featuring Ted Turner.

From the time Ted Turner burst onto the national scene, he represented American capitalism in its purest, most aggressive form. His father was a self-made millionaire who tolerated no expressions of weakness in his son, or, apparently, in himself. By his son's own description, the senior Turner overworked himself to the point where the growth of his billboard business worried him over the edge; in 1963 he shot himself to death.

When young Turner—then 24—found the business had been sold, he rallied his own forces, bought the company back, then springboarded his investment into a fortune reportedly worth at least $1.8 billion.

Turner purchased the Braves from Bill Bartholomay in 1976, presumably for no greater reason than to ensure programming for WTBS, then just an independent television station that he had operated in

Atlanta for five years. Later that year, the Federal Communications Commission approved an application by the Southern Satellite System to carry the WTBS signal across the nation, and the first superstation was born.

There was no indication that Turner had previously been a sports fan. In fact, his lack of involvement with athletics as a boy would seem to work against his susceptibility to its lure. Buying the Braves—and later the NBA Atlanta Hawks—appeared to be business decisions.

But Ted Turner, a hands-on businessman, moved to get things done in his own style. That kind of personality in sports draws the spotlight. A year after buying the Braves, while his team was mired in a 16-game losing streak, Turner prescribed a scouting mission for his manager, Dave Bristol, and proceeded to put on a uniform and manage his team. His tenure as manager lasted one day; National League President Chub Feeney banned him from the dugout.

Turner was just as direct about acquiring players. During that same spring of 1977, the Braves were charged by Commissioner Bowie Kuhn with tampering—for trying to lure Gary Matthews away from San Francisco. They were fined $10,000. After the season, Turner allegedly confronted Giants owner Bob Lurie, promising before several sports writers to pay "whatever was necessary" to sign Matthews. Lurie filed a complaint and Kuhn banned Turner from baseball until the following season.

Turner was getting a reputation for meddling, and helping to build one of the worst teams in the league. But ultimately good business was more important than the pleasure of expressing his personal will. And he had the money to survive that difficult transition, which gave him the opportunity to adjust to his new toy. By the 1980s, a more serious Ted Turner was in charge. From a 1986 article in *Sports Illustrated*:

> Virtually all decisions have been turned over to his general managers and coaches. No longer is it so important that the players be his buddies, no more does he spend hours in their company. . . . The Braves still have one of baseball's highest payrolls, but that is a vestige of earlier years when Turner seemed compelled to lavish long-term, no-cut contracts, many on nominal players he wanted to befriend.

Suddenly Turner was treating the Braves the way he treated his other business. He hired one of the game's most respected managers, Bobby Cox, and brought in John Schuerholz of Kansas City fame as general manager. Turner let them handle the baseball. As a result, the

Braves won the National League pennant in 1991 and 1992, and established themselves as one of the good, young teams in the game.

That is what it takes for this new breed of owner to be successful. Baseball is a funny game. The talents that make a successful car dealer or shipbuilder do not necessarily translate to baseball, but if owners without great baseball knowledge are to succeed they must apply sound business attitudes to their teams. They need to hire good general managers and field managers, and then let them do their jobs.

Bill Veeck knew business as well as baseball. Just as he used integration to bring Satchel Paige and Larry Doby to the Indians to help win a pennant in 1948, he used the new situation of free agency to bring Richie Zisk and Oscar Gamble to the White Sox for that one 1977 season before losing them to the open market. But it was always baseball first. Veeck's lifetime in the game allowed him to spot an exceptional baseball mind in an aging Class AAA utility infielder; he gave Tony LaRussa his first chance to manage, first in the minors and then with the Sox in Chicago.

We never answered the second question about success and failure in Seattle. But that kind of sense does not come quickly or easily. It takes time. And time now costs more than it ever has before. The top is a difficult place to learn baseball today.

Jeff Smulyan did not assume he knew enough about his new business to run the club; he hired experienced baseball men to make the decisions. Nor was he infatuated with the public attention. So with all of his know-how about marketing and his willingness to contribute money and energy to that franchise, why couldn't he make it work?

In the answer we find the new economics of sports. "Just too much working against us," says Smulyan now, looking back on his exercise in the Northwest. "For a baseball team to survive today, it must be able to generate revenues in five places: gate; other in-stadium interests like concessions; over-the-air broadcasts; cable; and that special convergence of the corporate community that supports stadium advertising and luxury suites.

"No individual flaw is fatal, but when you don't have any of them, it's fatal."

Smulyan knew all along that the 16-year-old Kingdome was not going to yield as much revenue as a new stadium; there wasn't much he could do about that. He concentrated his efforts where he could have an effect—improving the ball club and marketing it, all aimed at generating fan and community interest.

And it worked, as far as it could. The team got better, and attendance improved substantially. Then he hit a stone wall. "The final straw was our last TV bid," recalls Smulyan. "We were in first place at the time, and the ratings were way up. A 12, up from a 4 when we bought the team. But it didn't matter; the TV stations were still indifferent."

Before the 1992 season started, Smulyan was out of baseball. "The hardest thing to swallow was the lack of interest in the corporate community," he says today. "When the corporations aren't committed to the team, they don't buy the tickets, they don't buy advertising that induces the TV stations to bid on the games. That's what killed us."

Perhaps. Or maybe it was the combination of low corporate support with the small local television market, all of it happening in an area that lacks that historical connection to baseball of a Kansas City, Pittsburgh, or Cincinnati; smaller markets whose teams are most successful. Baseball is a funny sport. Certain markets, even small markets, have enough of a tradition with the game to support a franchise through the leanest of years. The community in Seattle may simply have lacked that tradition.

Or, just perhaps, Jeff Smulyan did not have enough money to continually pour into the Seattle team to compensate for those other problems. It will be interesting to see what happens with the team's new owners, a syndicate headed by Hiroshi Yamauchi, head of Nintendo of America.

2

Football

Compared to professional baseball—established even before Cincinnati's all-salaried Red Stockings of 1869—football was a stepchild in the new age of athletes for hire.

Pro football's starting date was 1895, but that was a ragtag start. Definition was a problem. An outgrowth of the enormously popular college game, the pros found themselves in competition with their better-known predecessor, and invariably came out second. To many fans, their game was little more than a duplication of college football with over-the-hill players.

The charge was not unfair. Pro teams were stocked with college stars who were paid for an afternoon's extracurricular activity. There were no contracts. Players went from team to team as their talents dictated their desirability. Understandably, the unstable rosters thwarted fan loyalty.

It was a blue-collar sport from the beginning, and teams formed where there was enough of an industrial base to lend support. In Ohio, teams started in Canton, Massillon, Akron, and Dayton; in Pennsylvania, it was Latrobe, Jeannette, and Greensburg. Getting into pro ball was not a big investment for an owner; a franchise in 1920 could be had for $100.

George Halas, who helped form the American Professional Football Association that year, called the game "a catch-as-catch-can affair" in his book, *Halas by Halas:*

> Teams appeared one week and disappeared the next. Players came and went, drawn by the pleasure of playing. If others came to watch, that was fine. If they bought tickets or tossed coins into a helmet passed by the most popular player, that was helpful.

Even baseball dabbled in football. The Pittsburgh Pirates fielded a team with ex-Bucknell star Christy Mathewson at fullback. Connie Mack coached a team of Philadelphia Athletics; Rube Waddell played "briefly" in each game, reportedly as little as one play. In the beginning, it was that casual.

Slowly, the pros began to separate themselves from the amateur game. They began playing on Sunday, leaving Saturday to the colleges. A few franchises with staying power were formed: Curly Lambeau organized the Green Bay Packers in 1921; Halas started the Chicago Bears a year later; the New York Giants were begun by Tim Mara in 1925.

But it was still a very young sport, waiting to be discovered by the American public. Players passed in and out of the game without leaving much of a trace; its stars—men like Frank Bacon and Fritz Pollard—were names only the most devoted fans recognized, names now faded by time. That was one of the problems—nobody was grabbing the public's attention. And then came Jim Thorpe.

Thorpe, a Sac and Fox Indian from Oklahoma, gained national attention at the Carlisle Institute, an Indian trade school in Pennsylvania. He played baseball, basketball, and ran track for Carlisle, and in 1911 and 1912 was an all-America halfback under the legendary football coach, Glenn (Pop) Warner. But his fame was not limited to the United States. Thorpe proved his extraordinary athletic ability to the world at the 1912 Olympics in Stockholm by winning the decathlon (ten track and field events normally competed over two days) and a five-event version, the pentathlon. When he returned from Sweden, he spent the next ten years playing professional baseball.

Jim Thorpe was just what professional football needed—a ready-made star. He joined the Canton Bulldogs in 1915. (That's right! Long before Bo Jackson or Deion Sanders, Thorpe played football and baseball in the same season—eight of them.) The impact was immediate. Previously averaging only 1,200 fans a game, the Bulldogs welcomed 8,000 customers to Thorpe's first appearance. The young American Professional Football Association—later the NFL—was so appreciative it made him its first president in 1920.

The league quickly learned Thorpe was better at playing than governing and replaced him the following season. But on the field, Thorpe embodied the spirit of the decathlon: He did everything, and he did it well. He ran with power and speed; he could punt, and drop-kick field goals from mid-field. He was a devastating blocker and a punishing tackler whose style was to dive at the ballcarrier, whipping his body around him and knocking him off his feet.

Thorpe was an early testament to the importance of celebrity to sports. But pro football needed even more; it needed to ignite the hearts of the American public. It needed Harold "Red" Grange.

Like Thorpe, Grange came to professional football with his reputation already made. Most of that happened in one October afternoon in 1924. Playing halfback for the University of Illinois, Grange scored four touchdowns in the first 12 minutes of a game against Michigan. The first came on a weaving, 95-yard return of the opening kickoff; another was on a 67-yard run from scrimmage down the right sideline; a third on a 56-yard punt return; and another on a 45-yard run.

Situation is crucial in sports, and the situation that day was ideal for maximum exposure. More than 67,000 fans were in Champaign to open the new Memorial Stadium. By day's end, they were dazzled, as the entire nation soon would be. It was the Michigan game that inspired Grantland Rice to dub Grange "the Galloping Ghost." Damon Runyon wrote: "The man Red Grange is three or four men and a horse rolled into one. He is Jack Dempsey, Babe Ruth, Al Jolson, Paavo Nurmi and Man O' War."

Grange—only a junior that Saturday—finished the 39–14 victory with five touchdowns, 402 yards on the ground and six completed passes, one going for a touchdown. He also held for the kicker.

He returned to play for Illinois in his senior year, but then joined the Chicago Bears after his final game, without waiting for graduation. His reason for leaving early was money. Within hours of his Illinois finale, Grange signed an elaborate contract that called for a $2,000-per-game guarantee and a percentage of the gate that rose from 10 percent to 40 percent depending on the size of the crowd. (For one game against a team of all-stars at the Los Angeles Coliseum in 1926, he earned a reported $49,000.)

There was not much time left in that 1925 pro season, but the Bears were determined to make the most of their new investment. Grange played his first game for the Bears against the crosstown Cardinals in Wrigley Field on Thanksgiving Day before 36,000 people.

Three days later the Bears played the Columbus Tigers before 28,000 at Wrigley, and in the next 12 days went on an eight-game tour, highlighted by drawing more than 65,000 fans to a game against the New York Giants at the Polo Grounds.

The tour was a marketing bonanza. It fixed Red Grange as the first football superstar and placed the sport in the consciousness of the American people as never before.

The Archetypal Owner

The man who lured Grange out of Illinois and into a Bears uniform was George Halas, founder and owner of the Bears, and the individual who was as responsible as any owner for the league's survival and first flashes of success.

A graduate of Illinois himself and an end for the Fighting Illini, he briefly played outfield for the New York Yankees in 1919, appearing in 12 games. The following year he helped organize a semi-pro team, the Decatur Staleys, for the Staley Starchworks of Decatur, Illinois.

Early football was full of operations like that, teams that represented companies in order to spread publicity and goodwill. The idea is not unique to football. Similarly conceived teams helped form basketball's early history, and in the 1950s and 1960s powerful Amateur Athletic Union teams—among them the Phillips 66'ers and the Akron Goodyears—played at a quality level between college and the NBA in the National Industrial Basketball League.

Staley Starchworks was pleased with the attention gained by Halas' team, but those were tough years. Tight money prompted the company to drop football after one year. Halas moved the team to Chicago in 1921, and was paid $5,000 by Staley to retain the team's name. He made halfback Edward "Dutch" Sternamen his partner, not only eliminating one salary but drafting another body to help support the franchise; Halas sold cars that first year, while vice-president Sternamen pumped gas. They renamed their team the Chicago Bears for the 1922 season, and an institution was born.

George Halas went on to be a force in the game, both politically in the league and on the field, reviving the "T formation" in 1940 and adding to it the "man in motion."

But in the early days of professional football, there were as many paths to the owner's box as men who occupied them. They are linked by how quickly the game became part of them and how long they remained committed.

- George Preston Marshall, head of a successful laundry company in Washington, D.C., had organized a basketball team to promote business. Halas convinced him that football would work as well. But the only available NFL franchise was in Boston. The year was 1932; the price, $30,000. Marshall shared the bill with two partners on a lark. He bought out his partners, renamed the team the Redskins and moved it to Washington, where it has flourished ever since. It was Marshall who urged the league to divide into two divisions with a playoff for champion. He introduced spectacular half-time shows, contributed the Redskin band—its members dressed in Indian outfits—and commissioned the Redskins song.
- Timothy Mara, a successful and respectable bookmaker in 1925 (when such a profession was legal), tried to purchase a piece of heavyweight boxer Gene Tunney and ended up buying the New York Giants instead, even though he knew nothing about football. To this day, the Mara family owns half the Giants and is still actively involved with the team.
- Earl "Curly" Lambeau dreamed of playing football as a kid. He grew up to organize a company team for a meat-packing firm that a small Wisconsin community later operated as a public non-profit corporation called the Green Bay Packers; Lambeau served first as player and then coach from 1919 until 1949, piling up six NFL championships along the way.

These were some of the pioneers who brought credibility and order to the young league. Through them and others, the league grew and prospered. By 1940 the price of a franchise was up to $100,000; there were ten teams, playing in two divisions. Compared to the disarray of its beginnings, the NFL seemed to have come a long way, but those first 50 years would later become known as pro football's dark ages.

The great illumination came in the 1950s with television, which quickly moved from a novelty to a social and economic giant, the idol to which all sports would forevermore pray. We will probe the importance of television to sports later. For now it is enough to say that in the American scene, television and professional football were the perfect marriage. Because of it, the sport enjoyed unparalleled growth.

When the Los Angeles Rams were sold in 1962, the price was $7.1 million, only slightly less than it cost the Miami Dolphins to enter the league as an expansion team in 1966. By 1993, $7.1 million would cover only *a fraction* of the contracts of the league's top quarterbacks. This kind of economics—as with the economics of baseball—vastly affected the people who purchased football teams in the 1990s.

Let us look at one specific football team, the New England Patriots. For 28 years, from the time they were created as a charter member of the American Football League in 1960 to 1988, the Patriots had one principal owner. Then, within four years they were sold twice, in 1988 and 1992, in both cases under stress.

For most of those seasons, the Patriots played well on the field. Back in the old AFL days, the team known as the Boston Patriots finished second in their division three times and once first. After the AFL and NFL merged for the 1970 season, they came in first or tied in their division three times, and in 1986 they earned a trip to the Superbowl. (That resulted in a 46–10 drubbing by the Chicago Bears.)

But winning did not spell success for the Pats. This was a franchise with real problems right from the start. The man at the top throughout those years was William H. Sullivan, Jr. His father, William, Sr., was a sportswriter in Lowell, Massachusetts; that put son Billy around sports all his life. He was in charge of public relations for Boston College and then the Boston Braves before briefly working as a heating company executive. Billy's friendships within the sports fraternity led to his entrance into the fledgling AFL in 1959. It took just $8,300 of his own money to become head of the group of nine investors who tallied up the $25,000 needed to join the party. (That was a bargain basement price compared to the NFL.)

Much of Sullivan's efforts over the next 28 years were devoted to retaining ownership of the club. He borrowed from banks and relatives, even raised $600,000 in the club's first year by selling stock to the fans. But it was a constant struggle. For years the team was homeless. Until 1971 when the stadium in suburban Foxboro was built, the Pats played all over Boston—in Fenway Park, at Boston University, Boston College, and Harvard. Eleven seasons as an orphan equalled 11 seasons of lost revenue from no home stadium.

Sullivan actually lost control in 1974, when his fellow stockholders forced him out as president. His response was to fight. With the help of his son Chuck, then an associate with a Wall Street law firm, he borrowed enough to buy out his opposition and return to power. Billy ended up with all the stock, Chuck with ownership of the stadium.

Setbacks from non-football ventures, one of the highest payrolls in football, and a lack of parking, concessions, and advertising revenues caused losses which ultimately led to the league's urging that the team be sold. An all-star list of potential buyers seemed close and then withdrew: Paul Fireman, chairman of Reebok International; former Transportation Secretary Drew L. Lewis; former U.S. Postmaster General Preston Robert Tisch; even developer Donald Trump.

All dropped out. Their reasons differed, but their scrutiny of the franchise's financial health surely helped shape their decisions. A 1988 article in *Business Week* called New England "the National Football League's great financial eyesore."

In another 1988 article, *Sports Illustrated* painted a gloomy picture:

> One set of documents obtained by *SI* shows that the team lost $11.9 million in fiscal 1987. Another set indicates that as of Feb. 15 of this year, the Patriots' debt had reached $49 million; that the Chuck Sullivan–owned Stadium Management Corporation, the company that runs Sullivan Stadium where the Patriots play, had debts of $52.6 million; that Chuck had debts totaling $22.1 million; and that Billy had debts of $2.1 million.

Stranger in a Strange Land

Who would buy into such a situation? The man who finally stepped forward was Victor Kiam. A pro football fan for 25 years, he admittedly knew little about the inner workings of the game.

Until 1988 when he purchased the Patriots, Kiam was known to most television watchers as the man in the Remington shaver ads, the guy who tried a new shaver and was, in his own words, "so impressed [he] bought the company." Prior to that, the Navy veteran was educated at Yale and the Sorbonne, and earned an MBA at Harvard. He sold bras and girdles for Playtex before becoming the company's vice-president, and later headed the Benrus Corporation.

In 1979 he purchased the troubled razor company from Sperry-Rand, using mostly borrowed money. His attitude toward success sounded remarkably like that of Jeffrey Smulyan.

"You buy a company cheap, cut costs, work hard, and eventually turn things around," he told *The Boston Globe* in 1988.

Kiam delivered at Remington. The company's sales rose from $43 million in 1983 to $300 million in 1988, according to *The Globe.* To achieve that, he reportedly eliminated 75 executive positions, slashed corporate perks, consolidated manufacturing at the Bridgeport, Connecticut, plant, and dropped the price of the shavers.

Unfortunately, things did not go that well with the Patriots. Partly that was Kiam's own fault. Like so many new-comers to team ownership, he was unable to bring the same cold commitment to efficiency to sports that made him successful in business.

But Kiam also inherited conditions about which he could do little. Most difficult to overcome was the situation with Sullivan Stadium. The facility was not part of the purchase of the team; it was then still owned by Billy Sullivan's son, Chuck.

In sports, a stadium is more than a place to play, as we will explore later. In short, it represents a major source of revenue. Concessions, parking, luxury boxes, money paid for the display of advertising—they all add up. And in the case of Kiam and the Patriots, they were adding up in somebody else's bank account.

The quagmire of Sullivan Stadium was no secret; it complicated any deal for the Patriots. Reebok's Paul Fireman had been interested in the debt-ridden team, but discouraged by the stadium's status.

Kiam says now, looking back, "There were many reasons why I didn't want to buy the stadium when I bought the team. In spite of the fact that today some people say it was not the right decision, I firmly believe it was. I would have purchased it, but at a much lower price than it was ultimately sold.

"Based on the objectives that could be achieved, paying more would just compound the difficulty already on the team. It was just too much money. Even today I think that was the right decision."

By August of 1988, the matter was in the hands of a trustee appointed by the U.S. Bankruptcy Court in Boston. According to Kiam, the court ruled out several agreements that existed between the club and the stadium; one team-to-stadium payment was called an inter-family loan and had to be repaid. Kiam says the team lost approximately $7 million from such court decisions.

Kiam's $19 million bid in late 1988 to buy the stadium out of bankruptcy was topped by a $25 million bid by the K Corporation, owned by Boston businessmen Robert Karp and Steve Kraft. Kraft had owned the Boston Lobsters, an entry in the now-defunct professional team tennis league, and at one point had expressed interest in purchasing the Patriots. One highly valuable asset of the stadium deal was the lease with the team, an arrangement negotiated between William Sullivan and his son and regarded by many observers as one of the worst in the NFL.

The financial relationship is assessed by Andrew Wasynczuk who joined Kraft and Karp in January of 1989, just after the K Corporation became the Foxboro Stadium Association, that name taken from the newly named facility:

> When the family was involved, the lease wasn't an issue—it was all the same pot. Whether the father or the son had the money, it didn't make any difference. But when you look at it as a stand-alone operation—when you try to separate the business and try to define the terms—we have a favorable lease, and the team has a less-favorable lease arrangement, compared to other teams in the league.

That arrangement not only earned the Patriots no money from concessions, parking, advertising, and the rent of the stadium—reportedly totaling $1.5 million a year—but also left Kiam with a yearly bill of $125,000 for the owner's box.

"We got wiped," says Kiam. "If we got a normal sharing of revenue, we would have had a better chance. But after the bankruptcy, we got nothing."

The stadium proved only to be the beginning of Kiam's problems with the big-time game of sports. The team finished 9–7 in 1988, tied for second in the AFC East for the second consecutive season. To increase revenues, Kiam raised ticket prices 17 percent. The fans were not happy. Season ticket sales began dropping, from 37,000 in 1988 to 18,000 for the 1991 season; over the same period, overall attendance fell by nearly 15,000 fans a game.

And the team began losing. The Patriots were 5–11 in 1989, and 1–15 in 1990. The losses brought new head coaches. Rod Rust replaced Raymond Berry after 1989, and Dick MacPherson replaced Rust after 1990. The estimated cost of buying out those two contracts was $5 million.

Then came the Lisa Olson affair. Olson, a reporter new to the Patriots beat for the *Boston Herald*, claimed members of the team sexually harassed her in the locker room in September of 1990. Specifically, she charged that three naked Patriots made lewd gestures and suggestions while she was trying to interview a fourth player. Accounts varied widely. Certainly Olson was in the crowded locker room after practice for a scheduled interview, and an incident occurred between her and several players. The rest of the story was covered in the national press the way celebrity sex scandals are covered by the tabloids, but the facts remained in dispute. Also disputed were comments about Olson charged to Kiam—which he denies. All of this came at a time when the public was increasingly sensitive to harassment of women in the workplace . . . especially one as charged as a previously all-male sports locker room. The coverage was aggressive, and Kiam took a lot of heat.

Olson brought suit against the players, the ball club, the owner, and several team officials, asking for monetary damages for sexual harassment, civil rights violations, intentional infliction of emotional distress, and intentional damage to her professional reputation. She eventually settled out of court for a sum reported to be $250,000; as a result, the full, accurate details of what happened will probably never be known.

So within two years of purchasing the controlling interest in the Patriots, Kiam lost money—"a lot of money," he says—was sued, and held up to national ridicule. This certainly was not what he had in mind when he got involved. In May of 1992, he sold his interest in the team.

Exactly what he did have in mind at the start was never made clear. Some who were close to him at the time felt he saw the acquisition as a good way to draw attention to himself and to Remington. That worked in the past; his television ads helped boost shaver sales. Kiam admits that was part of his thinking back in 1988.

"I felt that with any exposure I got, there would be some falloff benefit for Remington," he says. "Obviously, if you won, there would be more benefit than if you lost."

But promotion was not his only reason for buying a team. "I had been an ardent fan of the NFL for a long time, and I wanted to be part of it," says Kiam. "I felt it would be exciting and different, something that when I stopped being active in other businesses I could remain an active participant."

And while he examined the many complexities of the Patriots' situation before investing his money, once inside they proved even more numerous than he thought. He cites the more than 20 lawsuits pending against the franchise when he took over, from former stockholders, former players, and others. There was even the spectator who helped tear down the goalpost and was injured when the purloined post hit an electric wire; he was suing the Patriots. "As we overturned rocks," he says, "we found more worms."

If he were starting over, he says, he would structure his purchase differently, safeguarding the franchise against some of those suits, and holding the Sullivans responsible for the situation they had created with the stadium.

But maybe even that would not have saved him. Part of his problem, Kiam candidly admits today, was that he cared too much about the game and the team. "My emotional drive overshadowed the business sense of what I was doing," he says, explaining that he focused too much on trying to make a winner. Being in a field he did not know forced him to accept other people's judgment of how to accomplish that.

"By 1990 it became apparent to me that I was going down the wrong path," he says. That path had him committed to a level of stability that left the Pats with one of the older teams in the league, a team that was generating little success in 1990 and promising little improvement.

It was then that Kiam brought in Sam Jankovich from the University of Miami to reorganize the franchise. Jankovich attacked problems on many levels, from travel to negotiating players' contracts to who would be signed. Prices for meals were negotiated for road games along with room rates, individual incentives in contracts were ended, and the overall age of the team dropped from 12th oldest in the league to 27th.

These were part of the business of sports, very different from product-oriented businesses, an area where Victor Kiam excelled. "At Remington, if somebody were run over by a truck, I could step in and fill the job for a while," he says. "I couldn't do that in football. I had to rely on third-party decisions, and I was constantly getting hurt."

But professional sports is like no other business. Running a team does require a great understanding of the game, and of the people who play it and those who pay to see it, just as running any business requires an understanding of the product and the market in which it is sold.

But the complexities of operating a sports franchise are greater. There are the subtleties of the marketplace, endless competition for the customer's attention, and a volatile situation with labor. And to all of these considerations, sports adds an emotional element that makes calculating any outcome—from fan loyalty to an athlete's ability to play while hurt—all but impossible.

This is what makes sports such a risky business. But risk can be exciting.

3

The Second Generation

Stars of professional hockey and basketball today rival and often surpass in salaries and fame their counterparts in baseball and football.

Only in sports could such a rally have occurred.

The origins of pro basketball and hockey differ greatly from the giants that preceded them. The first was a brand-new sport, created only a few years before men were first paid to play it. The second was a national obsession in Canada; its appeal in the United States came later, and for a long time was limited to those regions close to the border.

But as different as the two sports are from one another, they share a season—winter—and a common thread meanders through their origins: The hockey that we know began in Canada, and basketball was invented by a Canadian.

No sport has seen a greater change since its beginning than basketball. It is likely that if superstar Charles Barkley were somehow zapped back to a basketball game in the 1890s, he wouldn't recognize what was going on. Never mind that players were well under six feet tall and white; anyone might anticipate that. More of a shock would be the seven players to a side, the baskets that were really bushel baskets with no backboards, and the rule that had the teams jump for the ball at center court after every score. Oddest of all, a high wire mesh surrounded the entire court.

Basketball was unlike any sport ever seen before. Baseball grew from the English game of rounders; football, from rugby. But basketball sprouted from nothing more than a seed in the fertile imagination of James Naismith, a visiting Canadian taking a course for physical training directors given by the Young Men's Christian Association in Springfield, Massachusetts.

Charged with getting some of his fellow students to exercise indoors during the harsh New England winter, he sympathized with their disdain of calisthenics and gymnastics. Naismith told the department chairman he could come up with an entirely new game and was handed the job.

That was 1891; the resulting experiment was basketball. The story goes that Naismith decided his new game would need a ball, because all the popular games of the age employed a ball. And it would have to be a large ball, since games with small balls required too much equipment. Most ingenious was the concept for goals; two boxes placed high up, he thought, one at either end of the court, to act as targets for the ball to be thrown or arced into. But he could find no boxes the size he wanted—18 inches square—and settled for peach baskets, forever saving us from calling his invention boxball.

The game caught on quickly, and was played at YMCAs across the country, the perfect season-filler after football in the fall and before baseball in the summer. But the organization decided it was too rough and banned it. Basketball addicts were left with no choice but to form their own teams. They sought out armories, gymnasiums, barns, dance halls, and anywhere else they could rent space, and charged spectators a small admission to cover costs. To protect their customers from balls flying out of bounds, netting—usually wire, sometimes string mesh—was erected around the court. It was called a cage, and basketball players forever more became cagers.

Suddenly, teams were playing basketball everywhere. It was easy to set up a game, especially compared to baseball and football—sports that required large teams, big parks, and lots of equipment. All basketball needed was a court, a ball, and two teams of seven players each. Even that got simpler; by 1898 a team was down to five players.

Almost from the start, it had a professional side, if professional means getting paid. Gatherings of enthusiastic fans quickly covered expenses, and the players pocketed the rest, anywhere from $5 to $15 a game. Everything was very loose; players had no contracts, and it was years before they were paid by the season.

While some teams formed and folded overnight, others became little dynasties. The Buffalo Germans claimed a record of 792–86 over their nearly two decades; the Troy Trojans didn't last quite as long, but once won 38 straight games, and won four consecutive titles in two of the leagues in New York State. Other leagues formed in Pennsylvania, New England, and the Midwest.

A lot of good basketball was played in America during the first third of the century, but it failed to achieve the stature of an "event" that quickly characterized football and baseball. There were no permanent leagues, no national championship, not even a schedule. The game was kind of a sideshow. Barnstorming to pay the bills was popular; games often accompanied dances and other social functions.

Leadership and vision were lacking. Early forces were promoters who, while perhaps athletic-minded, saw the game as a new and exciting way to make money. With no history and no role models, they were left to make up a script as they went along.

A Child to Lead Them

One the most inventive of these men was Frank Basloe, a Hungarian-born bundle of energy who became one of basketball's great ambassadors. Just 16 years old, this resident of New York State's Mohawk Valley turned his attention to the pro game in 1903. First he ordered fancy stationery, paying for it with savings from his paper route, according to Robert Peterson in his book on early basketball, *Cages to Jump Shots.* Then he contacted teams in northern New York, scheduling nine games for a team he did not yet have. Peterson reports:

> Now it was time to sign up his "Champions." Lew Wachter and Jim Williamson of Troy, both then in their late teens, and two youngsters from Herkimer agreed to play for $5 a game. Basloe himself was the fifth player. Borrowing $10 from his mother for the team's railroad fares

to the first game in Ogdensburg, Frank Basloe took off on his first barnstorming tour. He returned with nine victories and nearly $300 in his pocket.

Basloe and his teams—actually it was just one team, but it played as the 31st Separate Company, the Oswego Indians, and Basloe's Globe Trotters—prospered from 1904 until 1914, at first in northern New York and New England. As basketball's popularity spread west, they followed it to Pennsylvania, Ohio, Indiana, and Illinois. Basloe liked to get a guarantee of $100 a game, but was known to renegotiate that figure up during a game if the crowd was larger than anticipated.

And why not? There were no rules. Basketball was theater—traveling bands of athletes performing to make their living—athletic vaudeville. It lacked an identity that separated it from other forms of show business; sometimes it was unclear if it wanted to be a sport or a show.

One team that played the game hard was the Original Celtics. Not the Boston Celtics; they would come later. These Celtics came out of New York, and were the class of the sport from 1914 until the Depression. While there were many leagues forming in the East and Midwest in those years, the Celtics were mostly a road show, playing as many as 100 games a season, often before crowds of 4,000 and 5,000 fans who loved their accurate shooting and tight defense.

Other teams viewed the game differently. The Harlem Globetrotters started out playing earnest basketball in the late 1920s. But they were also talented showmen, and the popularity of their ball-handling routines eventually turned them into the clown princes of the game and the most successful barnstormers of all time.

Basketball by then had taken on the basic form it has today; five players to a side, with no protective netting. But the overall style of play was slow; they still tossed the ball up at center court after each score. Worse, the sport had no central structure. Major league baseball and football at that point already had national championships to climax their season. Early basketball resembled black baseball of the time, with league games accounting for a relatively small part of a year's total and most teams surviving from the money earned barnstorming.

Basketball's identity crises, its stilted rules, and lack of structure in the sport hurt its growth and its image. It simply wasn't taken very seriously. Rarely were games reported in the sports pages of *The New York Times,* already known as the newspaper of record and an unofficial granter of credibility.

But that was changing. Acceptance came first to the colleges, as rivalries developed across the country. It was further enhanced by key changes in the rules and by one player. The center jump was eliminated after the 1936–1937 season; that did wonders to speed the game. Then, on the West Coast, a Stanford player named Hank Luisetti introduced the one-hand jump shot. It may not sound like much, but a revolution had begun. Where teams had rarely scored 40 points, Luisetti himself scored 50 in a game against Duquesne.

By the 1940s, professional basketball was on its way. The faster game drew more public interest and college players added continuity. As was the case with pro football, fans were eager to follow the careers of college stars in the pros. Still missing was a league with stable teams and a set schedule.

That ingredient was finally added not from a love of sport, but a love of money. In the summer of 1946 the operators of some of the nation's major arenas decided basketball was ready. A group led by Walter Brown of the Boston Garden, and Al Sutphin, owner of the Cleveland Arena, created the Basketball Association of America. Within three years the BAA absorbed the existing National Basketball League to form the National Basketball Association (NBA).

All those arena owners in Chicago and New York and elsewhere were already making money putting on hockey games, along with ice shows, boxing matches, and rodeos. Basketball, they finally decided, had become enough of an attraction to help fill their arenas in winter when their hockey teams were traveling. What an irony: basketball—the true American game—receiving a hand up into professional respectability from hockey.

Sports and Money on Ice

Hockey got there first because it existed first. Some form was played in Britain in the early 1800s, brought to Canada by the army and codified with rules in 1867. Just when it became all-professional is less clear, and the origin of the Stanley Cup, today's symbol of dominance in the National Hockey League (NHL), provides little assistance. Though we know the cup was purchased in 1893 by Lord Stanley of Preston, the sixth Governor General of Canada, it was to go to the "champion hockey club" in Canada. Competing in those days were schoolboys, adult amateurs, professionals, and all manner of combinations of these.

The immense popularity of the sport on the frozen lakes of Canada eventually spread to the frozen lakes of the northern United States. One of Canada's early hockey greats, Fred "Cyclone" Taylor, played briefly around the turn of the century for a team in Houghton, then the center of a thriving copper industry in Michigan's Upper Peninsula.

But until 1916, American teams were forbidden to contend for the Stanley Cup. The Seattle Mets won the Cup a year later, though the team was stocked with Canadians. That trend has remained through today. The vast majority of NHL players—regardless of their uniforms—have always been Canadians, though the number of Americans has shown a steady increase.

Most who helped build the sport have also been Canadians. Tommy Gorman, who managed and/or coached more different teams to Stanley Cup championships than anyone else, was Canadian. Connie Smythe, who created the Toronto Maple Leafs and managed the team to a Cup championship in 1945, then in 1947–1949, and again in 1951, was Canadian. Frank and Lester Patrick, who together championed the growth of hockey in Western Canada, then individually coached and/or managed the New York Rangers, Boston Bruins, and Montreal Canadians, were Canadians.

There were also influential Americans behind hockey's growth, most notably Charles Adams, who created the country's first pro team, the Boston Bruins. And while James Norris, a pioneer in American hockey, was born and educated in Canada, he moved to Chicago at 19 years old and spent a lifetime enriching American hockey: He owned the Detroit Red Wings; one son, James D. Norris, was co-owner of the Chicago Black Hawks; his other son, Bruce, ran the Red Wings after his father's death in 1952.

Most of the big American names in hockey were wealthy men with an interest in sport and making money. Adams was a grocery magnate in New England; the Bruins got their name because the mascot for Adams' grocery was a bear. James Norris was a tycoon in grain, cattle, and shipping in the Midwest, and had interests in banking, railroads, and milling. Through their influence, the game prospered and the arenas in which it was played became temples to sport—and to commerce.

Professional basketball got the chance to prosper because it was part of that commerce. In 1946, the newly formed Boston Celtics played in Boston Garden, home of the Boston Bruins. The New York Knickerbockers played in Madison Square Garden, home of the New York Rangers. The Philadelphia Warriors would play in Philadelphia Arena, where the Philadelphia Rockets of the American Hockey League played.

The relationships were closer than tenants renting out space. Most of the corporations that owned and operated the hockey teams also owned the new basketball teams, sometimes with one man in charge.

This was the case with the Boston, New York, and Philadelphia teams. In some cities a virtual monopoly existed. For 27 years until his death in 1964, Walter Brown was general manager of the Boston Garden; for 18 of those years he was president of the Boston Celtics, and president of the Bruins for 13 years.

A good lease in a modern arena today can make the difference between a team earning a profit or not. In the 1940s, when survival was even more tenuous, a good relationship could determine if a team played that very night . . . or ever.

"I've read that Walter Brown didn't even like basketball," according to Gregory McQuade, who conducts historical tours of the Garden for the Bruins. "He bought the team because he wanted events to constantly fill out the Garden schedule.

"Once he brought the Ice Capades in, forgetting that his Celtics had a home game. Being a big skating fan, the Ice Capades started on time at eight o'clock, and the Celtics laced on their sneakers around midnight. But he was committed to their survival. The Celtics were on the verge of folding in those early years, and Walter Brown stepped in with his own money."

In today's high-priced world of sports, there are still many close relationships between the two sports. Basketball's New York Knicks and hockey's Rangers are owned by one company, Paramount Communications; Washington's Bullets and Capitals are owned by one man, Abe Pollin. The Rangers and Knicks, of course, play in Madison Square Garden, also owned by Paramount; the Bullets and Capitals play at the Capital Center, also owned by Pollin.

And there is another joint ownership in basketball and hockey—the Cleveland Cavaliers in the NBA and San Jose Sharks in the NHL. Both were purchased by the Gund brothers, Gordon and George III. At first glance, it seems to be an odd pairing: teams in California and Ohio. But it started in Cleveland, ancestral home of the Gund family.

The Gunds originally bought an NHL team based in Cleveland, the Barons. That name may not be familiar; it wasn't around long. The Barons began as the Oakland Seals in 1967. That was the year the NHL expanded from 6 to 12 teams. Some of those new arrivals found success. The Pittsburgh Penguins and Philadelphia Flyers would win the Stanley Cup; the Los Angeles Kings and St. Louis Blues would win respectability. But the Minnesota North Stars and the Seals won little.

The Seals especially had trouble. The team went into receivership in 1970, was purchased by Charles O. Finley and became the California Golden Seals, struggling every inch of the way. To avoid seeing the first franchise in their history fold, the NHL took over the team after two-and-a-half years, and sold it in 1975 to Mel Swig. Swig moved the Seals to Cleveland, and sold it to the Gunds in 1977.

The team—renamed the Barons in Cleveland—continued to do poorly, and was merged with the Minnesota North Stars in 1978. The unusual move had the NHL's blessing. Times were tough in the league. Competition from the rival World Hockey Association (WHA) drove up players' salaries and further taxed the weaker clubs. Even before the Barons/North Stars merger, the Kansas City Scouts—an expansion team—folded and transferred to Denver, pausing as the Colorado Rockies before moving to New Jersey as the Devils. The two leagues merged in 1979, four WHA teams joining the NHL.

But prosperity did not greet the hybrid Stars, and the Gunds wanted out. Under threat of moving the team, they worked a sweet deal: They would sell the team and be guaranteed the new San Jose team in the league's 1991 expansion, could select 20 unprotected young players from the North Stars, and also collected Minnesota's share of the expansion fees for both new teams in 1991, estimated to be $6.7 million. Meanwhile, the Gunds purchased the Cleveland Cavaliers in 1983. They also bought the Coliseum, where the team plays.

As is the case with so many owners of teams today, the Gunds had no history in sports before their first purchase. George III is a financier in San Francisco; Gordon, a venture capitalist in Princeton, New Jersey. Most of their money came from their father. *Forbes* estimated the family's worth in 1992 as over $1.6 billion, most of it coming originally from beer, coffee, real estate, and banking.

There does not appear to be a family interest in sports, and nothing in George or Gordon's background suggests either could run a successful franchise. But they learned enough in their Cleveland Barons/Minnesota North Stars experience to know they wanted to start afresh with an expansion team in California. And they had the money to absorb whatever that lesson cost. If they also learned enough to be successful in San Jose remains to be seen; the team began in the 1991–1992 season.

It is not too early to see their effects in Cleveland. They took a team that was historically one of the weakest in the NBA and made a dramatic impact. They accomplished that by making the kinds of moves that good businessmen make—they hired smart, experienced people to operate their new business. For general manager they selected Wayne Embry, a former NBA center who had been successful in building the Milwaukee

Bucks into a championship team in the 1970s. They hired Lenny Wilkens, also a former player, as coach; Wilkens lead Seattle to the league championship in the 1979–1980 season.

Improvement was slow but still impressive. In the 1991–1992 season the Cavs finished second behind Chicago in their division, and were runners-up to the Bulls in the Eastern Division playoffs. The change was not lost on their fans. The season the Gunds took over, the team averaged slightly fewer than 4,000 customers per home game. For the 1991–1992 season, that figure was up over 16,500.

The Cleveland Cavaliers and the Gunds are one of the nice success stories in sports. They prove that an owner doesn't have to be born and bred in a sport to succeed.

Of course, it must be noted that their success came in professional basketball, a sport with 5 players on each side and active rosters of 12. According to *Financial World's* 1992 report, operating expenses for the Cavs was only $29.2 million in 1991, compared with $46.8 million for the Cleveland Indians baseball team and $51.6 million for the Browns football team. Turning around an NFL franchise or one in major league baseball is a more formidable task.

But there are consistencies that run through all sports. One is the importance of a team either owning the place where it plays or having a good business relationship with those who do. It affects everything from the cut on concessions to the priority choices when filling out the building's schedule. The Gunds bought the Coliseum when they bought the Cavs, ending any of these conflicts. Even more important, the Gunds had enough capital to rebuild, and to stick around and enjoy the success.

Simply put, functioning successfully in sports today requires an enormous amount of money. It can be other people's money, but sufficient backing must be in place. And for those going it alone, a word of warning: Not any millionaire can play in this league. Professional sports has become a game for people with deep pockets.

Look at the owners of big-league sports teams. Nearly 25 percent of them are among the richest people in the country, names found right along with the Gund family on *Forbes'* list of America's 400 wealthiest people. A few of them—Larry Tisch, who owns half the New York Giants; Portland Trailblazers owner Paul Allen; and Ted Turner, who owns the Atlanta Braves and Atlanta Hawks—even made *Fortune's* billionaire list.

Success never comes quickly or easily in sports. Any franchise needs to be rich enough to fail first.

4

The Legacy

Professional sports sought prosperity through most of the first half of this century in the large centers of population: New York, Philadelphia, and Boston in the East; Chicago and St. Louis in the Midwest.

All four major sports were establishing themselves as business enterprises, trying to attract as many fans as possible. It was a matter of numbers. The pro game still appealed primarily to a working-class audience. But after seeking those people in the Cantons and Decaturs of the early years, leagues turned to the diversity of larger populations for enough support to help baseball and hockey and the other sports grow.

From the start there were exceptions. A few of those first franchises so fixed themselves in the hearts and minds of their communities that survival was guaranteed. That was the Green Bay Packers' story. Even today this eastern Wisconsin city has fewer than 90,000 people, not big enough to be considered for a franchise even in the 1940s or 1950s. It is also only the 67th largest television market in the United States, the most important factor in determining the worthiness of host cities in the contemporary world of sports.

The smart thinking in those years was the bigger the city the better, and load on as many teams as the population would support. New York had three baseball teams; Boston, Chicago, and Philadelphia, two each. All four had football teams; for a while New York and Chicago had two. Of course, they had basketball teams and hockey teams as well.

Somewhere between then and now, the big cities lost their control. Today, there are teams in Hartford and Salt Lake City, in Orlando and Portland and Buffalo. And those cities that don't have a team want one. Teams still have a greater chance of making money in the larger population centers, but even the smaller cities want to have a shot.

Look at who was bidding for the new NFL franchise, scheduled to begin play in 1995: Baltimore, Charlotte, Jacksonville, Memphis, Oakland, Sacramento, St. Louis, San Antonio, Nashville, Raleigh-Durham, and Honolulu. Raleigh and Durham together have fewer than 300,000 people. And St. Louis has been losing its population for a century. The fourth-largest city in 1900 and still number eight in 1950, St. Louis had fallen to 34th by 1988, its population of 400,000 less than half its 1950 total. The city had one NFL team, which it lost to Phoenix after the 1988 season, yet it pushed hard for another, to complement its professional baseball and hockey teams.

Part of the reason teams are in such demand is that sports have cleaned themselves up. Fans took their lives in their hands to attend a baseball game at the turn of the century. And while arenas and stadiums continue to have rowdy fans, management has taken action. Security has been increased and liquor sales controlled, with alcohol-free "family" zones created and sales stopped late in the game. Such efforts have enjoyed success. An afternoon football or baseball game is an activity the entire family can enjoy. An evening at the Great Western Forum or Madison Square Garden is considered a classy date, especially in some of the luxury boxes or special clubs.

But having a pro team in a city means more than providing another option for a Saturday night out. And while teams do generate revenue for a community, financial gain does not explain their appeal.

"It can't be because a major league team brings a town economic vitality," claims an article from 1992 in *Time* that discusses the threatened move of the Giants from San Francisco and that city's effort to keep the team:

> Teresa Serata, San Francisco's budget director, says she can document only a $3.1 million annual net gain from the Giants; the city's gross economic product is $30 billion, or 10,000 times as large. 'Opening a

branch of Macy's has a greater economic impact,' says Roger Noll, professor of economics at Stanford University. Besides, discretionary income is easily diverted. If there is no ball club, citizens will find another way to spend their discretionary income.

That Special Motive

So what is the attraction? Why are all these cities desperate for a team?

One big factor is civic pride. Places like Buffalo and Raleigh-Durham may have small populations relative to New York City and Chicago, but they think of themselves as metropolitan centers. And somehow, some time after flying beer bottles threatened the first baseball fans and cages protected the first basketball fans, professional teams became a badge of urban stature. Like having an art museum and a television station, and at least three pizza parlors that deliver within 30 minutes, no "real" city is now complete without a team.

Few cities have worked harder to land a major league baseball franchise than Buffalo. You remember Buffalo, the place with all the snow, the butt of all those Johnny Carson jokes on the old "Tonight" Show. The people of Buffalo are all too familiar with that image.

"Buffalo has had a chip on its shoulder for a long time about how it was perceived by the rest of the world," author Verlyn Klinkenborg told *The New York Times* in an article about the city's quest for more civic pride. Klinkenborg's book, *The Last Fine Time,* views changes in Buffalo through a family tavern.

It has gained some of that pride through its professional football and hockey teams, and with its 36th-place ranking it is the smallest television market to have two professional teams. But Buffalo has embarked on a near-religious crusade to land a baseball team. The showcase of that campaign was the building in 1988 of the $43-million stadium, Pilot Field.

Buffalo has a successful Class AAA franchise, the Bisons, known for its ability to draw large crowds without winning pennants. But they hunger for more.

"The dream that everyone in baseball shares is getting to the majors," says Robert Rich, owner of the Bisons. Rich, chairman of Rich Products, the frozen food company, is also the man behind Buffalo's effort. "It's the thing that everyone shares, including the shortstop in Appleton, Wisconsin, and every city with a minor league team."

Major league team—major league city. More and more people are making that leap of logic. Residents of cities with teams do. You can see it in the expression of those wearing team T-shirts, and caps sporting their team's logo. That look says "I'm from Toronto, home of the World Series champion Blue Jays, and I'm proud." Residents of cities pursuing teams long to experience that same feeling.

Can It Be Love?

It is mysterious, this connection between a fan and a team. Having a local team gives residents something of their very own to champion. And it's all so clean, unlike the tangled personal efforts in one's own life. Fans don't have the burden of performing well for big games, and aren't to blame when the team fails. Yet when the team wins, everybody shares in the victory.

So powerful is this bond that it often outlives the very athletes being adored. All across America, communities mourn the loss of sports teams. Brooklyn has never gotten over the Dodgers' flight to Los Angeles; it was forever reduced in stature by the team's move. Washington was so shaken by the loss of the Senators—twice—it continues to place itself in front of every line bidding for one of baseball's few expansions.

One of the saddest of all was the loss of Baltimore's Colts. Few cities ever expressed as much affection for a team as the people of Baltimore did toward their football team. And the team responded with eight division titles, three league championships, and a Super Bowl. Sellouts were the rule; 56 of them in a row in the late '50s and early '60s.

City and team seemed indelibly coupled. Players not only owned bars and restaurants in town, but many of them also lived there and were active in the community.

But after three straight division titles, the Colts dropped to 5–11 in 1978, the beginning of six years of frustration. And then on a March night in 1984, without any warning, Colts owner Bob Irsay had a fleet of moving trucks pull into the Memorial Stadium, packed away the Colts, and moved them to Indianapolis.

Quoting from Dan Shaughnessy's article in *The Boston Globe*:

> BALTIMORE—Employees reported to work and there was no furniture in the office—just a few telephones sitting on the floor. There was no equipment in the locker room, no weights in the weight room. The men from Mayflower were thorough. They even took the dumbbells.

Eight years later, the city had not recovered. The stadium was still there; flags along 33rd Street still read, "Give Baltimore the ball." Of the 34 branches of the Colts fan club, 22 remain. And the Baltimore Colts Band still plays all over the country, but no longer for the Colts team.

Baltimore is still a city in mourning. "I know it's not a matter of life and death, but when the Colts left, it was heartbreaking," John Zieman, president of the Colts band, told Shaughnessy. "I mean, the sun came up and Baltimore was still here the next day, but it took a while to get a grip on it. And I don't think some of us yet have a grip on it. Sundays now are empty. We feel violated."

These are strong sentiments, and their impact should not be diluted because the man expressing them happened to be tied to the team. That is a mistake non-fans often make, assuming that the intensity of team loyalty affects only those in one uniform or another.

Unfortunately, the people who run pro sports occasionally commit the same sin. They weigh the economic needs of team owners against the rights of the fans and grant permission for teams to change cities. The NFL ruled that way in 1984. After all, it reasoned, the Washington Redskins were just 30 minutes away along Interstate 95; Colts fans can root for them. Some did, but not the true loyalists.

Author and Baltimore resident Tom Clancy made his feelings clear: "I would rather sell my children to gypsies than root for the Redskins."

Sports. It is at once a business and an emotional experience, money and heart. Neither side of the duality can be dismissed, by the fan or the people in charge.

This very complexity helps attract owners who would seem to have enough in their lives without inviting the risks and aggravation of dealing with temperamental superstars, strikes called just before play-off time and a market already saturated by too many events. Yet they line up to take their chance.

In the pages that follow we will explore the forces that must be balanced for success. We will look closely at the entries on both sides of the ledger to see how they affect a team's ability to function in business and sports.

PART TWO

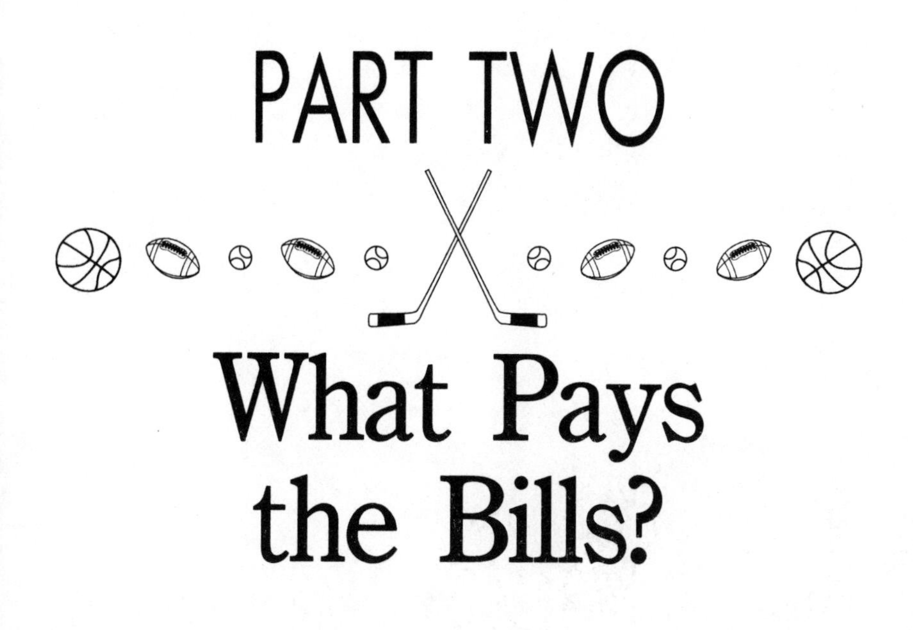

What Pays the Bills?

5

TV 1—Birth of a Giant

As the New York Giants and Baltimore Colts lined up for their National Football League championship game on the last Sunday of 1958, the number of fans awaiting the kickoff far exceeded the 64,185 gathered at Yankee Stadium.

The invisible factor was television.

The young medium had courted professional football cautiously for nearly a decade. Early evidence of a natural match was not conclusive. The Los Angeles Rams televised all of their games in 1950, only to discover attendance for the year was nearly half that of a 1949 season without coverage. Not until 1956 did the league sign its first network contract, and that came with safeguards reflecting the Los Angeles lesson: All games were blacked out within 50 miles of the host city.

Still, attendance throughout the league was up in those years since television began exposing the game to its wider audience, an impressive

11 percent in 1957. Fans across the country liked watching the quick, hard-hitting action from the comfort of their own living rooms.

But televising pro football was unfamiliar ground; no one was quite sure what lay ahead. The 1958 game was only the third NFL championship to be aired nationally, with neither of the first two qualifying as classics. CBS, hoping for cliff-hangers, got routs; New York demolished Chicago in 1956, 47–7, and Detroit was equally rude to Cleveland a year later, 50–14. The new NFL rule that so tempted television, calling for overtime to decide post-season games tied at the end of regulation, was relegated to pregame chatter.

And the 1958 title game began poorly. The Colts took a 14–3 lead into halftime, and threatened on their opening drive after intermission. Their march to New York's three-yard-line had CBS sweating; 21–3 would beckon another romp, and a flurry of channel switching. But New York's defense held, and moments later the Giants struck to make it a new ball game, 14–10.

The Giants went ahead in the fourth quarter, 17–14, on a Charley Conerly to Frank Gifford pass. But now it was Baltimore's turn. With 1:56 left to play, quarterback Johnny Unitas began picking the Giants' pass defense apart. He connected with halfback Lenny Moore, then end Ray Berry, and Berry again.

The Colts reached New York's 13-yard-line with seconds remaining. Steve Myhra's field goal tied the score and sent the game into overtime. The first team to score by any means would be the NFL champion.

Suddenly it was historic—pro sport's first sudden-death overtime. And television was there. People not even interested in football in 1958 would years later claim to have seen that game. It was an easy lie; they didn't have to be in New York, just at home, watching the game on television. What happened that afternoon dramatically impacted on pro football.

The Giants won the coin toss and chose to receive. But they could not move the ball, and punted to the Colts' 20-yard-line.

All eyes turned to John Unitas. The man who only three years earlier was playing semi-pro ball for $6 a game was suddenly at the center of professional football, the center of the entire American sports world.

Unitas proved unflappable. He handed off to halfback L.G. Dupre for ten yards and a first down. Dupre got three more on the ground, and Unitas passed to fullback Alan Ameche for another first down. Then, after another Dupre run, Unitas was sacked. On third and long, he looked downfield for Lenny Moore, but Moore was covered. Spotting Ray Berry, Unitas realized the end was short of the first-down marker. In-

credibly, as the Baltimore line held out the Giants, Unitas waved for Berry to go a little deeper, then calmly threw him the ball.

A 21-yard run by Ameche and 12-yard pass to Berry gave Baltimore first and goal at the nine, well within Myhra's field-goal range. But Unitas just kept hammering at the Giants' defense; a short pass to tight end Jim Mutscheller reached the one-yard-line. The next play has been immortalized by television, the images run over and over in the minds of football fans much too young to have seen it: Unitas taking the snap from center and jamming the ball into his fullback's gut; the Colts' line driving the Giants back on their heels; Alan "The Horse" Ameche, head lowered, charging untouched into the end zone.

What better way to promote a sport and a medium! It was the first glorious moment in a partnership that now, 35 years later, appears to have been conceived in Fort Knox.

Sports has qualities our daily lives lack. First, it is finite. Most of what we encounter began before yesterday and will not be resolved till past tomorrow. In sports, nearly every game has a winner and a loser—and real heroes, athletes who faced the challenge of the moment and drove on to victory.

Focusing on these qualities is what popularized the sports sections of newspapers early this century. Other than obituaries, only sports articles guaranteed readers a resolution. And no other section supplied a hero and a goat with each story. Radio came along in the 1920s to offer the same attractions, only faster. Fans no longer had to await the morning paper to thrill to the exploits of their favorite athletes. Dramatic pictures painted in the words of golden-throated announcers came streaming from wood-paneled boxes even as events unfolded.

Then came television—instant drama with pictures. But as good as TV sports was for the fan, it was more important for broadcasting. Sports was the perfect program for a medium desperate for something to put on the air.

The first carefully arranged demonstration of a television broadcast into a home was in 1930, a half-hour program beamed from two stations in New Jersey to the West Side of New York. The public was intrigued, but not excited. Something else was needed, something big and spontaneous. Combat was reshaping the world, in Ethiopia and then in Spain; that would have made for perfect programming. But it would be Vietnam before television could properly exploit war.

By 1939, technology had freed transmissions from the studio, landing anything remotely newsworthy on television. A fashion show; the visit to New York of England's King George VI and Queen Elizabeth; President Franklin Roosevelt's speech at the World's Fair in Flushing, New York. All were television firsts. But sports was better. Sports was news, and yet it was scheduled well in advance. And while everybody knew where and when an event was going to happen, the outcome was always in doubt. That would unfold in real time, before the eyes of the viewer.

On May 17, 1939, the first sporting event was aired, a collegiate baseball game between Columbia and Princeton, from Baker Field at the northern tip of Manhattan; Princeton won in ten innings, 2–1. In June came the first prizefight, Lou Nova's TKO of Max Baer in New York City. August brought the first professional baseball game, between Cincinnati and Brooklyn from Ebbets Field, followed by the first college football game, Waynesburg College at Fordham, and finally the first pro football game, with the Philadelphia Eagles visiting the Brooklyn Dodgers.

Were events of note only happening in New York? No, but all the equipment was there. Early television had managed to get out of the studio, but not out of town.

Successful as these early broadcasts were, it took more for television sports to impact upon the American psyche. A perfect combination of event and exposure was necessary to create an explosion of excitement. That explosion occurred first in baseball. It was 1951, when viewers of a rare national broadcast happened upon a play-off game between the Giants and the Dodgers. By chance, the game was one of baseball's all-time classics, won in the bottom of the ninth inning by the Giants when Bobby Thompson hit his dramatic home run off of Ralph Branca. Seven years later, a similar explosion occurred in football; that was Baltimore's overtime win in New York.

For both sports, it was history. And television was there, not simply to report it, but to present the entire spectacle, as if the viewer were at the scene. It was faster than the newspaper and more complete than radio.

Eventually, television would add another element, one that would ultimately change sports as nothing before had: It would pour money into sports and make the people involved rich. That spiral of activity began in 1946, with a $75,000 contract to locally broadcast games of the New York Yankees, then the most successful team in baseball. It was a modest beginning, at a time when television viewers were still too few to be important.

In his book, *Baseball and Billions,* Andrew Zimbalist reports:

> When NBC provided the first live network coverage of the World Series in 1949, fewer than 12 percent of U.S. households had television sets. By 1953 fifteen of the sixteen clubs had local television contracts, and ABC introduced the first network game-of-the-week format. The share of U.S. households with televisions grew rapidly throughout the 1950s, reaching 67 percent (34.9 million households) in 1955 and 87 percent (45.8 million households) in 1960.

According to Zimbalist, when the Yankees signed that first contract in 1946, radio and television combined contributed only 3 percent of major league baseball's revenues. That figure rose to 16.8 percent by 1956, and continued to increase through the years until in 1990 television money represented more than half of baseball's yearly earnings. By that year, 98 percent of U.S. households—or about 92 million—had at least one television set.

The story is nearly identical for football and basketball; broadcasting monies amount to about half—or even more—of their overall revenues. Only hockey, whose history with national television can only be described as spotty, has thus far been left out of the party.

A Game of Numbers

Like all business, broadcasting exists to make as much profit as possible. But early expectations in radio were modest: Create programming that people wanted to hear, and they would purchase radios. Not until the 1930s did advertising become part of radio. By the time television came along, the economic groundwork was laid.

Today, sports and television coexist in a high-priced equation. The leagues of the major sports sell the rights to broadcast their games for millions of dollars each season. The networks in turn sell advertising by the half-minute to sponsors on a national, regional, and local level. The sponsors, confident that sports reaches "the right" customers for their products, pay hundreds of thousands of dollars for their flashes of exposure.

The actual numbers are staggering. In 1992, the three major networks—CBS, NBC, and ABC—and cable's TNT and ESPN were entering the third year of four-year contracts with the NFL that brought the league about $3.6 billion over that period. At the same time, Major

League Baseball was in the middle of four-year pacts with ESPN and CBS that earned $400 million and $1.06 billion, respectively. Four-year NBA contracts with NBC and Turner—expiring in 1994—total $875 million. Hockey was not completely left out; the NHL's five-year contract with ABC and ESPN, signed in 1992, was worth nearly $80 million.

And those figures only represent revenue from national contracts, negotiated by leagues with over-the-air and cable networks. Deals cut between individual teams and local stations are crucial in sports, and weigh heavily on a team's financial success or failure. Big markets mean big money. It is no coincidence that the two biggest population centers—New York City and Los Angeles—have the wealthiest teams. According to *Financial World*'s 1993 report on team values, four of the seven most valuable professional sports teams were located in those cities.

Major League Baseball, because of the number of games in its season and its tradition of local coverage, does best. Local television, radio, and cable generated more than $350 million for the 28 teams in 1993. (The New York Yankees alone reportedly hold a cable TV contract that brings in over $40 million a year for 12 years.) Outside of pre-season games, no local television exists for the NFL. For the NBA, revenues from local radio, cable, and over-the-air TV come to over $100 million each year. And while hockey's local television figures are rarely released by individual teams, revenues ranging from $1.5 million in small markets to a high in the $10-million range for Boston and New York have been reported.

The change from 1950, when the networks first got involved with sports for thousands of dollars, to 1990, when their multimillion-dollar contracts constituted the single most important force in sports, occurred smoothly. The progression went from contract to contract, up the money ladder. And all along the way, everybody was benefiting. Teams made money; networks grew wealthy; sponsors sold more product; fans saw more games; and eventually, athletes got very wealthy.

How and why this mutual admiration relationship has existed is complex. To understand it, we look at one network—the American Broadcasting Company. For a little historical background on the ABC story, we turn to Benjamin Rader's book, *In Its Own Image.*

Rader describes the creation of today's network sports divisions as beginning with ABC in 1959. Before that time, sports came under news departments, and was forced to compete with that most favored entity for equipment, talent, and time. ABC placed an emphasis on sports programming that lifted it out of a subservient role, and the decision helped the network climb from third place in ratings in 1960 to number one in 1976.

The network accomplished this by placing creative people in responsible positions. Among them were sports enthusiast Tom Moore as head of programming, and Edgar Scherick, a sports programmer who helped create baseball's "Game of the Week" for NBC. And there was the Gillette factor.

An Offer They Couldn't Refuse

NBC, then the leader in TV sports, was eager to rid itself of its famed Friday night boxing because of the sport's unsavory reputation. The Gillette Safety Razor Company—the show's longtime sponsor—wanted another sports outlet and so promised ABC all the company's television advertising except what it had already contracted to NBC for the World Series. The figure was $8.5 million.

"That was more money than ABC spent on sports during the network's entire history," according to Rader. "The $8.5 million suddenly placed ABC in a position to bid for the rights to big-league baseball, pro football, and college football."

First came the acquisition of NCAA football for the 1960–1961 season, an association that still exists with the network today. Gillette money also initially financed "Wide World of Sports," which has become the longest-running sports series on television.

But ABC was doing more than adding programming, event by event. It was creating a formidable sports division that was strong and independent—something new in television. Much credit for the division's success went to Roone Arledge, hired by Scherick from NBC in 1960.

Arledge's skill at obtaining rights was unparalleled. ABC soon carried the Professional Golfer's Association championship, the U.S. Open, the U.S. Women's Open, the U.S. Men's Amateur, and the Amateur Athletic Union's annual track and field meet. He also became a master at dealing with the intricacies of Olympic politics and helped to make ABC "the network of the Olympic Games."

But nothing has brought ABC more attention for a longer period than "Monday Night Football." In 1993 this phenomenon of prime-time sports marked its 23d season. It's hard to imagine that the network had to be coerced into giving the program a try.

Prime-time football was the idea of Pete Rozelle, NFL commissioner from 1960 to 1989 and the man credited with carrying the shotgun for the arranged wedding of football and television. Rozelle realized that confining his product to Sunday afternoon doubleheaders threatened overexposure to one audience and denied exposure to others. He was able to persuade CBS to experiment with four Monday night games in 1966. Viewer response was strong, but the network was not convinced it would last. "Preempt Doris Day? Are you out of your mind?" CBS was reported to have said. NBC was equally unenthusiastic.

The powers at ABC weren't hot for the project either. But this was 1970; the network was still in third place in the prime-time ratings, though closer than it had been. And Roone Arledge had been successful in using sports to help cut the gap.

There was also the threat that Rozelle might sell his proposal to Sports Network Incorporated, the fledgling independent venture of Howard Hughes. Losing programming to another network is a major force in TV's decision making, then and now. Terms of the final deal reflected how much he wanted a contract with one of the major networks in 1970. While Hughes offered more money, Rozelle sold the 13-week package to ABC for $8 million, less than half the rate paid by CBS for its Sunday afternoon NFL games.

"Monday Night Football" was an immediate and immense success. It is difficult to know what part that success played in catapulting ABC to the top of the prime-time ratings by 1976. Other factors were the network's concentration on light comedy aimed at a young audience, especially "Three's Company," "Laverne and Shirley," and "Happy Days," the top-rated show of the time. But the impact of "Monday Night Football" is undeniable. Because of the length of games, the program represents more than 13 percent of ABC's weekly prime-time schedule. In times when it is difficult to come up with a 30-minute situation comedy that will last one season, ABC maintains a three-hour ratings provider that has been on the air for 23 years, and that ranked sixth in prime-time ratings in the 1991 season. That kind of prolonged success helped lead to Arledge's promotion to the president of ABC News. Today he is, obviously, one of the most powerful men in television.

But why should sports on television have such power? The primary reason is money—advertising money.

Sports delivers a specific audience for which networks can match specific advertisers. Research has shown that mostly men watch sports. Even the relatively primitive research of 40 years ago made that clear to the networks. That was why Gillette and breweries such as Pabst

Blue Ribbon, Miller, and Falstaff were so involved with early sports on radio and then television. These products are primarily for men, or boys looking forward to being men. Gillette ran special promotions at World Series time, one year packaging tiny baseball encyclopedias with their shavers, another year a small 33 r.p.m. record of historic baseball events. Many a boy started shaving early just to get such a prize.

Today advertising research is more exact, permitting a more narrow targeting of markets. The new level of accuracy in ratings hurts baseball; ratings tell advertisers the sport "skews old." This means baseball appeals more to the "35 and older group" of men, who are less attractive to many clients since they buy less.

Pro football is more attractive because the men watching that sport are within that 18-to-49 category most attractive to advertisers. Gone as a constant major player is Gillette, although it resurfaced early in 1993 to introduce a new line of products; the breweries remain. Automobiles are big, as are the manufacturers of athletic shoes.

With "Monday Night Football," the ante is raised even higher. The majority of professional football is played in the afternoon; Monday night is prime time—the most important part of the television schedule—the period when advertisers pay the highest fees to get across their message. "Monday Night Football" is the only regularly scheduled prime-time sports event on television.

"I do not think there is any question that the most glamorous package in all of network sports is 'Monday Night Football,' " says Dennis Swanson, president of ABC Sports since 1986, when Arledge was appointed head of ABC News.

"Our position with 'Monday Night Football' vis-a-vis the rest of prime time TV has actually improved in the last few years. There have been fewer defections by viewers . . . to the expansion of all the other options, than there have been from other entertainment programs in prime time.

"We realize we're competing in prime time against some of the strongest entertainment vehicles the competition can throw at us. We are not in a protective environment where it is just sports viewing in the afternoon," Swanson says.

Certain phrases in Swanson's statement jump out, and refer to factors that spell success and failure in television. "Defections of viewers" and "competing in prime time" are major considerations for every network today. These considerations created a condition approaching war among the three major networks, especially in the 1960s and 1970s. Toward the end of that period, cable TV joined the fight.

Pro football was the hottest property. The feeling was that no network could survive without some piece of the pro football pie. This gave staggering leverage to Commissioner Pete Rozelle. Each contract was bigger than the one before. In 1977, dealing with the networks separately, he negotiated a four-year package worth $656 million. Each team in the league earned nearly $6 million a year, which was more than their gate receipts for the same period. And it didn't stop there. Four years later, Rozelle negotiated a five-year deal worth $2 billion; this earned each club $14 million annually.

There are many reasons why professional football has made such a perfect match with television, and why the union of sport and medium are such an attractive package for advertisers. First, as we have seen, the demographics are good; football fans are the people advertisers want to reach.

But it goes further than that. Football really needs television. The game is not easy to follow in person, especially in huge stadiums that place fans far from the action, for three hours and often in poor weather. Television, with its many camera angles, its telephoto lenses, instant replay, and slow motion, has the technical equipment to dissect the game. And as the game has become more complex, with its multiple formations and masking defenses designed to deceive and confuse the offense, television provides experts to explain what is happening; the three hours it takes to run the single hour of playing time also affords infinite time for such discussions.

And football has made an effort to make this marriage work as well. Official time-outs increased over the years, providing more commercial time units to sell. When television's instant replays showed too many wrong calls by officials, the league experimented with an instant replay of its own to review the officials, then abandoned the rule in the light of severe criticism. As the television audience went from small black-and-white screens to giant color sets, uniforms got more colorful; players' names appeared over their numbers, helping to keep the viewer more informed.

Even the league schedulers get involved. From the very beginning of "Monday Night Football," the league promised to provide exciting matchups for its prime-time showcase. And that promise is as good today as it was in 1970. Look at the 1993 season: 1992 playoff teams filled 27 of the 36 available spots in the 18-week schedule, beginning with a matchup of the two teams that won the previous two Super Bowls, the Dallas Cowboys and Washington Redskins.

"All of the national broadcast games are strong," says NFL Commissioner Paul Tagliabue. "We made a concerted effort [to build up] all the national games."

But possibly most important, the sport had the right people in charge when it counted. Bert Bell, the NFL's first commissioner, watched the slumping attendance in Los Angeles after the Rams experimented with unlimited television broadcasts, and became a staunch proponent of the blackout rule. Pete Rozelle, his successor, had a masterful understanding of TV's potential power. While other sports permitted their teams to negotiate television contracts individually, he fought Congress and his own league for a better way.

The Broadcasting Act of 1961 permitted professional sports franchises to negotiate the sale of national broadcast rights as a single economic unit. And nobody did that better than Pete Rozelle, main champion of the act.

Not only did negotiating for the league give him unprecedented leverage with the networks, thereby bringing the teams more money than they possibly could have earned on their own, but by subsequently splitting the money equally among the teams he kept the entire league healthy and helped negate the effect of large market/small market pressures. This kept teams like Green Bay and Minnesota competing with the New Yorks and the Dallases.

The NFL's television policy was important in the 1960s and 1970s, and crucial in the 1990s, a time when large market/small market pressures were gravely felt in other sports. All four of the major team sports share national television contracts, but the impact is greatest in football, where that revenue constitutes such a high percentage of the teams' yearly income—an estimated 64 percent in 1992. Local TV, on the other hand, which is almost never shared, is virtually meaningless in football; an average of about $400,000 per team comes from local preseason broadcasts. (Baseball does share its receipts from pay television.)

The money generated from local TV in baseball, basketball, and hockey, as we'll see, often spells the difference between the haves and the have-nots in those sports.

Rights Fees Soar

The beginning of the rapidly increasing television contracts can be traced to the Broadcasting Act of 1961, not only for the NFL, but for all of pro football. Rights fees rose because of it, and the resulting revenues had a direct bearing on the success of the new American Football League (AFL), which began playing in 1960. It was television money that enabled the AFL to compete with the NFL for airtime as well as top players coming out of college.

"Rozelle ignited the spiraling inflation in television contracts by negotiating an annual $4.5 million contract with CBS in 1962," reports Benjamin Rader. A two-year, $14-million pact signed in 1964 accelerated the issue.

"Within only two hours of learning that CBS had won the NFL rights, Carl Lindemann, head of NBC Sports, sat down in the offices of the American Football League," says Rader, describing the negotiations that led to NBC's funding the AFL in 1964 to the tune of $42 million for five years. It was a contract, he says, that was five times what ABC had been paying, and that "overnight . . . wiped out the bush-league image of the AFL."

And it was only the beginning; the contract numbers for the 1970s and 1980s indicate that. As ABC's Swanson makes clear, the concern over remaining competitive with the other networks for desirable programming is never far from the minds of those running ABC, NBC, and CBS.

" 'Monday Night Football' and the NFL are special," says Swanson. "It is tough to find vehicles from an advertising standpoint, to reach 18- to 49-year-old men, and 'Monday Night Football' has been the number-one 18- to 49-male vehicle in all of television."

And yet, as rights fees continued to skyrocket, somewhere in the 1980s the mechanism that made it okay to spend whatever was necessary to keep inventory suddenly got rusty. ABC read the signs early.

It happened with the Olympics, an event with which that network had become closely associated. And with good reason. ABC's coverage of the games in 1968, 1972, and 1976 were major factors in the network's rise to the top in prime-time ratings. The individual most responsible was Roone Arledge. His ability to secure rights, and the scope and expertise of his productions, earned the praise of the world and the rewards to his network.

But for the 1980 Summer Games in Moscow, the cost of rights was up to $85 million; CBS purchased them, but the boycott ended their involvement. ABC re-entered the competition in 1984 by bidding a staggering $225 million for the Summer Games in Los Angeles and $91.5 million for the Winter Games at Sarajevo. For 1988's Calgary

Olympics, ABC bid again and won the rights, but they cost $309 million. The Games were an artistic success for the network and an economic disaster.

Dennis Swanson says of buying the rights to sports programming:

> It's not a complicated process. You figure out how much money you think you can generate from the broadcast and then you figure out what it will cost you to produce. You build yourself in a little profit line and what is left is what you have to bid. If that does not get it done, then you should walk away.
>
> ABC Sports built a great reputation over a number of years through its involvement with the Olympics. Though it was fun to go to Calgary and produce the Games, we lost millions of dollars even though the Games received high ratings.
>
> We tried to buy both Olympics in 1992 for $500 million, but we were outbid. We have gotten to a point where 80 cents of every dollar we spend at ABC Sports goes to rights fees. We could cut a camera here or drop a graphic there but it doesn't have much effect.

ABC's bowing out of Olympic coverage was not the only effect of the incredible expense of broadcasting the games in a slow economy. NBC, which paid $400 million for the Barcelona Games, suffered heavy losses in 1992, largely due to the network's disastrous experiment with TripleCast. As a result, any use of Pay-Per-View or basic cable for 1994 is expected to be only for minor events.

Those kinds of figures, and the havoc they would wreak, were anticipated by the International Olympic Committee (IOC), and led to its changing the very schedule of the games. In October of 1986 the IOC voted to divide the games into alternating two-year cycles, starting with the 1994 Winter Games in Norway. "This was done for a variety of financial reasons," said *Sports Illustrated* in 1987, "but mainly to ease the troubles that American TV networks have had in getting advertisers to buy time on their sports programs—not just the Olympics, but all sports programs."

More and more, we see business driving sports.

6

TV 2—Growth to Success and Trouble

The decision to purchase rights for a particular event, as ABC's Dennis Swanson suggests, is not a complicated matter. But neither is it so simple. A network starts with the appeal of that event. Obviously, the more attractive the event, the easier it is to sell.

" 'Monday Night Football' is unique. It's appointment television—people plan their weekly schedule around it. And it's prime time. No other sports event has all that going for it."

The speaker is Bill Cella, vice-president of sales for ABC Sports. His job is to sell ad space for "Monday Night Football," along with the rest of ABC's sports lineup. To do it well—like any good salesman—he must understand what makes his product desirable. Only then can he market it to the right customer.

"All NFL is great, but none of it has the cachet of 'Monday Night Football,' " says Cella. "The viewer is upscale, with a lot of disposable income. We sell demographics, and the demographics of 'Monday Night Football' are good: mostly men, 18 to 49. That means young families with more buying power, rather than 50 and older viewers on a fixed income. That's what the advertiser wants, a viewer who can afford to buy whatever products are being sold."

What other events are particularly good? The Super Bowl, of course; that is in a class by itself. The properties in ABC's schedule that rank with "Monday Night Football," according to Cella, are the Rose Bowl, U.S. Open Golf, the Indianapolis 500, and horse racing's Triple Crown, especially the Kentucky Derby.

"The Kentucky Derby is one of the most expensive events we sell," says Cella, pointing out that while it costs an advertiser $250,000 for a single 30-second unit of "Monday Night Football" and about $180,000 for a unit of the Derby, CPM, or "cost per thousand viewers," for the race is higher.

"This is a CPM business," he says, explaining that he has 18 three-hour games to sell each season of "Monday Night Football," and only three 90-minute races in the Triple Crown. In the "cost efficient" terms of television, "Monday Night Football" comes in at a CPM of $15 to $16, while the events of the Triple Crown are $18 to $19.

And who buys? Even the Budweisers and Millers have found the airtime of the Triple Crown too rich to breathe. Such heady stuff is left to automobile advertising, to luxury items, airlines, insurance companies, and computer manufacturers.

"Horse racing is one of the most upscale sports we have," says Cella. "It's a preferred audience. While it skews older than pro football, which could be a problem, it is very upscale, which is good."

Unlike teams in competition, advertisers purchasing television time for high-profile events are not playing on a level field. It's business, and in business regular customers always get the best deals. Regular customers here would be the ones who purchase multiple units in each event of the season. Television calls these customers "franchise advertisers."

"All car companies and all beer people pay a similar rate," says Cella. The others fluctuate, depending on frequency. What event and when they want to advertise also affects their rate. Inventory is more expensive around the holidays, when everyone wants his product before the public, than it is early in the season.

And conditions in which a spot runs change the price of a unit. Exclusivity is especially costly. If Nike wants to be the only running shoe for a half or a quarter, that costs more. Car companies do that and so do beers. Anheuser-Busch has had exclusive exposure at various times in recent years on all pro bowling broadcasts on ABC and NBC, for Wimbledon and the French Open on NBC, for all boxing, for the NBA on TNT, and for several track and field competitions on ABC. Miller has had exclusivity for the Indy 500 on ABC, for pro basketball on CBS and TBS, and Major League Baseball on NBC.

Networks sell time based on a projected audience for that program, and what percent of the entire television-viewing audience that number represents. The greater the share that is expected, the more costly the unit of airtime. "Monday Night Football," for example, usually gets a 16 or 17 rating. The number in a rating represents the percentage of total U.S. households with television sets, estimated by Nielsen in 1992 to be about 93.1 million. Just what share of active viewers that number represents depends on how many sets were in use at the time the broadcast is aired, but a 17 rating might translate to 25 percent or even 30 percent of the viewing audience. That's good, and one reason a "Monday Night Football" commands $250,000 and more a unit.

Special conditions also increase the value of an event. Take the 1993 Sugar Bowl. During November, anyone who purchased a unit in the 1993 Sugar Bowl expected to pay $100,000 per 30-second unit. But as the game drew closer, it became clear it could be the star attraction of New Year's Day, pitting the number-one-ranked University of Miami Hurricanes against number-two-ranked Alabama. The game determining that matchup was the Southeastern Conference championship, played between Florida and Alabama on Saturday, December 9. Any advertiser who bought time by the close of business on Friday, December 8, still got the $100,000/unit cost. But on Monday, after Alabama defeated Florida and set up number one versus number two, a unit of the Sugar Bowl cost $200,000, or more.

All events are sold that way, though the scale is usually smaller. The greater the projected audience, the more expensive the time. And in certain situations, networks even guarantee specific ratings. Not for everyone, but for some franchise advertisers; the beers and automotives, the big ones, who buy two, three, or more units on each date during a season. These people sometimes get a little insurance policy.

"If one of those advertisers, back when we carried the whole baseball season, bought three 30-second spots a game over the 26-game regular season, I might guarantee him a three and one-half rating," says Cella. "If those games didn't deliver and there was a shortfall at the end of the season, I would balance that out by giving him free units in another telecast, or some other event."

Of course, nobody got a guarantee for the Sugar Bowl; nobody gives guarantees for big, single events. It's just too chancy. Anything can happen to affect the ratings of one game.

In a Class by Itself

The exception is the Super Bowl. Nothing seems to affect the popularity of the Super Bowl. It is the biggest single event in all of American sports, the object of an estimated $8 billion worth of gambling around the world. Certainly it is the biggest recurring event on television. The game is so big that the rights are rotated; each year a different network carries it.

The Super Bowl was not born big. It wasn't even called the Super Bowl, not officially. That was the name used by the press as the second Sunday in January of 1967 drew closer. Roman numerals weren't added until Super Bowl V; I–IV were christened retroactively. What seemed most important back in June of 1966 was that the war between the rival American Football League and National Football League was over; it ended six years of competition for players that threatened bankruptcy for several of the weaker franchises. A game between the league champions was just a natural extension.

That first game, between the NFL's Green Bay Packers and AFL's Kansas City Chiefs, attracted only 61,000 people to the Los Angeles Coliseum, leaving 31,000 seats empty.

Things built from there. Every Super Bowl thereafter has sold out. The appeal to television audiences sets records. Of the 30 most popular shows ever to air, half are Super Bowl games. According to NBC, the 133.4 million who watched "some portion" of the 1993 game between Buffalo and Dallas made it the most watched program of all time, but that claim is hard to verify. "They use total viewer figures, a grossly inflated number," says Larry Hyams of ABC research, who says that the finales of "MASH," "Dallas," and "Roots" rate higher than any of the Super Bowls. "It's usually done by household ratings."

The 1982 game between Cincinnati and San Francisco earned the highest rating of any Super Bowl, a 49.1 for an audience share of 73. That means that 73 percent of the television sets in use that Sunday were tuned to at least six minutes of the Super Bowl. While "MASH" drew a rating of 60.2, "Dallas" a 53.3, and "Roots" a 51.1, no other sporting event comes close. But all those figures were compiled a decade ago, when fewer homes in America had television sets. Those ratings may have been higher, but they meant fewer viewers.

Because those numbers are so big, networks are able to charge advertisers awesome amounts during the national holiday that has become known as Super Bowl Sunday.

The early games were played in the afternoon, but kickoff is now early evening—6:18 EST in 1993—to get the bulk of the action in prime time for maximum exposure and maximum revenue. While a normal NFL broadcast is three hours, by the late 1980s, considering pregame and postgame festivities, the Super Bowl had stretched to twice that time. The price of airing a 30-second spot depended on where that spot would run, with projected rating numbers determining the charge. During the game, with a rating of 40 or 42, the price is highest; coming in at some early part of the pregame hoopla is lower.

"Our top rate was $875,000 for a 30-second unit during the game," says Cella of ABC, which last carried the game in 1991. "Not every advertiser can afford that, but there are six or seven different ways of packaging it. We broke up each time period—from 4 P.M. to 5; from 5 P.M. to 5:45; from 5:45 to 6, finishing with the postgame show from 9:30 to 10 P.M.—and priced each time period differently.

"You might price the 4 to 5, with a rating of 10 at $125,000. That way somebody can be part of the telecast, and have his 30-second spot run as part of the Super Bowl," he says. Cella estimates that ABC billed "close to $56 million" for the 1991 Super Bowl.

Such figures have left some companies out of Super Bowl Sunday; it's just too rich for their budgets. And for others, all the hype—the money and the ratings—place the Super Bowl in a special category, one in which they need to be included.

"The Super Bowl is the most watched sports event of the year," Thomas E. Clarke, Nike's vice-president of marketing, told *The New York Times* in 1992, "and as a company that made a name for itself in sports and fitness, it's very important for us."

And it's important to be seen in a specific light. All manner of new spots are created for the broadcast, because research shows that "an average of 60 percent of Super Bowl viewers agree that the ads they see are more interesting than commercials during prime-time programs," according to *The New York Times.* "And 54 percent can recall a Super Bowl spot, compared with an average of 23 percent for a conventional commercial."

Nike made a new commercial for the 1993 Super Bowl, and Anheuser-Busch had special spots. Master Lock went a step further; it's their only TV spot of the year. The lock company reportedly spent its entire annual ad budget on one 30-second ad.

And what does having all this on your network cost? Plenty. The four-year package signed in March of 1990 between the NFL and television—that's the three networks, Turner, and ESPN—brought a reported $3.6 billion into the league. ABC's share of the bill was $950 million. In return, ABC received the rights to the 1991 Super Bowl, "Monday Night Football," and to first round AFC and NFC wild card games.

The big question: Is it worth it?

The answer—from a business perspective—seems unclear. The NFL is not the hot ticket it was throughout the 1970s. This last decade has seen a drop in its popularity. According to Joan M. Chandler, writing in the 1991 collection of essays, *The Business of Professional Sports,* the three networks lost an estimated $50 million on pro football in 1985. The 1990 jump in rights fees made that figure seem like prosperity.

Exactly how much they lost is a hard question. The networks complained loudly, but actual numbers were scarce. The NFL's television committee got a chance to examine the networks' books during the summer of 1991. *Sports Illustrated* reported that Art Modell, Cleveland Browns owner and the committee's chairman, estimated the loss on pro football would reach $260 million over the course of the contract.

The situation with baseball is no brighter.

When CBS signed its $1.1 billion deal with Major League Baseball in 1989, the predictions from the economics observers were doom. And sure enough, CBS lost money. How much depends on whose accountants are reading the books. *The Wall Street Journal* said in October of 1990 that CBS "could have a loss in excess of $75 million on this first year of its baseball contract." *The Sporting News* put the 1990 loss to be "at least $100 million, probably $120 million and conceivably up to $150 million." *The New York Times* said the network's loss on baseball for the same year was $55 million after taxes. By the time the contract was drawing to a close, during the summer of 1993, the generally circulated figure was $500 million for the four years.

The high rights fee paid by CBS angered a lot of people at the other networks. The feeling was that CBS accelerated the already inflationary spiral in bidding for sports, a pattern many feel endangers the entire system. The entire industry shook at the prospects of what lay ahead. The networks felt themselves losing control of their own programming.

"We were investing enormous sums in major sports properties, and at the end of the day we had nothing to show for it," says Ken Schanzer, executive vice-president of NBC Sports, the network whose 40-year association with Major League Baseball temporarily ended with the CBS contract. "We owned no equity, and if those properties decided to go somewhere else, our investment was gone."

One response from NBC was to add sports it could control to its schedule—made-for-TV events such as professional beach volleyball, three-on-three basketball, and celebrity golf. The network was at least part-owner of all three events.

But a network didn't have to be directly burned by the CBS negotiations to feel the heat from the process of rising costs and an unstable market. Everybody was being affected.

"Rights fees are a significant element in our profit equation and we think today they are simply too high," says Swanson of ABC. "We have said they are too high all along and we have proceeded to stay out of most of the high-stake negotiations as a result.

"Because of high rights fees, we walked away from Major League Baseball and the Olympics, both properties which we were previously involved with."

Just Too Expensive

Does that mean escalating rights could someday see ABC walk away from "Monday Night Football"? Even back in 1986, Swanson told *Sports Illustrated* that the high costs of rights had the network considering "pulling the plug" on its long-time winner. Joan Chandler reports that ABC's losses in 1985 of "around $20 million" put the show in danger.

But the rights have risen considerably since then, and nothing but the NFL has been on ABC's Monday night fall schedule for 23 years. Why? Because ABC still considers it important—perhaps not as the great money-maker it once was, but important in other ways.

"Because of the ratings and attention it gets," says Swanson. "From a financial aspect that would not be the case."

This brings us to the gray area of television economics: When is programming that isn't making money not actually considered losing money? When it earns the network prestige and helps attract viewers for other programming.

"It's a very competitive business," says Cella. "Prime-time NFL is unique. It does a consistently high rating, and it's very upscale. We don't want to lose it.

"And yet it is a tough decision. That last go-round almost didn't happen. Our company had to take a hard look at the rating strength it adds to prime time over the course of the fourth quarter, with its sweep month in November. Sweeps are very important to the local stations; they had to weigh how the affiliates would react to losing it."

That particular part of the year is important to everybody. The fourth quarter includes the holiday buying season, the crucial time for advertisers. And while the new television season begins earlier in the fall, it is in November—the famous sweeps—when the popularity of the shows is evaluated.

And beyond the actual numbers, certain programming has such prestige that a network might decide to retain it on the schedule to maintain its image of strength, even if that decision costs it money. For ABC, "Monday Night Football" appears to be one such program. Remember, ABC is already "the network of the Olympics," with no Olympics.

"This is not just a sports decision," says Cella. "It's a corporate decision."

The point that ABC is making is that no program can be viewed on its own, but must be seen as part of the overall schedule. As Roone Arledge used a broad selection of sports to help ABC move from third among the networks in 1960 to first in the mid-1970s, ABC used sports to hang onto its position of second in the 1990s.

Sports not only draws viewers, which helps ratings; it also gives the network an opportunity to promote its other shows. News programs accomplish the same goal, and news—both national and local—is very important to the networks and their affiliates. But you can schedule just so many news shows. The theory has always been that you can't have too much sports. But that is changing.

A new way of thinking was what made CBS spend $3.5 billion between December of 1988 and March of 1990 for the rights to televise the NFL, Major League Baseball, the NCAA basketball tournament and the 1992 and 1994 Winter Olympics. Some call this the "big event" theory, and it is more popular today than ever.

"Once cable started to grow a decade ago and regular-season events began to multiply," CBS vice-president Jay Rosenstein told *The Sporting News* in 1990, "we realized the network's function was to focus on big events. At the culmination of each season, all those fans who watched are drawn to the finals, and there's only one place to watch it."

Clearly the big event was CBS's goal in purchasing baseball. Their contract called for only 16 regular games during the 26-week season, but also the All-Star Game, and, especially, the league championship games and the World Series.

How well the theory works in practice is hard to say. Was the money CBS lost from baseball and those other sports offset by its rise in the ratings? After many years as the prime-time leader in the 1970s and early 1980s, it had fallen behind NBC and ABC in the 1988–1989 season, figured from mid-September through April. The network found itself again atop the ratings race for the 1991–1992 season, and held on to that spot for 1992–1993.

But CBS apparently did not feel the investment was worth repeating. When the new contract was being hammered out in the spring of 1993, NBC and ABC were the active participants. And the lessons of the previous four years were not lost on the networks involved. That new contract continued to point toward emphasizing "the big event" and gaining maximum exposure for every broadcast.

NBC and ABC ended up sharing the six-year contract, which called for only 12 regular-season broadcasts, none before the All-Star Game and all at night. That was four fewer than CBS televised on Saturdays between April and September, and down 14 from what NBC aired in 1989. The regular-season and playoff games would also be broadcast regionally, a ploy taken from the NFL and college games. Showing games involving local teams to that region increases ratings, but cuts out fans of teams viewing from outside that region. Only World Series games in the post season will be aired to all viewers in the country at the same time.

Economically, the new contract was revolutionary. For the first time, baseball received no rights money up front. Under the agreement for the joint venture, a new corporation would be formed to sell advertising for all the games shown during the regular- and post-season. The working capital would be provided equally by the networks and major league baseball, with a nine-member board of directors acting as overseers—

five from baseball and two from each network. All revenues with would be shared, with baseball getting 80 to 90 percent, depending on the amount of advertising sold.

Each team earned about $10 million under the CBS contract, and an additional $4 million from ESPN. That figure will drop considerably, but how much is impossible to accurately predict. Most experts in 1993 projected an annual per-team figure—including monies from ESPN's more conventional rights deal—of about half the revenue of the previous agreement.

Progress for Basketball and Hockey

One by-product of CBS's effort seemed to be the ending of their nearly two-decade association with the NBA. While it is impossible to know exactly what CBS executives were thinking, *The Sporting News* saw a clear connection.

"Using high-profile sports events to promote new prime-time shows was one reason CBS basically traded its NBA rights for NBC's rights to baseball telecasting," wrote the weekly sports journal in December of 1990. "While the league playoffs and the World Series occur just before the all-important fall sweeps period, with November ratings dictating upcoming advertising rates, the NBA's postseason occurs in the late spring, just before summer reruns."

Professional basketball did not exactly suffer from the divorce. In November of 1989, the NBA agreed to a four-year, $600 million contract with NBC. The new deal nearly tripled the league's old CBS package, which brought $176 million over four years. The NBA also signed a four-year contract with TNT for a reported $275 million, which runs through the 1993–1994 season.

The combination of agreements represented a stunning accomplishment for the NBA. Remember, the sport got a slow start in the hearts and confidence of the money men in sports. It was 1953 before the league had its first contract; 13 games for $39,000, with the Dumont Network. Then it suffered through a period of decline in the 1970s. But a drug agreement between the league and the union—with the stiffest penalties in pro sports for athletes convicted of abuse—and the emergence of such stars as Magic Johnson, Larry Bird, and Michael Jordan helped its public image and its overall popularity.

The new contracts were a direct result. Not only did they mean more money, but more exposure: more regular-season games to be broadcast than under CBS, up from 16 to a minimum of 20 and as many as 26. All games would be in prime time or on weekends, and there would be up to 30 playoff games. It was a deal that proved profitable for the league and the network.

In April of 1993, on the eve of the NBA's playoffs, the league agreed to a new four-year pact with NBC. The agreement was a 25 percent raise—up to $750 million—and a revenue-sharing plan.

"When we signed the last contract, there was awesome speculation about how we'd do," Dick Ebersol, the president of NBC Sports, said when the agreement was announced. "We anticipated a modest profit, and we've exceeded that."

In an unusual expression of cooperation between network and league, NBC shared the financial records of its basketball telecasts with the NBA. This led to an agreement splitting the revenues between both sides after NBC attains a certain level of gross advertising sales over the four-year contract.

NBA teams get an additional boost from local television contracts. Even a market the size of Seattle—14th in the nation—contributed an estimated $4.1 million into the SuperSonics' account for local rights in 1992, while the Detroit Pistons pulled in $10.1 million, and the Los Angeles Lakers a whopping $19.3 million.

So where was hockey in all this picture? For a long time, half in and half out.

Hockey has not profited from national television as the other major team sports have. Some charged the NHL with poor organization and a general ineptness in promoting its sport. Others point out that hockey does not enjoy the same roots south of the Canadian border that its rival sports do.

It may be a combination of both factors, and an illustration of how different hockey is from the other sports.

The league had no significant history of national television exposure for its regular season games from 1975 until the contract signed in 1992 with ESPN and ABC. During most of that period, this represented official league policy.

"We principally emphasized that our teams develop their local market," said then-NHL President John Ziegler in 1991. "As cable opportunities grew, we went to an umbrella approach with national cable; first at USA Network, then to ESPN and then to SportsChannel America."

While the major networks were negotiating multimillion-dollar, multiyear contracts with football, baseball, and even basketball in the 1980s, hockey stumbled along with low-paying agreements. ESPN carried the National Hockey League games for three seasons, beginning in 1985–1986, at a fee reported to be about $8 million annually. SportsChannel took over then, and for the next three seasons averaged $17 million for the rights; that fell for the 1991–1992 season to only $5.5 million.

The absence of a broad, aggressive schedule on national networks reflected the nature of the league, which reflected the kind of sport hockey is.

"This is a very regional sport—saying national doesn't mean very much," says NHL Vice-President Skip Prince, in charge of television and team services. "The National Hockey League was for a long time an amalgam of local markets, all of which worked in concert to have a league."

For the purposes of broadcasting, at least in the United States, it has been difficult for the league to behave as any more than a loose confederation, according to Prince, because there is little national interest in the game.

"My question is," he says, "are there *hockey* fans here, or *team* fans? Would national exposure to a game in which there is not current interest on a national basis be any more than putting on a long and expensive infomercial?"

In Canada, where hockey is the national sport and the interest is intense, there is national television exposure, with fees paid to every team by the Molson Breweries.

And in this country, the place of national television has been filled by televising games regionally to the fans who are most interested. And the teams, individually, have prospered from that approach. The best cable contract the league ever negotiated could not compare with hockey's local television deals. Those numbers are tightly controlled, but in 1992 *The Boston Globe* reported the Bruins annually earned "a little less than $6 million" from local radio and television; *Crain's New York* put the Rangers' local revenues that same year at about $4 million. A league average seems to be about $4 million per team, which makes hockey the only major league sport with more income from local broadcasting than from national contracts.

The five-year rights agreement signed in the summer of 1992 with ESPN and ABC may only have totaled $80 million—that's just $16 million a year—but it suggested some stability for the future. *The Sports Industry News* described the arrangement:

> The cable channel will offer a weekly Friday game during the regular season plus the playoffs. Up to five games would air on ABC, with ESPN

> buying the time and the NHL helping line up sponsors. The network games will be scheduled on weekends in tandem with ABC's college basketball offerings.

Perhaps most important, the new contract got hockey back on network television, a critical first step in introducing itself to the American sports fan. And perhaps the size of that first step—small—is good for the sport.

"I don't think we're network-ready right now, and won't be for a couple more years," says Prince. "Before we are, we have to be damn sure the sport is ready to be exposed, with a passel of young stars, and an audience that understands the game and the nature of its rivalries."

Of all the major team leagues, the NHL has the least success in promoting itself or even governing itself. After a year of strife in 1992, highlighted by a ten-day players strike that threatened the Stanley Cup playoffs, John Zeigler, then the league president, was forced to resign. In choosing its first commissioner, the NHL turned away from its own sport to Gary Bettman, who had been third in command at the NBA for 12 years. The league also hired as senior vice-president Steve Solomon, who had been ABC's senior vice president of sports planning and administration. Both moves reflect the NHL's need to improve its visibility with American fans. Bettman says:

> There is much we need to do to improve the look of our games. One of my goals is to get more exposure for the NHL on network television. I don't view that in the short-term as a financial issue as much as I view it as a means of building our fan base.
>
> I believe that knowledgeable hockey fans don't have trouble watching the game on television because they know the game and understand its strategy. What we need to do is become more user-friendly for our casual fans. With this, we can more readily expand our fans base and our audiences.

Too Much of a Good Thing?

Talk to the people selling time for sports events on television today and they all say the same thing: Their job has gotten a lot harder. And the reason is simple. There's so much out there.

Let's look at a typical Sunday television lineup in New York in December, 1992:

10 A.M.	(MSG) English Soccer
12:30 P.M.	(CBS) NFL
12:30 P.M.	(ESPN) Soccer
1:30 P.M.	(SC) NBA
4 P.M.	(NBC) NFL
4 P.M.	(ABC) Golf
6 P.M.	(ESPN) Golf
7:30 P.M.	(ESPN) College Basketball
7:30 P.M.	(MSG) NHL
8:05 P.M.	(TBS) NBA
9:30 P.M.	(ESPN) College Basketball
2 A.M.	(MSG) Tennis

The average television household receives approximately 33 broadcast and cable channels, many of which carry some kind of sports. There are occasions when as many as ten sporting events are telecast at the same time.

It is a sports television explosion, and it has all happened in the last decade. Baseball broadcasts alone, including cable and free television, have increased dramatically from the 1,777 games in 1982. In 1990, there were 7,500 hours of various sports programming on all television; that's 20.5 hours of sports every day, 365 days a year.

More events means more competition for the viewers' attention and for each advertising dollar. And the clutter on the stations is compounded by the clutter of excessive advertising plaguing every event. The 1990 NFL contract with the networks allows them to sell 56 units of advertising per game; that's 28 minutes of commercials in a three-hour broadcast.

Some of the responsibility for the massive numbers of sports shows on the air falls with networks themselves. After the success of televising major sports became evident in the 1960s, the networks began looking around for other, less obvious sports to air.

ABC's "Wide World of Sports" came early, and proved how successful such efforts could be. There were serious segments—on the British Open Golf Tournament and track meets around the world—and less serious segments. Demolition Derby was a "Wide World" staple, along with spots on cliff diving, barrel jumping, and wrist wrestling. Some of the programming even brought the show's judgment into question. Through frequency of exposure and verve of promotion, "Wide

World" lifted daredevil Evel Knievel and his death-defying motorcycle jumps to star status, and in the process lured countless youngsters to fly through the air on their bicycles.

But the most important impact of "Wide World" was the redefinition of what constituted sports on TV. Suddenly screens all over the dial were filled with events never before considered worthy of airtime. "Wide World" spawned "The American Sportsman," where celebrities were seen hunting or fishing around the world. Later came "The Superstars," with noted athletes competing against one another in running, bowling, bicycling, and weight lifting. That was so successful it led to "The Women Superstars," "The World Superstars," "The Challenge of the Sexes," and even "Celebrity Challenge of the Sexes."

"There seemed to be no end to synthetic sports," Benjamin Rader tells us in the pages of *In Its Own Image,* adding that one "Celebrity Challenge" show featuring a tennis match between Farrah Fawcett and Bill Cosby drew a 49 percent share. And then he quotes from Robert Wussler, president of CBS Sports in 1978: "I've got ideas for telecasts in envelopes piled as high as this building. I'll bet 25 percent of them are good ones."

It was a happy time for sports television. The networks were giving the people what they wanted and making money, all at little cost to themselves. And while they appeared to have the airwaves to themselves, there were already signs of incursion. A few independent networks carried events on national hookups. One was Howard Hughes's Sports Network Incorporated, which carried some UCLA basketball games and mounted a brief challenge for "Monday Night Football."

The real beginning of the end of the networks' monopoly of sports television was the launching of the first communication satellite in 1974, which led in 1977 to sports on cable around the country. Ted Turner's WTBS in Atlanta carried Braves baseball and then Hawks basketball. WGN in Chicago carried the Cubs and then the White Sox. WOR in New Jersey carried the Mets.

And in 1979 the Entertainment and Sports Programming Network was born, now officially ESPN. The network was founded by William Rasmussen, an individual with an idea, who had just lost his job doing television and marketing for the Hartford Whalers of the old World Hockey Association; funding came from the Getty Oil Company. Rasmussen believed that America had enough sports addicts to support 24 hours of broadcasting a day. He hitched his idea to a newly orbited satellite that in those early days RCA "couldn't give away."

The early years were lean for ESPN. Starting with only 2.7 million customers, the channel showed slow-pitch softball, women's billiards, rodeos, and tape delays of college football. According to a 1989 article in *The New York Times*, it lost $100 million from 1979 to 1984. ESPN marked its first profit in 1985; by then it was seen in 30.2 million households.

Its turning point came in 1984, when ABC bought ESPN in two separate transactions, the second and larger purchase set at 85 percent in a $202 million deal with Texaco. Texaco had inherited the cable company when it purchased Getty Oil in February of 1984 for $10.1 billion. ABC later sold off about 20 percent of the network to Nabisco; Nabisco then sold its stock to the Hearst Corporation in November of 1990. ESPN served 60 million customers in 1992, or about 63 percent of the households in the country.

To one degree or another, the station would come to offer everything the big networks did—no Super Bowl or Triple Crown, but Major League Baseball, the NFL, the NHL, and lots of college football and basketball. It offered items once seen only on the networks, such as the NHL's All-Star Game and the Pro Bowl, as well some never seen elsewhere: aerobics and other fitness shows, monster truck races, and drag boat racing. For continuity, there were rodeos and billiards. It all spelled competition for the networks.

"It's been tough to sell sports ever since the mid-1980s because of the proliferation of products," says Bill Cella. "Turner and ESPN had come on board with all these shows. They started off slow, but as they began to hire people away from the networks, the quality of what they were selling improved."

The difference in audience size remains a big selling point for the networks. A 16 rating for "Monday Night Football" delivers to close to 15 million households, many of them occupied by youngish men with money to spend. ESPN still cannot claim that.

"But these shows are still reaching men and the advertiser can accomplish a lot without paying the same price he's got to pay at an ABC," says Cella. "He can go to Turner or ESPN, where units are $60,000 compared to $250,000 for 'Monday Night Football.'

"The buyer's got to make the choice, but now there are a lot more choices. Buyers have the opportunity to spend their money in many more places," Cella says.

Help from New Areas

Ever since the dawn of the 1980s, each new rights contract between the leagues and the networks has raised cries that the fees escalation cannot go on. The increased inventory of sports on television coupled with the decreased advertising revenues in a flat economy contributed to network losses that eventually supported those dire predictions.

In an effort to stop lost advertising dollars tied to pro football, the networks went directly to the NFL for relief. The league seemed sympathetic. At first there were headlines about a suggested $28-million-rebate, or $1 million from each team. That never happened. Instead the NFL decided to spread out the season, playing the 16 games over 18 weeks; they would give each team two weeks off during the season, thus giving the networks two more weeks in which NFL games were played, and two more weeks to sell advertising. But this just created more inventory in an already saturated market.

The negotiations added fuel to the argument that the day of free sports on TV was fast coming to an end, and that pay-per-view would fill everyone's future. This system, whereby customers order directly from their cable company for specific events and pay for each viewing, has been the subject of conversation since the 1970s. By the 1980s, some hockey and boxing matches were available. It had not caught on as was predicted. A few baseball teams offered games on a pay-per-view basis as of 1992—Los Angeles, San Diego, and Minnesota were among those that tried it—but their success was limited. And pay-per-view's big test, the 1992 Olympics from Barcelona, flopped. The heavily promoted "Triplecast" attracted less than 20 percent of the paying customers necessary to break even, making the project a $100 million loser.

Its primary appeal thus far has been for boxing and other one-time events. *The Sports Industry News* reported in September of 1992 that for the Julio Cesar Chavez–Hector Camacho super lightweight bout Showtime Event Television signed up almost 800,000 households. That was a 3.6 percent buy rate, yielding a pay-per-view gross of about $20 million based on the $25 average price. "The percentage represents a reasonably successful sales effort for a fight outside the heavyweight division," said the weekly newsletter.

ABC tried pay-per-view for college football in 1992. The network projected 25,000 national buys for over the three-month season, reportedly making fewer than half that many sales. But it was enough for ABC to try again in 1993; the price was $8.95 to watch one of three telecasts on any Saturday, or $59.95 for the 12-week package.

Critics of pay-per-view suggested that the extra charge for something exotic may work, but that Americans were reluctant to pay for what they've always gotten for free. This certainly proved to be true in the case of baseball in 1992; the San Diego Padres had little success charging $7.95 for an individual game on pay-per-view, or $3.75 per game in a package of 50. And when the subject of paying to see the Super Bowl or the World Series comes up, those same critics point to a Congress committed to defending the public's right of access to sports over the airways.

While some in television fretted about the future, others have confronted the problem of costs more directly. First CBS with the 1993 Masters, then NBC with the Ryder Cup, separated the two events from their other golf offerings, giving sponsors product exclusivity for fees reported to be $1 million each in the case of NBC and the Ryder.

ABC worked out an $11-million package for its coverage with ESPN of the 1994 World Cup with the U.S. Soccer Federation. The plan called for a few high-profile sponsors; Canon, Coca-Cola, Fuji Film, Gillette, and MasterCard are among them. Sponsors get exclusivity, but ads run in a non-obtrusive fashion. Logos will be displayed with the time and score during play, and all commercials are scheduled to air pregame, postgame, and at halftime. There will be no commercial interruption during games.

Television cable companies across the country have also moved aggressively into local and regional sports broadcasting. The largest, and the oldest, is the Madison Square Garden Network (MSG), a division of Paramount Communications, Inc. It owns the rights to Knicks and Rangers games; the teams are also owned by Paramount. The network entered into a 12-year, $500 million contract with the Yankees to broadcast 150 games a year, beginning in 1991. MSG put 108 games on cable in 1993, and aired 50 over local station WPIX, the Yankees' longtime outlet. (The network bought time on WPIX and sold the commercials.) The remaining four games in the 162-game schedule were reserved for national network broadcasts.

The sports have looked to economize, too. Several NBA teams have taken on the production of their own broadcasts instead of selling those rights to the local stations. Their efforts have contributed to steadily rising revenues from local radio and television. According to *Broadcasting Magazine,* the figure has more than doubled from $63 million for the 1987–1988 season to approximately $130 million for the 1992–1993 season. Some baseball teams have tried the same tactic. Seattle, with local television revenues in 1991 of $1.1 million, the lowest in the league, cleared close to $3 million in 1992 by producing its own broadcasts and splitting games between two stations.

At the same time, the networks have begun to turn over some of the responsibilities for producing sports to third parties. For years a lot of car racing and special events like the "Skins Game" on television were produced by Ohlmeyer Productions. Don Ohlmeyer had produced sports for ABC and then NBC before forming his own company; in 1993 he was made head of NBC's West Coast operation. Much of the golf on television is produced by Jack Nicklaus. And an ever-increasing amount of college basketball is televised through the efforts of an independent production company called Raycom.

The Rays of Raycom are Dee and Rick Ray, of Charlotte, North Carolina. During the same 1980s that saw networks' profits from sports dwindle and even disappear, the Rays built a neat and successful little empire, all on the back of sports.

Their approach was simple: While the networks had their eyes on the large picture, showing one game to the entire country, the Rays thought small, selecting games of high regional interest.

"Often it was just the local team playing locally," says Rick Ray, "a Louisville playing in Louisville or a Memphis State playing in Memphis, and those games did tremendous, a 25-to-30 rating. Try that over six states and it might be a 2."

Raycom used that approach to build itself from a two-person operation in 1979 to the nation's top sports syndicator today. That first year it sold three packages to television; in 1992 they supplied more than 400 events.

Rick Ray came out of television, first as a cameraman and then a program manager. He persuaded his station—WCCB-TV in Charlotte—to carry a Alaskan basketball tournament that featured North Carolina State in 1978, and everyone was pleased with the success. When no local team was represented the following year, the station opted out. Ray hung in.

"I knew that in every market there were at least two or three stations that would take college basketball, but there wasn't enough of it being produced," recalls Ray, speaking of the time when cable was just getting started.

So in 1979, at the age of 30, he went into business for himself. He sought the help of a local agency to sell advertising and began producing basketball games. Ray and the ad agency have been together ever since; he and agency boss Dee Birke were married that same year. She is now president of Raycom, while he serves as CEO. The firm has 76 employees and $65 million in annual sales, and maintains offices in New York, Chicago, and Dallas, in addition to the headquarters in Charlotte.

Among Raycom's television events are college football's Kickoff Classic, Freedom Bowl, and Blockbuster Bowl; basketball from the Atlantic Coast; and Big Eight, Big Ten, Metro, Pac-Ten, Southwest Conferences, as well as Southwest Conference football.

But how can relatively small Raycom succeed with sports while the same product is dragging down the big networks?

Partly it is Raycom's approach of thinking regionally, airing one game with regional appeal in the area most interested, and scheduling two other teams in a locale where their fans are located. Later they progressed, putting on a conference game-of-the-week in the area of that conference. It was a natural evolution, since conferences are set up geographically. Most Big Ten schools are in the Midwest; most Southeastern Conference schools in the Southeast.

"Of course the NFL has always been regional," reminds Rick Ray. "The local team is on in its market. That's one reason that professional football is so huge." It is also an approach that Major League Baseball went to for the 1994 season in an effort to shore up that sport's sagging television ratings.

But there is more to Raycom's success. They profit from being small. They pay less for rights than an NBC or CBS would, about 25 percent less, and they use non-union, free-lance crews.

"There is a cadre of free-lance talent out there that's quite sizeable," says Ray. "These people are good, and they're well paid. A cameraman may make $500 or $1,000 a day, but that's still less than union. That bottom-line cost is triple what we end up paying."

Those numbers play well in North Carolina, and also in New York. As a result, Raycom entered into a relationship with ABC in 1992, paying the network $1.8 million for six weeks of airtime to put on 26 college basketball games. The contract was a lifeline for ABC. Nielsen ratings for its college basketball had dropped to a disappointing 3 in 1991, while rights fees to the colleges continued to climb.

"We lost millions last year," ABC Sports programming director Tony Petitti told *The New York Times* in 1992. "This takes all the risks out of college basketball."

The deal was good for Raycom as well; it gave it the national sell that added even more credibility to its programming and syndicating efforts. Most of the mechanism was already in place. It had the collegiate and conference contacts to secure the necessary rights, and also had the connections to sell the advertising. Ad sales of $10 million was its goal.

"We did better than that," says Rick Ray, who is quick to add that the first year was not perfect.

"We found some weaknesses in the upper Midwest and the East, but we've addressed that," he says. "We bought some Notre Dame games to help in the Midwest, and some DePaul games. And we added the University of Massachusetts to help in Boston."

It's the old Raycom theory: regional help for regional problems. And it's the kind of thinking that television needs if it is going to continue making money in an ever-tightening market with more choices for the viewer.

7

Radio, First and Always

While the money contributed by radio to professional sports is dwarfed by what comes from television, it is nonetheless substantial.

Radio payments in 1992 for professional football teams totaled more than $49 million. Baseball's figures include about $13 million for 1992's share of the national four-year, $50-million contract with CBS. Local team rights range from a low in Seattle of $500,000 to a high for each of the New York teams of $5 million; the Boston Red Sox' local deal earns them about $3.8 million annually. NHL and NBA teams guard their figures, but a survey reveals that hockey radio is worth from about $500,000 a year to the New Jersey Devils to $1.5 million for the New York Rangers. The range is similar for basketball, with contracts for the New York Knicks and the Detroit Pistons worth about $1.5 million.

But the worth of radio broadcasts is greater than the money they generate. In many ways, there would be no television sports without radio. The subject here is progression, and not so much the progression of technology but of cultural patterns.

Radio began with baseball. The first game ever aired was played August 5, 1921, at Forbes Field in suburban Pittsburgh. The station was KDKA; the announcer, Harold Arlin.

In his well-researched and passionately written chronicle of sports announcers, *Voices of the Game,* Curt Smith speaks of the 26-year-old pioneer of sports broadcasting. Arlin had already begun giving baseball scores over the air, and the day following his historic trip to Forbes Field, he would become the first man to broadcast a tennis match.

> In an era that bespoke extravagance, Harold Arlin spoke without self-puffery and sham. "I was just a nobody, and our broadcast—back then, at least—wasn't that big a deal," he said two years before his death, on March 14, 1986, at ninety, of a heart attack, in Bakersfield, California. "Our guys at KDKA didn't even think that baseball would last on radio. I did it sort of as a one-shot project, kind of addendum to the events we'd already done."

Smith does not view Arlin's afternoon at Forbes Field so lightly. Read his words carefully:

> His vehicle was known as "wireless telegraphy"; his microphone was a converted telephone. He was a Westinghouse Company foreman by day and a studio announcer by night, a Brigham Young sighting the Great Salt Lake. In a contest of seven walks, twenty-one hits, and one hour and fifty-seven minutes (final score: Pirates 8, Phillies 5), he christened the sculpted pageant of baseball broadcasting—a sacrament, looking back, bathed in consequence, but on that late-summer afternoon, dwarfed by the age's Gullivers, of almost Lilliputian concern.

Not everybody—not even every avid sports fan—would see the first game to be announced over radio in such a light. But Smith was responding to what has moved so many fans listening to sports in the years since that August afternoon. That is the ability of a good announcer to capture a moment of excitement and send it hurling through space to wherever the listener happens to be, at whatever the time of day or night.

This ability to recreate sports action, along with all of its attending emotional ties, has had great impact on sports and fans. We will deal with this element later, for it is crucial to the bond between fans and their favorite teams and players and therefore to the business of sports. For now, it is enough to explore how that connection has impacted more directly on our subject.

Radio Sports Without Commercials

At first, baseball broadcasts had no sponsors. As we have seen, they began as a technological gimmick, then became a lever to draw people's attention to the game. It was the same with pro football; it needed to introduce itself to the American public. Several teams had local radio for their games in the 1920s; Chicago's Bears and Cardinals; and the Frankford Yellow Jackets, based in a suburb of Philadelphia.

But no one was quite sure where radio fit into the overall landscape of sports. In baseball, Chicago Cubs owner William Wrigley was convinced that radio was a positive force. He declared Cubs Park—as Wrigley Field was known then—free and open to all radio stations. By the mid-1920s as many as seven local stations could be carrying the same game. Before the end of the decade, there was radio in Philadelphia, St. Louis, Boston, and Cleveland. But not everyone supported the broadcasts. In 1934, all three New York teams banned radio accounts of their games, fearing they were hurting attendance.

No such debate engulfed the World Series. It became an immediate sensation from its first exposure, and was unchallenged as a sports spectacle until overtaken by television coverage in 1949. The first Series broadcast was in 1921; the first play-by-play, a year later. According to *In Its Own Image*, by 1926 *The New York Times* considered the broadcast "such a pioneering venture that it carried the entire narrative in its sports section."

And it was all free. Sponsorship of games did not begin until the 1930s. In 1934, Mobil Oil began sponsoring the Detroit Tiger games; the average annual revenue from radio at that time was about $1,000 per team. It was also in 1934 that baseball commissioner Kennesaw Mountain Landis signed a contract with the Ford Motor Company to broadcast the World Series for the next four years for $400,000. All three major networks—NBC, CBS, and Mutual—carried the game simultaneously.

The games were major broadcasting events, to which the entire nation listened. And the men who brought them to life over the airways were stars. For nearly three decades, from sports radio's beginnings in the 1920s until the arrival of television in the 1950s, these were some of the most popular personalities in the country. Led by such men as Graham McNamee, Ted Husing, and Bill Stern, they were the Pied Pipers of their day, whisking the attention of sports fans away to a land of heroic athletes competing in all the greatest of events. Through their near-hypnotic deliveries, millions of people were introduced to the sports and the athletes of the day. And the men behind those deliveries became as famous as the events they covered.

McNamee was probably the most admired, even loved. Trained as a singer, his baritone voice would fill with emotion at just the right instant of a fight or a ball game. His work on the 1923 World Series brought more than 1,700 letters of affection within five days to WEAF, his station in New York; in 1926 WEAF became the flagship station for the new NBC. After his work on the 1925 Series, close to 50,000 letters came to McNamee.

Stern, who had many detractors in the business—some called the CBS announcer difficult, others mean—had a manner of broadcasting that turned every ball player into a hero, every hit into a Ruthian blast. He used that same fanciful approach in his popular radio program, "Colgate Sports Newsreel." According to the Benjamin Rader book, the program "deliberately falsified reports of athletes and sports events for dramatic effect."

But while these men were immensely popular with radio listeners, they were at the mercy of their sports. No career better reflected this than Ted Husing's. Husing was one of the best for 20 years. CBS's first national sportscaster, his work had a quality of harmony and balance, and the ability to evoke a distant scene. "You could smell the autumn when he broadcast," former athlete and announcer Marty Glickman told *Sports Illustrated* in 1990; "you could see the rustling of the leaves, you could feel the wind howling through the stadium."

And unlike some of his contemporaries, Husing was a reporter. None of this phantom lateral to correct a misidentified ball carrier; Husing reported what he saw. But he was also blunt, and that was costly. His description of a Harvard player's performance as "putrid" got him barred in 1931 from that university's football games; calling umpiring during the 1934 World Series "some of the worst I've ever seen" got him barred from the 1935 Series.

Both those events rated full-column articles in *The New York Times.* Husing was that important because radio broadcasting was that integral a part of the American scene.

Radio's Trickle-Down Effect

The nationwide fame generated by network broadcasts helped make the local sports coverage popular and lucrative. In 1939 the Dodgers abandoned their radio ban and signed a contract with General Mills for the rights to their home and away games for a price reported to have been between $70,000 and $77,000.

Sports became important to radio. As was the case with early television, radio needed sports to help fill out its schedule. Between 1945 and 1950, a period of rapid growth in America following the war, the number of locally operated radio stations doubled, and sports—especially baseball—was a popular source of programming. Towns and cities without their own teams could still pick up one of the many networks formed by teams; in the late 1940s and early 1950s the St. Louis Cardinals had one of the largest regional networks, carrying their games over some 120 stations in nine states. Starting in 1950 and continuing for the better part of two decades, the Mutual Broadcasting Company carried a live baseball game daily, Monday through Saturday, over as many as 500 stations across the country.

The importance of these broadcasts to each franchise far exceeded the money derived from selling the rights fees. The clear, sharp voice of the announcer created for the listener an exciting world that lifted fans out of their own circumstances and, for at least a few hours, carried them into the heart of a big-league ballpark. This created team loyalties that lived for years, even generations, turning the listeners into loyal fans. These fans would often travel hundreds of miles to see a game and, even more importantly, they would express their loyalty by buying T-shirts, yearbooks, and other revenue-producing items.

Much more than in television, the radio announcer is an integral part of this process. With no visual image to contradict him, his voice is the only reality. What does this have to do with the business of sports, you ask? It's simple. Good announcers can help hold attention during boring games when the fan's team is hopelessly behind after the fourth inning or in August when his team is 20 games out of first place. They do it by building relationships with their listeners—there isn't a fan in the world who, while speeding through stations, won't stop at the sound of his or her favorite announcer. That is the kind of connection that builds ratings, win or lose. And ratings, as we have seen, is what attracts advertisers.

Even today, with television dominating our sports coverage, radio lives. And there are still radio announcers who have the ability to latch onto the mind and hold it captive for the duration of a game. Instead of that process happening on a national scale, the communication is very personal, forming a link between a voice without a face and a listener out there somewhere in the dark. Unlike their predecessors, the network announcers who lived and worked in celebrity, these men often perform in obscurity. Often their importance to the game and the fans they serve is never explored until the end of their careers.

When Ernie Harwell was told that the 1991 season—his 32d of announcing Detroit Tigers games—would be his last, the furor caused by local fans literally shook old Tiger Stadium and the city of Detroit; "We want Ernie!" chants even erupted at Joe Louis Arena during Red Wings games. (After purchasing the Tigers in 1992, the new owners rehired Harwell.) When Red Barber died in 1993 at the age of 84, the man who had been the voice of the Cincinnati Reds and New York Yankees but most notably of the Brooklyn Dodgers was mourned by an entire nation of fans; every television network carried a tribute. When Marty Glickman retired in 1992 at the age of 75, after four decades of broadcasting New York basketball and then football, a city stood in respect. And George Vecsey, writing in *The New York Times*, tried to put the man and his ability into perspective:

> With his Nedick's persona, Glickman has been in the greatest tradition of the local announcer, the voice who sounds like home: Cawood Ledford broadcasting the Kentucky Wildcats. Harry Caray sputtering "Cubs win!" The Fordham Angeleno, Vin Scully, wafting from transistors all over Dodger Stadium. Bill White trying to elicit something rational out of the Scooter [Yankee announcer Phil Rizzuto]. Radio does this best. It is personal, and it requires a bit of imagination.

That is the essential point about sports that can never be forgotten: It is always personal. Yes, for the people making the big decisions, the owners and the managing partners and the general managers, it is business. Yes, for the athletes and the coaches and the scouts, it is athletics and tactics and strategy. But for the fans, the people who attend the games and tune in on radio and television, who buy the products and carry the banners, it's personal.

All-Sports Radio

Because people's attachments for their teams are so personal and generate so much emotion, there is a whole new kind of radio station: All-sports radio.

Sports talk shows have been around since the 1950s. From New England to Miami to the West Coast, fans could vent their frustrations about their latest sports irritation by dialing the local call-in program.

Then in 1987 came Jeff Smulyan and his brainstorm—all-sports radio. Actually, the form first appeared a year earlier in Denver, at KMVP-AM, but lasted only two years. Smulyan showed more perseverance. And when he purchased WHN, changed the name to WFAN, and transformed the programming, he created a revolution. WFAN hung onto the Mets broadcasts, and filled in the open air with sports news, interviews, and call-in comments from fans. All-sports cost more in operating expenses than WHN's mixture, but Smulyan was confident from the start of its success.

He was right. After a slow start, WFAN became one of the most successful radio stations in New York by the end of 1990, generating revenues of $20 million to $24 million a year, or almost 10 percent of the $300 million market for radio advertising in the city, according to *The New York Times.* Smulyan made history when he created the format, and he made history four years later when he sold the station for $70 million. *Broadcasting Magazine* said it believed that was "the highest ever paid for an AM standalone—approximately 10 times WFAN's $7 million in cash flow on $20 million in annual revenue."

But it proved to be more important than that. WFAN was the beginning of an all-sports epidemic on radio. In Boston and San Diego and Philadelphia, all-sports now gives fans a place to complain and praise their teams well into the night. In 1992 alone, four major markets—Chicago, Los Angeles, Minneapolis, and St. Louis—started their own all-sports stations. By the summer of 1993, there were more than 50 stations around the country with all-sports radio formats, according to *Radio Business Report,* the Washington-based trade journal.

That year also saw the launching of the ESPN Radio Network. It hit the air with an affiliate base of 150 stations covering all 50 states, and within less than a year was heard on 240 stations. Compensation between ESPN and its affiliates was by barter. The network paid no affiliate compensation and retained 100 percent of advertising revenue from the commercials aired on its programming; in return, the affiliates got highly rated programming which attracted listeners to their own programming.

"We focus on breaking news and interviews with the marquee names in sports and notable analysis," says Kevin Young, executive producer of the network that makes liberal use of the personalities on the television side of ESPN. Not surprisingly, many of its affiliates were among the new all-sports stations.

The programming patterns for all-sports radio is similar from station to station. They couple play-by-play with call-in shows, interviews with athletes, and lots of sports news. Results have been mixed.

WFAN struggled at first; its early years saw losses of $7 to $8 million. The station turned the corner when Smulyan and his Emmis Broadcasting purchased WNBC-AM in New York, and moved WFAN from its old spot on the dial—1050—to the preferred 660, where WNBC had been aired. The signal was stronger there, and WNBC owned the rights to New York Knicks basketball and New York Rangers hockey; WFAN was already broadcasting the Mets games, and later picked up the New York Jets football and St. Johns basketball.

The WNBC deal added the perfect starter to WFAN's formula, "Imus in the Morning," starring the irreverent and popular Don Imus. By the summer of 1990, WFAN was the number-one rated station among males, aged 18–54, in the New York market. That strength was only aided when it supplemented its sports programming with ESPN.

Boston's WEEI also started slowly, but has been less successful in finding its audience. Owned by the Celtics, the station carries all Celtics games and Bruins matches (when they do not conflict with the basketball.) It carries ESPN on weekends, and mixes in other syndicated sports programming with its own sports talk shows. But while Boston is known as a good sports city, WEEI was perpetually cost-cutting from the time the station was created in 1991.

San Diego's XTRA became the first all-sports station on the West Coast when it converted from talk radio in 1990. The station was also the first all-news station in 1961, and one of the first stations in the country using the "beautiful music" format. It found success with neither. According to *The New York Times,* XTRA lost $2.5 million the year before trying all-sports. But it did better with its mix of San Diego Charger football, Los Angeles Kings hockey, and San Diego State University football and basketball. Other than some syndicated sports overnight—not ESPN—all of its programming is local, a combination of sports news and call-in.

The lesson seemed clear. All-sports radio was, by itself, no panacea as a source of revenue. Just as it was with owners of teams, station managers had to put good performers in their lineups and know how to market them.

What this new phenomenon did was give us an insight into Americans and their feelings about sports. With all the events on radio and television, a great number of fans still had a need to talk about their teams, in season and out, winning or losing.

It's like a really good ball game; when it's over, nobody wants to leave the stands.

8

Through the Turnstiles

In the days before television, professional sports earned money based on their appeal, and the appeal of the teams and athletes that played them. These qualities were measured each day, by the fans who showed up to buy tickets.

As late as 1950, approximately 92 percent of the revenue for all major team sports came from attendance and its close relation, concessions.

Our world has grown ever so complicated since then. But even with all the money generated by radio and television, and by ever-expanding marketing departments, teams cannot survive for very long without putting spectators in the stands. Even television, hungry for programming, shies away from half-full stadiums and arenas. All those empty seats make the viewer—and the advertiser—wonder why he showed up.

Sports understands this reality, and does a pretty good job of attracting people. About half the adult population of this country attends at least one sports event every year, and the average is eight events.

Who are these people, and what sports do they like?

Using statistics compiled by Gallup, a 1991 article in *The Christian Science Monitor* said that while baseball was America's favorite sport well into the early 1960s, at that point football's popularity began to soar. It moved to first by the end of the decade, and has held on to its 35 percent share of American's affection; baseball was second at about 20 percent, and basketball third at 15 percent. (*The Monitor* didn't mention hockey.)

The survey found baseball was much more popular among men over 50, and football and basketball did best among those 18 to 29 years of age. Women like football less then men, but prefer it to baseball, two to one. Among black sports fans, basketball ranked first at 35 percent, football second at 33 percent, while baseball pulled in only 10 percent.

And then *The Monitor* article offered this analysis:

> Baseball is the one professional sport an academic or writer can claim to love without risk of having his 'practicing intellectual' card revoked. But in the public at large, the college-trained like baseball the least and dote most on football. Those who haven't graduated from high school are, predominately, baseball's biggest fans.

How has the world outside sports affected who's attending games and who's staying home? Baseball and football games have been around long enough in sufficient numbers to suggest that depends on how forceful outside events are.

World War I cut sharply into baseball attendance, which was then only about 3,000 to 5,000 a game; fans flocked back to the parks after the armistice. Attendance built steadily toward an average of more than 8,200 per game, until the Depression, when fan interest fell to a 15-year low, fewer than 5,000 a game during the 1933 season. Once the nation got back on its feet, so did baseball, and the numbers began to grow. There was a drop in attendance during World War II, followed by a strong recovery. There was serious fluctuation from 1967 through 1972, while Vietnam tore the country apart, and then another recovery. The recession of 1981–1982 and the nation's current economic woes had little effect.

Football also struggled through the Depression, then picked up in 1935. It lost fans the year after World War II broke out, hitting a five-year attendance low in 1942 of 16,144, but in 1943 shot up to 24,228.

NFL gates dropped off when the AFL began playing in 1960. They recovered, rose and fell and then picked up again after the merger, settling in to a period of growth in 1978. Professional football set a record for average attendance in 1990 with 62,321.

Trouble within a sport always makes waves. A dip in baseball attendance in 1981 was attributed to fan dissatisfaction with the players' mid-season strike. The National League average dropped from 21,733 in 1980 to 19,498 in 1981, then rebounded in 1982 to 22,127. The same pattern showed in the American League, attendance dropping from 19,389 in 1980 to 18,780 in 1981 and then jumping the following season to 20,353. And the only interruptions in football's recent steady growth were represented in 1982 and 1987, two years in which there were strikes.

The matter of how ticket prices effect attendance is not so easy to trace. In 1977, the average football ticket cost $9.67; hockey and basketball in their 1977–1978 season, $7.87 and $6.76, respectively. The average baseball ticket in 1977 was only $3.99.

Fourteen years later, the average football ticket was $26.50, the average basketball ticket was $25, hockey was up to $29, and baseball came in at $9.40. Those sound like big increases and they were; the biggest jump was for hockey tickets, 268 percent. But those were years of inflation. A copy of *Sports Illustrated* went from $1 to $2.95. Over that same period, the price of the best seat of a Broadway show rose 242 percent, from $17.50 to $60.

The jump in ticket prices didn't seem to have much of an effect on attendance. The three most expensive teams to see in the NBA in 1991, according to *Team Marketing Report*, the sports marketing newsletter, were the Lakers, Knicks, and Bulls; they were also three of the top seven teams in home attendance. The most expensive regular-season baseball experience—that's the $112.83 paid by a family of four, complete with tickets and all the normal extras at a Toronto Blue Jays game (see "The Concessionaires" in Chapter 9) was also the most popular. The Blue Jays led all of sports in tickets sold in 1991, with over four million. The most expensive NFL ticket, the $35 for an average seat to watch San Francisco, did not keep the 49ers from placing second in attendance in their conference, and fifth overall in the league.

Hockey, again, needs a longer explanation. As was the case with television, attendance for the NHL was a problem in the early 1990s. The reason may have been increased prices, the lack of television exposure, labor problems that led to a strike in 1992, or a combination.

While the league showed a modest increase of 5.8 percent in 1991–1992, that was after registering a 2 percent drop from 1990–1991. And key teams saw attendance fall early. The Rangers rallied after the first of the year to show an increase, but Boston and the New York Islanders never did recover. Affordability could have been a factor. Top price for the Rangers was $65; the expansion San Jose Sharks, with the third-lowest attendance in the league, had a top of $50.

What seems evident about ticket prices is that they reflect more the economy of the times and city where the franchise is located, and less the quality of the team. It was expensive to watch the 49ers and Redskins in 1991 because San Francisco and Washington are two very expensive cities, as is New York, whose Mets had the top price in baseball that year. And while Toronto is not such an expensive city, their SkyDome did cost $532 million in Canadian dollars to build.

Oddly, raising ticket prices does not seem to affect overall attendance. The fans will pay the additional money. But while attendance figures do not fall after prices are raised, there is a theory that certain fans are denied access by the higher prices, and being replaced by others. Who is being shut out, and what this costs sports, will be approached later.

One thing is certain: A bad show is no bargain at any price. Having the cheapest ticket in baseball was not a selling point for residents and visitors of Cleveland. The Indians, with the worst record in the majors, drew fewer fans in 1991 than any other team, just over a million.

What does attract fans? We know winning attracts fans best. We know faithful supporters will always come, since deep-seated personal allegiances are often held from childhood and seem immune to erosion from losing seasons. And we've learned that what is new usually attracts, at least temporarily; new stadiums draw big numbers, and expansion teams often do well early. (The expansion Charlotte Hornets and Minnesota Timberwolves took turns leading the NBA in attendance in the 1988–1989 and 1989–1990 seasons respectively, their first seasons; Minnesota's average of 26,160 fans and a total of 1.07 million set a league record. Then there are baseball's Colorado Rockies. As of the 1993 All-Star break, the new expansion team was last in the National League West standings and first in attendance for all of baseball. By season's end, the Rockies had hoisted themselves out of last place and into sixth, and set an all-time home attendance record, 4.48 million.)

Winning, however, is the only guarantee. In 1990, when the New York Giants and Buffalo Bills were on their way to the Super Bowl, they led their conferences in attendance; the Toronto Blue Jays set an attendance record in 1992 on their way to their first World Championship. Even the hope of winning draws people. After four woeful seasons on the field and at the box office, the New England Patriots in January of 1993 hired former Giants coach Bill Parcells, who had led New York to two Super Bowl wins. The fans responded immediately. The announcement came midway through a Thursday; 260 season tickets were sold that afternoon, and on Friday a Patriots one-day ticket record was set with 701. It lasted till Saturday, when 979 season tickets were sold.

Drawing People to the Game

But no team can remain new forever, and no team can win forever. Other factors must be working to draw the fans in on a continual basis, fundamental factors that remain constant whether the team wins or loses and are irrespective of the comings and going of favorite players. The act of going to a game must be made to be viewed by fans as a positive experience. "We can't expect people to come to the ballpark and only be satisfied with a win," Jeff Smulyan said when he owned the Seattle Mariners. "They've got to feel good about that evening, win or lose. That's the challenge."

Smulyan dealt with that challenge in a modern way, making sure the Kingdome was safe and comfortable for the fans, providing family sections, even offering entertainment at games other than just baseball—fireworks and rock music on special nights. It was all part of creating an attractive environment for the fans.

The foundation of that environment is a comfortable, attractive facility. It must have the basics: it must be clean, with plenty of washrooms and plenty of parking. If possible, the seats should be comfortable and offer a good, unobstructed view of the game. It is an advantage to have an overall attractive look. Unique is even better. The Houston Astros, with one of the worst teams in baseball in 1965, set its all-time attendance record that season; people came not for the team but to see the newly opened Astrodome.

These elements are important in every sport. But with baseball, the look and feel of the ballpark seem to have a greater impact on the overall experience. With no clock to restrict it, baseball is a game that stretches unchecked over a period of time. This makes the visual characteristic of a park very important.

One never hears about the aesthetics of RFK Stadium, where the Washington Redskins play, or even Madison Square Garden, home of the Knicks and the Rangers. But a ballpark is different. People write poems to ballparks, sing songs about them, and put their pictures on calendars. Architects argue about the relative beauty of their facades, and how they fit into the landscape of the city. The Smithsonian Institution even has a tour each year of the nation's best ballparks. The stars of that tour are the few old parks left.

In 1993, the only three ballparks built in the pre–World War I era remaining in baseball were Chicago's Wrigley Field, Boston's Fenway Park, and Detroit's Tiger Stadium.

Two of those were shrines. Fenway, with its quirky angles and its famous left field wall, The Green Monster; home to Ted Williams and Jimmie Foxx and Tris Speaker.

And of course, Wrigley. Wrigley Field is arguably the loveliest ballpark in baseball. Cloistered among apartment buildings and houses on the north side of Chicago, it was built in 1914 as Weeghman Park; the Cubs moved in two years later. And while it has been fortified, altered, and often expanded, it continues to speak for an earlier time in American sports, a time when ball players read *The Sporting News* instead of *The Wall Street Journal*, and singing "Take me out to the ball game" meant an afternoon in the sun.

Yes, Wrigley's field is grass, its stairs and ramps unmotorized, its scoreboard controlled by men who change big numbers as each run crosses home plate. Until 1988, all play stopped when the sun went down. The Wrigley family, who owned the team from 1921 until 1981, first claimed that light towers would destroy the beauty of the park, then said that night-game traffic, noise, and lights would be intrusive to the residents of the park's residential neighborhood. Pressure from television led to lights, for limited dates a year—no more than 18—but primarily so that postseason games could be scheduled at night, during prime time.

Visually, the park is very satisfying: double-deck grandstands escort the foul lines nearly all the way out in right and left fields before the top deck falls away, exposing the lower tier; the outfield walls begin in the corners, run straight for a few yards, then dip in to accommodate the bleachers. Those walls, of course, are covered in summer with bittersweet and ivy.

Lines, rising and falling in perfect harmony, set off by brilliant colors: the lush green of the grass, a mixture of five strains from Kentucky to protect against blight; and the brownish-red of the base paths, pitcher's mound, batting area, a blend of sand and clay from New Jersey.

The effect is not lost on Cubs fans, or on visitors to Chicago. Though a team of limited success, the Cubs are always well above the league average in home attendance. While they won the Eastern Division in 1984 and again in 1989, they finished higher than fourth only two other times since 1972, and haven't been to the World Series since they lost to Detroit in 1945. Yet through the 1970s the club averaged 1.5 million a year in home attendance, and in the 1980s the figure was closer to two million, all in a park that seats only 38,710.

"This park is a major attraction," says Harry Caray, the Cubs' popular announcer. "It is, without question, the best place in baseball to watch a game. And everybody knows it. Even if the Cubs are losing, they'll come, just to spend a few hours at Wrigley.

"Every game, 25,000, 30,000. When the weather's really good, 35,000. There's just no place like it," he says.

What about those lights, Harry?

"That's a crime," he answers. "They never should have done it. Not even for one game. This is baseball as it was meant to be. In the daytime, on real grass."

Caray should know what he was talking about. On opening day, 1993, he began his 49th season as an announcer and 12th with the Cubs. He had already spent ten with the crosstown White Sox, one with Oakland, and 25 with St. Louis. His point was that for many Americans, watching baseball in the surroundings that could be described as "classic" has value—emotional value, and for the home team, commercial value.

It is an attitude that is catching on. Both the new Comiskey Park in Chicago, opened in 1991, and the Rangers stadium in Arlington, to be ready in 1994, use traditional facades. And Baltimore's new ballpark at Camden Yards was designed with the overall look of an old-time, urban park; a brickwork structure set in a warehouse neighborhood, its playing field asymmetrical as a modern testimonial to the individuality of playing fields of the past. Rarely has a stadium been more eagerly anticipated. Few were disappointed. *Boston Globe* columnist Bob Ryan, after his first visit to Baltimore during the 1992 baseball season, wrote:

> BALTIMORE—The first story I ever read about this place was in the *Sunday New York Times* of Nov. 19, 1989. The piece was not in the Sports section. It was in the Arts section, under the sub-heading of Architecture/Design.

> Architecture critic Paul Goldberger was ecstatic. He had seen the design of a baseball park to be constructed in the Camden Yards section of downtown Baltimore, and he spoke of this edifice in terms so exuberant as to be incredulous. Surely, I thought, no ballpark could be *this* good.
>
> "This is a building," wrote Goldberger, "capable of wiping out in a single gesture 50 years of wretched stadium design, and of restoring the joyous possibility that a ballpark might actually enhance the experience of watching the game of baseball."
>
> We fortunate people in Boston already have such a ballpark, of course.

Ryan went on to extol the virtues of designing a ballpark to fit into its urban environment. He was writing a love letter to Camden Yards and Fenway in one column, praising their ability to provide a satisfying place for baseball to be played while, at the same time, communicating the sport's uniqueness and its traditions.

"What Camden Yards demonstrates beyond dispute is that the old can indeed meet the new if intelligent people wish to promote the marriage," Ryan says toward the end of his column.

But not everyone favors such a union. When they built the SkyDome in Toronto, they wanted ultramodern, and they got it. With its Jumbotron scoreboard and 11,000-ton pop-top roof, the SkyDome has been a major attraction and curiosity since it opened in 1989. Toronto set a major league home attendance record in 1991 with 4,001,527, then topped that in 1992 by cramming in another 26,791 people. The appeal of the new stadium was enhanced significantly by the Blue Jays driving toward becoming the first non-U.S. World Series champion. According to *Financial World*, the team had the highest gate receipts in all of sports in 1992.

And what were some of the other teams at the top of *Financial World*'s list in 1992? The Boston Red Sox and Fenway were number five, right behind Toronto in overall value, and the hapless Cubs were but a slip away, ninth in overall value among baseball teams. All have succeeded in creating an enticing experience out of attending a ball game, and the uniqueness of their ballparks is a major factor.

A Little Sideshow for the Fans

But unique is hard to come by. Sports have traditionally used all manner of levers to stimulate attendance. They're called promotions. Any sport worried about filling the house uses them. They are rare in the NFL, especially among teams like the Giants that sell out every game, and less rare in the NHL and NBA, both with franchises struggling with low gate receipts. The Golden State Warriors, with low arena revenues, gives free pizzas to fans whenever the home team scores at least 120 points.

Baseball, with the longest schedule—and therefore the most seats to fill in any one season—is the most aggressive sport at employing promotions. Some have been around for so long, and have become so much a part of the game, we forget they were instituted only to attract larger crowds.

When major league attendance crashed with the Depression, down to six million in 1933, it was time to get resourceful. Taking a lesson from the movies, which used double features to lure customers, baseball introduced the scheduled double header that season. (Until 1933, teams only played two games in one day to make up for dates lost to rain.) Baseball's most famous promotion was the All-Star Game, begun in 1935. Pitting the best players in the National League against the American League stars, it was originally played in the spring, to reawaken the fans at the beginning of the long season.

Even night baseball began as a gimmick. One day after the first All-Star Game, on the evening of May 24th, President Franklin D. Roosevelt threw the switch to illuminate baseball's first night game played in Cincinnati; the Reds beat the Phillies, 2–1, before 25,000 fans. The game was also the first event ever broadcast on radio by the young Mutual Broadcasting Company, later to introduce the Game of the Day.

In his 1978 book on baseball promotions, *Hit the Sign and Win a Free Suit of Clothes from Harry Finkelstein*, Bert Sugar writes:

> There were six other night games that year in Cincinnati, often accompanied by fireworks displays, marching bands, and field meets between the two clubs.
>
> The fans loved it. The seven games drew an average of almost 18,000 fans, more than three times the attendance at an average major league game in 1935.

Ladies Day was tried first by the Cincinnati Reds in 1889, after they discovered that an unusual number of women attended games when the pitcher was the handsome Tony Mullane, known as "the Apollo of the Box." On those days, the club admitted women free if they were accompanied by male escorts. Other clubs adopted the promotion, but it died out, to be reintroduced for good by the Cubs in the mid-1920s.

Bat Day was begun in Cleveland in 1952 by Bill Veeck, certainly the king of baseball promotion. Now Bat Days are standard fare, along with Ball Day, Batting Helmet Day, and anything else management can think of to attract paying customers.

Other promotions have shown less of a universal appeal, but were successful for the home team when spotted in the schedule. In 1993, to celebrate the visit of the bald Charles Barkley to Houston, the Rockets granted free admission to their game against the Phoenix Suns for any man who would have his head shaved at the game; women getting shorn received season tickets. (Volunteers totaled 200, including 12 women.) The Mets employed a more conservative approach when Darryl Strawberry was still in New York; on Strawberry SunDay, fans received prepackaged strawberry sundaes upon entering the park.

The Appeal of Luxury Boxes

By their nature, promotions can have only a limited effect. All they can do under the best of circumstances is fill the house, and that cannot be relied upon. Even if there were a way of filling every seat, that would not be enough. Several NFL and some NBA teams regularly sell out, and yet the search for additional revenue goes on.

This quest is made even more urgent by the great economic changes in sports. "When I first came into football in 1953, it was not a business, it was a fun thing," said the late Carroll Rosenbloom, owner of the Los Angeles Rams, in 1977. "My payroll for my players and my coaches and everybody else might have been a quarter of a million dollars. For Chrissakes, today you're paying a player that much—one player." In terms of NFL economics, 1977 was light-years ago; the average salary in football was $55,288. By 1991, the league average was $430,000. And that 1953 payroll of $250,000 had by 1991 grown to $22.1 million in player costs for the Rams.

To cover those kinds of increases, teams had to become more resourceful. And while the first actual cut in baseball or football contracts did not come until the MLB's 1994 agreement with ABC and NBC, such an occurrence was long anticipated. No potential source could be overlooked by the teams. Stadiums were already holding 60,000 and 70,000 people, and arenas 18,000 and 20,000; building larger did not seem in the offing. Ticket prices were moving up as quickly as would seem acceptable; the rate of increase from 1991 to 1992 for a family at a game was about 8.8 percent. Something else was needed. Something special; something expensive. The answer has been the luxury box, or skybox.

Luxury boxes are those fancy rooms inside stadiums and arenas that allow corporations and some private individuals to entertain clients and friends while also watching events. They're always up high, often around press-box level, and usually equipped with closed-circuit television for close-ups of the action. And if the game isn't so exciting, there is often cable television, complete with movies. Of course there is a wet bar, and caterers offering everything from hot dogs to caviar and champagne.

Every facility built within the last 20 years has luxury boxes, and most of the older ones have been retooled to include them. Some can be bought—the good ones at Texas Stadium cost $1.25 million—but a lease arrangement is more typical. That costs a mere $30,000 a season at Texas Stadium, up to $43,500 at the Superdome in New Orleans, and a top of $215,000 at Madison Square Garden. But New York can't touch Toronto's SkyDome, where the top price for a luxury box is $250,000 per year.

How much money does such luxury seating generate? That depends on how many of these little palaces are occupied. According to a 1991 article in *The Wall Street Journal,* the potential annual revenue for Madison Square Garden is $15 million. The Bradley Center in Milwaukee brings in $3 million a year to the Bucks, and the Palace, $11 million to the Detroit Pistons.

But who gets all these millions? This depends on the agreement between the team and the facility. Generally, even in publicly owned stadiums, money from luxury boxes goes to the team, since often the team built them. But in Toronto, Montreal, Pittsburgh, and San Diego, the stadiums get the revenue. Teams playing in their own parks—such as the Dallas Cowboys—keep everything. Teams playing in stadiums and arenas owned privately by someone else—the Celtics, among them—most often get nothing.

Whatever a team earns from luxury boxes, it keeps. Regular gate attendance in the NFL is shared, 60 percent for the home team and 40 percent for the visitor. For Major League Baseball, the split in the American League is 80 percent to the home team and 20 percent to the visitor; in the National League, the split is 91–9%. Hockey and basketball teams keep all the money from home attendance, except for the 6 percent of NBA ticket revenues going to the league. But revenue from luxury boxes are exempt from such agreements, making them even more appealing.

Luxury boxes are a relatively new idea. They began not as ways to boost profits but as personal indulgences in comfort. It appears that the first skybox was ordered by Judge Roy Hofheinz, the original owner of the Houston Astros and the man who built the Astrodome. However, to be historically correct, we must recall that A. G. Spalding installed 18 private luxury boxes with armchairs in his new stadium in Chicago in 1883, and when Bill Veeck owned the St. Louis Browns in 1952, he turned a set of offices in their home field of Sportsman's Park into an eight-room, three-bedroom apartment, and moved in.

Judge Hofheinz clearly had something a little different in mind. Built when the Astrodome was constructed in the early 1960s, his suite had its own bowling alley and even a chapel. The Judge's accommodations sparked the imagination of another Texan, Lamar Hunt. After the Dallas Texans of the American Football League moved to Kansas City and became the Chiefs for the 1963 season, Arrowhead Stadium was built, and Hunt set a new standard for in-stadium apartments: two floors, four bedrooms, a game room, a living room with fireplace, just so the owner didn't have to get up and go home after watching a game.

The wretched excess of a rich owner, you say! Perhaps, but it was soon to be shared with any fan who could pay the bill. James A. Michener, in researching his 1976 book *Sports in America,* visited a skybox in an unnamed stadium. Here is his report:

> I would like to invite you into one of the more luxurious suites in one of the recently built stadiums. It is on the forty-yard line, about halfway up the side of the stadium. It consists of two large rooms plus bar and bathroom on one level, three bedrooms and two baths on the next level above. The entire floor area is covered with expensive carpeting from Belgium, on which have been placed massive pieces of Renaissance furniture providing seats on the main floor for some sixty guests. The wall decorations are paintings from Europe, mirrors with heavily carved frames imported from Europe and tastefully arranged scenes from former football seasons.
>
> The bar was imported from London, a stupendous affair along which forty or fifty of the guests can stand comfortably. At convenient spots are pull-out tables on which guests can place their trays while dining from the lavish smorgasbord. The upstairs bedrooms are done in French provincial style with ornate furnishings of considerable value. The bathrooms are marble and gold.

Somewhere between the introduction of skyboxes as a private haven and their being offered to the public—credit for the first commercial use belongs to the Dallas Cowboys' then-owner Clint Murchison in the late 1960s—these luxury accommodations became the gleam in every owner's eye. Luxury boxes went on to become the driving force behind the hunger for new stadiums in the 1980s and 1990s. But not every franchise could afford a new facility, and the need for more revenue was so great none could afford to wait.

Profit Through Addition

All over professional sports, the answer was reconstruction. They did it at Comiskey Park in Chicago, while waiting to build their new stadium. Atlanta Falcons owner Rankin Smith added 36 luxury suites to Fulton County Stadium while negotiating for his new stadium to be built. They did it at Yankee Stadium and Wrigley Field, and at Fenway Park, though none of those stadiums are about to be replaced.

The income from those efforts hasn't discouraged anybody on skyboxes. White Sox owners Jerry Reinsdorf and Eddie Einhorn added 36 skyboxes under the upper-deck roof of old Comiskey Park in 1983 and 1984. Two suites were reserved for single-game rentals at $2,200 a day. The other 34 leased for $45,000 a season, 28 under a five-year contract and 6 on a single-season contract.

If Reinsdorf and Einhorn needed any more incentive in their long push for a new stadium, these numbers provided it. They finally got their new facility in 1991, a $150-million mixture of traditional baseball design and the latest amenities. The new park pays homage to its predecessor with the sculpted pattern of old Comiskey's windows on the new facade. Management also brought over the old infield dirt, truckload by truckload. And the two parks have virtually the same attendance, about 44,000. But new Comiskey has 82 skyboxes, with per-season rental ranging from $60,000 to $90,000 each. That was supposed to deliver $5 million in revenue to the Sox each year, but the latest estimate was between $6 million and $7 million.

Regardless of the vintage of the park or arena where their teams play, few franchises could afford to function in the 1990s without skyboxes. New York's Shea Stadium now has 45 that lease for about $65,000 a season, and generate about $3 million a year. The 60 skyboxes at Denver's Mile High Stadium go for about $80,000 a season, and can generate $4.25 million annually.

A 1991 article in *Forbes* listed some of the lease prices of facilities around the country. The bargain of that list was Kansas City's Arrowhead Stadium, with skyboxes available for $14,000 a season of Chiefs football. Luxury boxes at Jack Murphy Stadium in San Diego rented for $29,000 to $49,000 a season; at Candlestick Park in San Francisco from $24,000 to $60,000 for the baseball season and $40,000 to $80,000 for football; and Houston's Astrodome, $25,000 for the baseball season and $15,000 to $45,000 for football.

The old caveat, "let the buyer beware," applies to renting skyboxes. Those prices do not always necessarily include the right to watch the game. Believe it or not, tickets are sometimes extra.

The skyboxes at new Comiskey Park come with tickets, but tickets are extra at Giants Stadium, and that's after paying $95,000 for a season in New Jersey. Leasing a skybox at the Astrodome includes 18 tickets to each game, and five parking spaces. At Shea Stadium, the ticket bill for each box is $17,000 per season.

Many strings are tied to signing up at Toronto's SkyDome, according to a 1991 article in *The Toronto Star*:

> Each owner of the 161 luxury boxes must buy Blue Jay tickets (16 per box at $21 each for every home game) as part of the contractual agreement. Argo [Toronto Argonaut football] tickets are optional. Hiring a host/bartender at $80 a game is mandatory, as is buying food and alcohol through SkyDome suppliers.

Baseball's two most revered parks—Fenway and Wrigley—have added some imaginative wrinkles to skybox thinking. In addition to Fenway's 44 suites, there is the 600 Club, an air-conditioned section of 600 theater seats behind home plate, complete with restaurant and bar. For only $23,000 a season, fans get a set of four club seats. No, tickets are not extra.

Wrigley Field added 67 skyboxes for the 1989 season, each accommodating 12 to 15 people. Most of them rent for $45,000 to $65,000 a year, but three "sky sweeps" are intended for daily corporate or private rentals. The price is $1,750 per game, plus the cost of food, which must be ordered through the stadium. As little as two days' notice is enough.

Of course none of this new construction is of any value to the home team if they either do not own their stadium, or if they have a poor arrangement with those who do.

That was why Jerry Jones, after purchasing the Dallas Cowboys in 1989, borrowed heavily to acquire the $75 million to purchase Texas Stadium and some 30 acres of practice facilities. He knew back when his team was 1–15 and only 90 of his skyboxes were in use that he was going to turn things around. And when his 1992 team went to the Super Bowl—and all 120 skyboxes were leased or sold—it would be he who reaped the profit. (Just a little incentive to build 70 more units for the 1993 season. Even regular seats will cost 20 percent more, and for 1994 about 4,000 end zone seats will be turned into "club seating," each equipped with a television set to improve the fan's view of the action.)

But what about the owners without Jones' resources and business sense, struggling to make a profit with limited revenue from their stadiums or arenas? Or even worse, those franchises gaining nothing; that was the case with the New England Patriots. Their names fill the bottom of *Financial World's* 1992 ranking of professional sports teams listed in order of value—richest teams at the top, with the main reason for their placement beside: New Jersey Devils, poor lease; Washington Capitals, no stadium revenues (even though team and stadium have the same owner); St. Louis Blues, no stadium revenues. And the lowest-ranked NFL team was the Patriots, whose owner even had to pay to use the owner's box.

Garden of Dreams

Basketball and hockey arenas have not been left out of skybox mania. Milwaukee's Bradley Center, home of the NBA's Bucks, has 68 suites, at $35,000 to $55,000 a year. The Palace in Auburn Hills, Michigan, home of the Pistons, has 180 suites, ranging in price from $30,000 to $120,000 a year.

And then there's Madison Square Garden. The most recent Garden—at least three versions preceded the current structure now occupying the two blocks of New York City between 31st and 33rd Streets—was completed in 1968, at a cost of $116 million. In 1991 it underwent $200 million worth of renovations. Among the changes was the addition of fixed outlets selling food, beverages, and souvenir merchandise from the original 109 to 171. By adding new restrooms and enlarging existing facilities, individual accommodations for women increased from 87 to 147, and for men from 182 to 223. They also replaced the old seats, and at the same time installed a special section of approximately 2,200 courtside or rink-side seats priced at $75 per game. Called Club Seats, they come with floor service: attendants register food and drink orders on hand-held computers and return with them "in a matter of minutes," according to the Garden.

Even more ambitious, and more lucrative, was ripping out the Garden's old skyboxes and replacing them with new ones, now called luxury suites. A 1991 article in *The Wall Street Journal* explained why and how:

> The old skyboxes generated just $2 million a year from leases. The new suites, when fully leased, should reap nearly $15 million. There are three times as many of them—up from 29 to 88—at much higher lease rates. The skyboxes went for $90,000; the suites are $140,000 to $190,000. [For the 1992–1993 season, those prices were up to $155,000 and $215,000.]
>
> Part of the difference is in the accouterments: one wet bar, three TVs, one buffet table, three mahogany-paneled walls and two tiers of six comfy seats facing the arena. One TV carries up-to-date statistics on the game below. The buffet table can be heaped with fancy catered food.

One of the advantages of leasing a skybox at Madison Square Garden is the variety of events, ranging from professional basketball and hockey to rock concerts, the International Cat Show, and the Westminster Kennel Club Dog Show. Twelve tickets for every Garden event come with the box, which is fitted with 12 theater seats and four stools at the bar. Box holders also have the option to purchase four additional tickets for the bar stools.

The hefty price on leasing the Garden skyboxes and the required three-year commitment caused some resistance initially. But even in the slowed economy, before the 1992–1993 season opened for the Knicks and Rangers all 86 boxes that could be leased were taken. (One box is kept back for renting on a daily basis, and another is used by Madison Square Garden's own television network.)

Not all the luxury suites around the country are doing so well. Reports out of Minneapolis, at the Target Center, where the Timberwolves play, indicated that the arena was experiencing difficulty getting leases renewed for the 1992–1993 season. And things reportedly were slow at San Diego's Jack Murphy Stadium, home of the Padres.

There were even some problems at Toronto's SkyDome, even with that new record in attendance at Blue Jay games. It wasn't just the cost of leasing the skyboxes, ranging from $120,000 to $250,000 a year, but the additional operating expenses. The cost of tickets, food, liquor, and staff easily added another $100,000.

The result, according to *The Toronto Star,* was a rash of ads in a special baseball edition of their newspaper during the 1991 season, offering boxes for Blue Jay baseball or Argo football games.

"A night watching Canadian Football League action could be yours for about $1,500 (although many owners said they couldn't give away Argo tickets)," said an article in *The Star.* "A date with the more popular Jays starts at $2,000."

The problem, the article said, was hard times.

"Buying into a 10-year lease looked like a solid investment when the dome opened in 1989," it reported, "but some of the smaller investors who have had to lay off company employees and slash budgets are being crippled by bills for wining and dining clients and friends."

Though the research is pretty convincing that spending by sports fans is immune to economic business cycles, this is old thinking, more valid when most fans came to the game with their buddies and sat in "regular" seats. That thinking breaks down in this era of luxury suites.

More times than not, luxury suites are business-related. And few businesses are immune from economic cycles.

9

While the Games Play On

The most obvious sources of revenue at sporting events—after the price of the tickets—are food and drinks, then souvenirs and parking. Viewed individually, these seem incidental, but taken together they rival the cost of getting in the door.

Each year the *Team Marketing Report*, the Chicago-based newsletter, surveys all the teams in professional baseball, football, and basketball to determine just what it costs for a typical outing. ("We don't do hockey because we just haven't found that to be as much a part of the American life as the others," according to Noah Liberman, associate editor of the monthly *Report*.) The publication figures the cost for an entire family of four, including average prices for tickets, two beers, four hot dogs, four soft drinks, two souvenir twill caps, two game programs, and parking.

Less than half the cost of taking your family to a baseball game goes to tickets, while the higher cost of football and basketball make those tickets about two-thirds of the total.

The *Marketing Report* tells us that in 1993, baseball continued to be the best family value, with the average outing costing $90.87. This compares to an NBA game in the 1992–1993 season for the same family of four at $158.17, and an NFL game in 1992 for $163.19. The most expensive outing in baseball, as noted earlier, was a Blue Jays game at $116.11, compared to $77.31 for a Cincinnati game at Riverfront Stadium. Tops in the NFL was the 49er's games at $205, down to a Bengals game at $139.37. For the NBA, four at a Knicks game spent $217.36, and at a Denver Nuggets game, just $117.80.

Traditionally, in the stadiums and arenas of America, the core of these edibles are peanuts, popcorn, hot dogs, and beer. Of these, the most important—and the item with the most history—is beer. Not by coincidence did professional baseball grow up in the last third of the nineteenth century with close ties to breweries. In Cincinnati and St. Louis, in Baltimore and Brooklyn and New York, team owners also owned saloons, distilleries, and breweries.

But those ties were subtle at first—until 1881, that is, when a St. Louis tavern owner named Chris Von der Ahe altered the course of sports. History is not clear on the progression of events. But apparently Von der Ahe observed that taverns near Sportsman's Park did a booming business when the local baseball team, the Brown Stockings, were playing. He offered to sell his beer right in the park, but was denied permission. After the Browns faded from the National League in 1877, the man known as Vondy invested $500 to ensconce the Browns in the newly formed American Association in 1882. His passion was not baseball but commerce. He built an amusement park beside the ballpark, complete with horse races, bands, and a beer garden. It wasn't long before he was selling his beer at the games.

An important lesson was firmly implanted in the other owners' minds. Money was to be made by selling the lucrative brew. And before long, selling beer in the stands was common. Another St. Louis resident ushered the union of beer and baseball into the modern era. That visionary was the president of Anheuser-Busch Breweries, August A. Busch, Jr.; the team, the St. Louis Cardinals of the National League.

When Busch had his company purchase the Cardinals from Fred Saigh in 1953—Saigh had been found guilty of income tax evasion and ordered by Baseball Commissioner Ford Frick to sell the team—the beer tycoon claimed publicly that he was saving the team for St. Louis. The fact that Cardinal radio broadcasts were sponsored by a rival brewery, he said, was immaterial. "I am going at this from the sports angle and not as a sales weapon for Budweiser Beer," he told the press upon announcing the purchase.

In truth, according to *Under the Influence*, a 1991 book by Peter Hernon and Terry Ganey on the Anheuser-Busch dynasty, Saigh was the one dedicated to keeping the team local; his agreed selling price to Busch was $3.75 million, a half-million less than he was offered by a group in Milwaukee. And as for Busch's lack of interest in beer sales, the book reports these words delivered to his board of directors: "Development of the Cardinals will have untold value for . . . our company. This is one of the finest moves in the history of Anheuser-Busch."

One Long Beer Commercial

Busch jumped into his new role with enthusiasm. He reveled in the celebrity, traveling with the team and making judgments on each rival franchise. He demanded that they replace the existing advertising at Sportsman's Park with "a single sign—a huge Anheuser-Busch eagle," according to *Under the Influence*. "Other signs popped up later, along with the incessant playing of the Budweiser theme song, the prancing Clydesdales and the relentless product hawking that transformed every Cardinals game into one long beer commercial."

And it worked. The Cardinals have become one of the more successful baseball franchises, both on the field and off. While they have won only one World Series in the last 20 years, they made it to the fall classic on two other occasions and were rarely out of the division race. Meanwhile, Anheuser-Busch continues to solidify its position as the country's top-selling beer, responsible for about 44 percent of all beer sales.

And the sales campaign at Busch Stadium continues. In a 1978 *Sporting News* interview, Busch boasted of the growth in sales during the Cardinals era from under 6 million barrels a year to 35 million. *Under the Influence* offered the following paragraph:

> A decade later those barrels had more than doubled, due in part to the fact that every Cardinals broadcast was a nine-inning advertisement for Busch and Budweiser. In the new Busch Stadium there were signs that flashed, signs that revolved or fluttered, and if you caught the game on

> radio or television, the team's beer-selling sports announcers never let you forget that Budweiser, Busch and Michelob and an assortment of lights and drys were the finest brewed in the world.

Fans at Busch Stadium see no beers other than those brewed by Anheuser-Busch. That is the goal of every marketer—exclusivity of presentation. As we learned in Chapter 6, advertisers pay extra to be the only product of their kind during a quarter or a half of "Monday Night Football"; for certain events, they can buy the whole show. And at least in their own park, Anheuser-Busch has the market to itself.

The task is not so easy when it comes to selling beer at stadiums and arenas. Concessionaires handle the food and beverages at almost all sports facilities. They make decisions on what will be offered based on what sells and what kind of deals can be cut with distributors. And while Anheuser-Busch controls which beer is sold at its own park, that power does not extend beyond the walls of Busch Stadium.

Why such a battle over beer when it comes to sports? Because in the eyes of the marketing apparatus, sports fans and beer drinkers are as close as if they were joined at the hip. In a 1988 article entitled "Sports and Suds," *Sports Illustrated* published some enlightening numbers about these Siamese twins.

> Statistical curves indicate that the age of maximum beer consumption and the age of maximum sports involvement are the same, both for men and for women. Peak beer-consuming years are 18 to 29, as are the peak sports consuming years—for both participants and spectators. Among males 18 to 34, there is a core group of drinkers whose consumption is so phenomenal that even though they make up only 20 percent of the beer-drinking population, they consume an estimated 70 percent of all beer drunk in this country. Though the industry doesn't make a public point of it, these supersudsers are obviously an enormously important audience—and most easily reached with sports-associated salesmanship.

And what does all this mean to the individual teams? That same 1988 article surveyed the previous season at Riverfront Stadium, home of the Cincinnati Reds. *SI* found that the Reds sold 12,610 barrels and 35,365 cases of beer, which, in the article's words, "works out to nearly a pint for every man, woman and child among the two million plus who attended the 81 Reds games played at Riverfront Stadium." It figured the sales for the year, after taxes, of $4,635,514. And after sharing the revenues with the stadium concessionaires, the Reds get 33 percent—and give 10 percent to the city—ending up with just over $1 million. A small bit of that went to liquor; mostly, it's beer.

The Concessionaires

It's easy money for the Reds, and for most ball clubs. All they have to do is clean up the paper cups that fans drop at their feet. Everything else is handled by the concessionaires, outside companies hired to do the job. In virtually every case, the team or the stadium manager contracts with a concessionaire to handle the food. The concessionaire pays rent on the space used; purchases, prepares, and sells the food and drink; and then pays back a percentage—usually between 25 percent and 35 percent of the business. The percentage on souvenirs is usually higher.

It's big business, and the names of the companies in it are big. ARA Leisure Services, of Philadelphia, with 15,000 employees; Sportservice Corporation, of Buffalo, New York, with 28,000 employees; Volume Services, of Spartanburg, South Carolina, a division of Canteen Corporation, with 10,000 employees.

And there's Harry M. Stevens, Incorporated, of Cranbury, New Jersey—the first in the business. It is a name that is almost as closely associated with arenas and stadiums as the items it sells.

Bert Sugar's *Hit the Sign and Win a Free Suit of Clothes from Harry Finklestein* tells us that the concessions industry officially began during the summer of 1887 in Columbus, Ohio, when Harry Mosley Stevens went to a baseball game and found the scorecard he purchased unreadable. According to Sugar, Stevens marched into the front office and offered the club $700 for the privilege of printing and selling intelligible scorecards. Soon he branched out to food, and by 1894 he was in the big leagues, selling peanuts and soda pop to the fans at the Polo Grounds in New York. Sugar recounts:

> One day, during a cold and windy Giants game, he noticed his soft drink sales were lagging. Employing the same spur-of-the-moment hustling that had first gotten him into the business, he sent his vendors out into neighborhood stores to buy up all the frankfurters and rolls they could find. He boiled the franks, split the rolls to form a bed and sold them to the chilled spectators, with the slogan that still rings up sales to this very day: "Get 'em while they're red hot."

Today Harry M. Stevens' 22,000 employees staff the Astrodome in Houston, Shea Stadium in New York, Fenway Park in Boston and more than 20 other big-time facilities. The company's revenues of $190 million in 1991 made it one of the country's largest concessionaires.

More than Hot Dogs

A revolution has taken place in the concession business since its early days, when a visit to the ballpark meant snacking on peanuts or Cracker Jacks™, when vendors carried buckets of Coke bottles in ice and hot dogs were boiled in a kettle under the stands.

The seeds for the big change were planted not in the major league parks but on the country roads of America, where minor league operations struggled to make an extra buck by selling local favorites at the park. Because the only fully developed minor league system in this country supports major league baseball, and because it has been going on for so long, it is those franchises that have added variety and interest to the food of sports: spicy hot chili dogs in the Double A park of the Chattanooga Lookouts in baseball's Southern League; Flying Burritos at the games of the Durham Bulls, Single A team of the Atlanta Braves in the Carolina League; Haid's famous white Coneys—sort of a bratwurst, heavier on the veal and pork than the beef—at McArthur Stadium in Syracuse, home of the Triple A Chiefs.

A few big-league parks carried on that tradition from the start. One was old Comiskey Park, which resembled a carnival more than its straight-laced cousins: Kosher hot dogs were sold from pushcarts with red canopies; snow cones in grape, strawberry, root beer, lemon, and a neon-blue raspberry were available at little steel stands; a portable steamtable pushed up against a wooden picnic table held bean burritos and beef burritos, tacos and tostadas; and two ladies made fried dough from scratch.

Old Comiskey Park is gone, but the new park just across the street has most of the same items. The reason is that Sportservice, the concessionaire that operates it—and operated the old one as well—knows that boring is out and diversity is in. Today, big-league parks across the country reflect that same philosophy.

- At Anaheim Stadium, the California Angels' home field, dishes include sushi, lasagna, spaghetti, and pasta salads.

- At Cincinnati's Riverfront Stadium, home to the Reds, fans can purchase barbecue in a pita pocket in addition to traditional favorites knockwurst and bratwurst.
- At County Stadium, home of the Milwaukee Brewers—another place where sausages are popular—national choices include Polish, Italian, and Bavarian, as well as bratwurst, conventional hot dogs, and Kosher franks.
- At Three Rivers Stadium, where the Pittsburgh Pirates play, they sell chicken freshly cooked on a rotisserie.
- At Tampa Bay Stadium, home of the Buccaneers, chilled peanut butter and key lime pies are the desserts of choice, washed down with mineral water and flavored spring waters.
- At the Los Angeles Coliseum, most recently home field to the Raiders, shrimp salad and Oriental chicken salad are but side dishes to the famous La Pizza Loco, a Southern California original that features such Latin toppings as chorizo sausage, refried beans, bacon, and even jalapeño peppers.

And just as in the general population, where people are concerned about the calories and fat in what they eat, fans want healthier foods. And they can get them. Along with all those fatty sausages are chicken items in a variety of forms, fish sandwiches and salads, and pasta salads and regular salads.

For snacking, some parks offer popcorn popped in no-cholesterol oil, and no-fat and no-cholesterol yogurt. At the Hubert H. Humphrey Metrodome in Minnesota, the weight-watchers special is low-fat frozen fruit whip. Of course, lite beer has been around for years.

What does all this cost? That depends on where you are eating it. According to figures compiled by *The Team Marketing Report* for its yearly Fan Cost Index, the cheapest hot dog in baseball in 1993 was at a Reds game, $1; the most expensive, $3 at Yankee Stadium. Draft beer ranged from $2 for a 12-ounce cup at Busch Stadium to $3.60 for a 12-ounce cup at the Hubert H. Humphrey Metrodome in Minnesota.

Soldier Field, where the Bears play, had the most expensive hot dog in the NFL at $3.25; the $1 dogs at Cincinnati and Philly games were the cheapest; beer ranged from $2 for a 12-ounce cup in Miami to $4.25 for the same size at a Rams game. Top price for a hot dog in the NBA was $2.95 at a Knicks game in New York, down to $1.50 at several arenas.

These are average prices. The new specialty items cost more. That sushi at an Angels game cost $5.50; lasagna was $4. At County Stadium, the Kosher frank was $2.75, $1 more than the regular hot dog. That usually means more profit, making the new products very popular with concessionaires. The use of brand names at stadiums also grew in popularity in the 1990s.

But a word of warning to concessionaires around the country: Don't forget the old favorites while rushing to embrace those new menus. That happened to Marriott when it took over food service at Dodger Stadium.

Marriott Stadiums and Arenas, concessionaire for the Delta Center in Salt Lake City, Dallas Reunion Arena, and Sun Devil Stadium in Tempe, Arizona, added Dodger Stadium in 1991. The firm spent $10 million over the winter renovating stands and adding 32 fast-food outlets. Marriott was very excited about bringing the wonders of Taco Bell, Pizza Hut, and TCBY Frozen Yogurt to the fans at Dodgers Stadium.

Of course, there would still be hot dogs. But, according to an article in *Adweek,* Marriott slipped up when the company switched from grilled wieners to steamed.

> But you do not mess with the famous Dodger Dog. Hundreds of fans protested to Dodger management, to Marriott headquarters and to local media. Fans decried Marriott as a tradition-killing villain intent on foisting fast food on a captive audience.
>
> "They're turning Dodgers stadium into a (bleepin') minimall," said one fan. "I want my old hot dogs back!"

Adweek went on to say that Marriott admitted blundering when they eliminated the Dodger Dog, and hurried to install grills at eight locations around the Stadium. At the same time, the concessionaire defended fast foods.

"We did surveys and studies," Marriott spokesman Rick Sneed told *Adweek.* "Consumers have asked that branded fast food be in the ballpark. We just didn't realize how many people wouldn't like the steamed dogs."

Most stadiums and arenas around the country had less difficulty introducing the branded concept. Besides the facilities serviced by Marriott, Gold Star Chili is now available at Riverfront Stadium, Kentucky Fried Chicken and Burger King products are at Montreal's Olympic Stadium, and Mile High Stadium in Denver sells Domino's Pizza.

What Makes 'Em Buy

How much any of this sells—and ultimately how much the club gets—depends primarily on how many people attend the event. Big events naturally attract the best crowds. At the 1991 Super Bowl in Tampa, Volume Services reported more than $800,000 worth of business. The Portland Trailblazers pulled in more than $600,000 from the three games played at home in their 1990 NBA playoff games against Detroit, according to Fine Host, the concessionaires at Memorial Coliseum.

Every game is not a Super Bowl or a playoff. But the eating and drinking go on, no matter what is at stake on the field, court, or ice. And while the receipts at the end of the season rarely make headlines, they do affect the financial health of the concessionaire and the club. Every game has a pattern. Tita Cherrier works for ARA Services; sales patterns are a hobby of hers. Cherrier says:

> Some things are real simple. The better the game—the closer the score—the longer the people stay and the more they buy. If the home team scores right off the bat, the fans tend to remain in their seats, waiting for something else good to happen. But if the visiting team scores, that's when they leave to get something to eat.
>
> People buy more at day games. Most of them eat before going to a night game, but a day game means lunch. And while bad weather keeps people home, those who come eat, and they eat what's hot—hot dogs and hamburgers, hot chocolate and coffee.
>
> On Sundays we sell a lot more of your basic ballpark fare. It's a family crowd; they eat hot dogs and peanuts and Cracker Jacks™ and ice cream. Sunday's not a good day for beer.

On Their Own

While nearly all big-league sports facilities enter into agreements with outside contractors to handle their food and drink, a few do it themselves. This is rare in stadiums; Montreal's Olympic Stadium is one of the few. Among the arenas, Maple Leaf Garden in Toronto has an in-house operation. And so does Madison Square Garden in New York.

The Garden used Harry M. Stevens until 1991. Under their agreement, Stevens operated the only restaurant—the Penn Plaza Club—provided food for the 29 skyboxes, and ran the 104 food stands. The restaurant menu consisted of steaks, chops, and fish; the stands, the standard hot dogs, pizza, peanuts, and such.

Then, while making plans for their $200 million renovation, the people who run the Garden—Paramount, the same people who own the Knicks and Rangers—decided to take more control of their property. First they decided to take over the cleaning, which had also been contracted out, and then they decided to handle the food.

"We decided to take the food to another level, to go on our own and be masters of our own fate," says Bob Russo, the Garden's executive vice-president and general manager. "If we were going to invest a lot of money in renovating this building, why leave it to others to run. When you're a step removed, it's hard."

The added responsibility required hiring 40 or 50 full-time people, but employing about 800 part-timers. Overall, the Garden has a full-time staff of 350; in addition, workers are called in as needed from a group of between 2,000 and 2,500. The renovations gave Paramount two restaurants instead of one, 87 luxury boxes instead of 29, an additional 64 food stands, and more than 2,000 club seats entitled to service.

The changes are more elaborate in the new main dining room, the Club Bar and Grill, which offers pastas, stuffed pork chops, fish and seafood in a variety of forms. And there is an expanded menu at all the stands; pastrami and smoked turkey sandwiches, salads, as well as hamburgers and hot dogs.

"The food has improved dramatically," says Russo, adding that serving quality meals in that setting is not easy. "People are usually late coming in. They want to eat and get out for the start of the game at 7:30. We end up getting 150 people who want to be finished and out in 45 minutes. It's tough to give them a fine dining experience in 45 minutes, but we've been able to do it."

Russo says the Garden is very happy with the change. Profits are up, though he declines to say how much. "If you're not splitting with a partner, and you see everything that's coming in—when you know what you're paying for labor—you can do a better job. And we do."

The Writing on the Wall

A less obvious source of revenue inside ballparks and arenas is the advertising. Signs can cover the walls, or be more subtle. Check the clock; some product has probably bought the space around it. Look at the scoreboard; something is usually being sold on top of all those numbers.

Including advertising in programs, scorecards, and inside stadiums and arenas, teams add between $.5 million and $5 million a year to their budget. And it's been going on for a long time.

Scanning through photographs taken at ball parks from the turn of the century on offers a glimpse into the past of sports in this country. Behold a fluid tableau of American commerce and industry: Mail Pouch tobacco, Lifebuoy soap, and B.V.D. underwear; Coke, Pepsi, and Budweiser; Regal shoes and Morisco cigarettes. The famous Spalding & Brothers sporting goods can be seen in an 1886 photo of the original Polo Grounds; Albert Spalding was a player, manager, and powerful force in baseball's early days. And what old Dodgers fan can forget Abe Stark's 3-foot high 30-foot long offer stretching beneath the scoreboard at Ebbets Field: "Hit Sign Win Suit"?

The flavor of those old ads is sadly gone from today's stadium and arena advertising. But today there is volume. A 1992 study by Ernst & Young of 105 professional franchises in 44 cities in the United States and Canada revealed there were more than 4,400 stadium signs representing nearly 1,400 advertisers.

The study, which included advertising in yearbooks and scorecards as well as external stadium signs and those in concourses, revealed that food and beverage companies account for about 38 percent of all ads. Two companies—Anheuser-Busch and Coca-Cola—accounted for about 40 percent of that total, and nearly half of all NBA advertising. Nearly 30 percent of advertising fell into the category of consumer products and service, and 13 percent into that of media and communications companies; most of this is advertising by television and radio stations. About 11 percent was by companies offering business products and services, and the final 9 percent by local or national retailers.

Hockey was the sport most actively embracing stadium advertising, especially Canadian hockey, with an average of 82 signs in each arena, 22 percent more than around American ice. The sport is ideal for the medium, with all that dasher-board space surrounding the rink, and the action happening right in front of it. The NBA was second, the NFL third, and baseball last.

"The Major League Baseball average was weighed down by Chicago's Wrigley Field, which has no signage," read Ernst & Young's report. Also lowering the overall average was Dodger Stadium. Only four signs—all Union 76—had been on display there since the stadium opened in 1962. But in 1993 they were replaced by Coca-Cola. "Economics was the biggest factor," says Bob Graziano, Dodger vice-president finance.

The 1993 baseball season also saw a new leader in quantity of stadium signage, as Baltimore's Oriole Park at Camden Yards replaced Candlestick Park. The new total was 65, well below the overall leader. The sports facility with the most signs was Le Colisée in Quebec, home of the NHL's Nordiques, with 113; America West Arena, home of the NBA's Phoenix Suns, was second with 95.

Purchasers of stadium signage generally do so with the television camera angles in mind. The more desirable spots are those likely to be seen routinely during a game's telecast, such as beneath the scorer's table in basketball or on the scoreboards that face the television camera in hockey. This was no doubt the inspiration for the new backstop signs that appeared in 1993 in Tiger Stadium, Milwaukee's County Stadium, and Joe Robbie Stadium in Miami. They are visible on every pitch shot from the center-field camera.

With virtually every game today being broadcast somewhere, stadium advertising signage receives significantly more exposure than it did years ago, when generally only the attending fan could be counted on to receive the advertiser's message.

Exactly what each club gains in revenue from stadium and arena advertising is difficult to determine, even if the clubs were willing to disclose that information. One source had Microsoft paying $300,000 for its sign at Toronto's SkyDome in 1990, and only $30,000 for their display in Seattle's Kingdome. When an anti-smoking group sued New York City over the Marlboro cigarette billboard at Shea Stadium in 1993, we learned that Philip Morris paid about $250,000 a year for space. And according to a 1992 article in *Amusement Business*, total signage deals at the America West Arena—home of the NBA's Phoenix Suns—was worth $3.5 million that year. The Coca-Cola deal at Dodger Stadium was worth millions, acknowledges Bob Graziano, without being specific. "It was a significant amount of money."

But those arrangements are rarely simple. Packaging is the more common rule. The ad for a television or radio station may be part of a package that includes the sale of broadcasting rights. A beer ad could be part of the stadium's deal to sell that product. Or it could even be more complicated.

Doug Ross, president of Madison Square Garden Network and the man who sells advertising space in the Garden, says, "We have a sponsor deal with Coke, and it's worth seven figures a year." But Coke didn't buy just a sign. They bought a package that included: the sign, the right to be the only soft drink sold at the Garden, advertising spots on MSG Network, and sponsorship of programs at the Garden. "Virtually all" of the advertising sold at the Garden is by package, according to Ross.

"Let's look at what Coke wanted," he says. "They wanted to be identified with these teams, this network, and the building. The best way to do that is to sell the product here, to have the sign, and then to continue that connection, so that when the fan goes home and watches TV, the Coke commercial is on."

People who buy just one sign or an ad in the program, insists Ross, don't get the full impact of what sports advertising offers.

It is, in other words, similar to the rest of the sports business: forces of persuasion tied to plans for commerce, all in an endless web of buying and selling.

Once there were signs mounted on the front of the upper deck or spotted on the outfield wall, offering a bonus for the ball player and diversion for the fans: "Hit This Space and Win $200" or "Hit The Toilet Seat and Win $20." Now they are part of deals involving millions.

Nothing in sports is simple any more.

10

Far from the Madding Crowd

Our professional sports have become so much a part of American life that teams and athletes don't even have to play a game to generate revenue.

In season and out, people spend billions of dollars on baseball hats and football shirts, and on jackets and gym bags and coffee mugs bearing the logos of hockey and basketball teams. And that doesn't even count all the money shelled out by advertisers to get superstars to eat breakfast food on television or drive cars or drink cola.

This game is called licensing, and although far from the field of action, it's worth a fortune.

As it applies to the world of sports, licensing is the official granting of permission to use an image to stimulate sales. That image can be as individual as Wayne Gretzky's picture on a trading card or as general as the NHL shield on a polo shirt. Using either one without written permission is illegal; using either one legally costs the licensee money.

The practice has been around a long time. Baseball players at the turn of the century were paid by the early trading card companies for the right to use their image. (These arrangements were not without incident. When Sweet Caporal cigarettes included Pittsburgh Pirate shortstop Honus Wagner in their 1910 series, Wagner objected. The man known as The Flying Dutchman chewed tobacco and puffed happily on cigars, but he did not want to appear publicly to promote smoking. He demanded that the company withdraw the cards, and it did. But a few escaped, creating one of the great collectors' bonanzas of all time. A Honus Wagner card was sold at auction in 1991 for $451,000.)

How much Wagner was supposed to get from Sweet Caporal is lost to history, in much the same way that the sums players today receive from such deals are lost to a maze of contractual agreements. In this modern world of high finance, of buying and selling rights, the player doesn't own that particular piece of the pie. It belongs to the league, or to the player's union. They own the image of the player in his official uniform, and negotiate the rights to card companies. This is the arrangement in all the professional team sports, though the exact details differ. The athletes receive whatever deal has been hammered out by their representatives.

But there is no question as to the huge amounts of money that are generated by the sale of licensed sports items. According to a 1993 article in *The New York Times,* retail sales of all licensed sports merchandising grew from a $5.5 billion business in 1985 to $12.2 billion in 1992. Major League Baseball's part in that was $2.4 billion, with the NFL close behind at $2.1 billion.

A Future in the Cards

Trading cards make up an important part of that action, especially in baseball. The only reason baseball leads in that list of licensing sales is because of cards, which is only fair; they were first on the scene.

The cards were introduced in 1887, in cigarette packs. Bubble gum cards came along in 1933, issued by the Goudey Gum Company. The Bowman Gum Company entered the business in 1948, not only with baseball cards but also with sets of NFL and NBA players cards. Theirs was truly a ground-breaking expedition in commerce, but the birth of the card business as it exists today was waiting to happen.

Tobacco was part of that story as well. The Shorin family was in the tobacco business early this century in Brooklyn, New York, but business was not good. In 1938 they created Topps Chewing Gum, Inc. Gum was a natural choice; it could be distributed through the same wholesale network as tobacco. In 1949, as part of an effort to promote sales, Topps issued its first set of gum-backed cards, The Hocus Focus Magic Cards. The set included 19 baseball players, who happened to be under contract to Bowman. The lawsuit that followed caused Topps to temporarily exit the baseball card business. They then bought out the Bowman Company, and reentered the business for good in 1951.

A year later, when Topps came out with their 1952 "wax packs," cards wrapped in waxed paper with bubble gum and selling for 1 cent and 5 cents, the modern era of baseball cards began. The cards caught fire with kids across the country, and a bond of sports and collecting was formed that has become a major industry today.

Some 40 billion new cards are created each year. Adults and kids alike invest in them, banking on the market value appreciation that cards have shown over recent years. And while profit is a prime motive for many, there are still plenty for whom the attraction is what it was back in the 1950s—a way to get closer to the game of baseball.

But even at the start—yes, even at a penny apiece—cards meant profit. For the people in charge, those trading cards were always big business.

Topps' early encounter with the law taught them to be more careful when they reentered the business in 1951. Marvin Miller, former head of the Major League Baseball Players Association, describes the company's policy toward contractual arrangements with players in his book, *A Whole Different Ball Game.*

> Topps had signed contracts with almost every major league player and many minor league hopefuls as well. A player received $5 to sign and $125 a year for each year he played in the majors for exclusive use by Topps of his photo for trading cards, either sold alone or sold in conjunction with a confectionery product. Players didn't get a percentage of sales. Nothing, not even free bubble gum.
>
> . . . Topps had, in effect, a perpetual reserve clause. After a player had been in the majors for two years, Topps would give him a contract renewal—a check for $75—insuring that the player was always three to

> five years away from being free of the contract. Even worse, Topps maintained that the contract provided that while he was under contract with them, he couldn't sign with another company even if the second company's contract was not to be effective until after the Topps contract had expired.

Miller, who left his job as chief economist and assistant to the president of the Steelworkers Union in 1966 to become head of the ball player's union, called the situation "a microcosm of the position the owners had the players in with the reserve clause."

Miller approached Topps to draw up new terms, but the card company was happy with the old ones. "There will be no change," Miller reported then Topps president Joel Shorin as saying. "Topps has the players signed to contracts, and I don't see what you can do about it."

Like any good union man, Miller moved to respond by organizing. He instructed the ball players to refuse to sign their Topps renewals; by the end of the 1968 season he was meeting with the card company on a new contract. The new terms, according to Miller's book, brought double the payment, from $125 to $250 per player, and 8 percent on sales up to $4 million a year, and 10 percent on sales above that.

"The royalties in the first year came to about $320,000," says Miller. He goes on to describe how Topps' monopoly over card sales would later be broken, then adds this point about royalties: "Almost 25 years later, with five trading-card companies under contract, [they] stand around $50 million a year."

And how big was the trading card business in 1991, when Miller made that statement? Estimates varied, but the retail market for baseball cards was close to $1.3 billion, according to one card manufacturer.

No other sport even approaches that. The figure for football card sales in 1991 was about $300 million; basketball, perhaps half that. The greatest popularity for hockey cards is in Canada; one U.S. manufacturer, Upper Deck, even produced a French-language set for the 1990–1991 season. (No figures were available on the income from NHL cards.) Pro basketball players received only about $5,000 in 1991 from the league in card revenue; the NBA owns all licensing rights under their collective bargaining agreement.

The NFL's history with trading cards is not as rich as baseball's, and football's cut of the card pie is much smaller. But neither factor limited the volume of debate over the rights for those cards. During the six-year war that began in 1987 and raged between the NFL and the NFL Players Association, the two forces battled over control of the market.

There were attempts by the union to solidify its bargaining position with card manufacturers by getting members to sign a "Group Licensing Agreement," attacks by the NFL that the agreement was illegal, and suits filed by the union against its own players for cutting individual deals with the NFL Properties, the licensing arm of the league. The following account from *New York Newsday* in June of 1992 gives an idea of the circus:

> As of Friday, NFL Properties had paid 678 players to cancel their group licensing deals with the union and sign separate, more lucrative agreements with Properties.
>
> The "NFL Quarterback Club," a group of 11 NFL quarterbacks, for example, guarantees each of its members $500,000 over five years for the use of their faces on a card set. The payments for other players range from $10,000 and up to $100,000 for the quarterbacks, based on the marketability of the players involved.
>
> NFL Properties also outflanked the union by signing top rookie prospects before the draft. Properties gave two-year, $150,000 contacts for first-round prospects; two-year, $100,000 contracts to second-rounders, and two-year, $50,000 contracts for third-rounders.

All of this high-level negotiating ended when the new contract was agreed upon at the end of 1992, and the union got control of card contracts. In light of all the other control that the league retained, it was a minor point of compromise.

A Major Offensive in Licensing

Notwithstanding trading cards, the NFL has been the most aggressive of all pro leagues in its licensing efforts. The sales of jackets, key chains, pajamas, caps, baby bibs, and anything else you can imagine that might sport an NFL logo now rings up over $2.1 billion worth of retail sales, netting about $200 million to the league.

The force behind all this is NFL Properties, the licensing and marketing arm of the pro football league. It was created under Pete Rozelle in 1963, as much to promote the league and protect the league's logos and trademarks as it was to sell souvenirs. At the time, those were primarily little player dolls with bobbing heads. Prior to 1982, profits were donated to charity. NFLP, as it is known, still contributes to charity—$13 million since 1973, according to their own records—but it now has both feet planted firmly in the marketplace.

A large reason for NFLP's success is its ability to recognize its diverse consumer base and respond to it with varying products and strategies. And it does not hurt that the beginning of the NFL season mirrors the back-to-school rush, and that the play-offs coincide with the Christmas season.

NFLP is into everything. About 350 manufacturers are licensed to produce more than 2,500 items that are league-connected. There are also over one hundred corporate sponsors, who paid an estimated $50 million in 1992 to use the NFL logo. Then there's publishing and special events on television, and the new football theme park. Called the NFL Experience, this league promotional event shows up at the Super Bowl to engage younger fans and fantasy players; it is similar to Major League Baseball's FanFest, held during the week of the All-Star Game, and the NBA's All-Star Jam Session.

The man given most credit for the explosion of football capitalism was John Bello, who until September of 1993 was the president of NFLP; Bello brought marketing experience from General Foods and Pepsi to his position at the NFL in 1988. Part of his success came from his passionate belief that the NFL is "magical" and that by offering even a little piece of it to the public he is stimulating their lives.

"The NFL is more than just a game or a sport," he said. "It's America's magical institution which transcends sport. It's an ongoing narrative, a drama which invites its fans to participate."

NFL Properties, Bello believed, could help accomplish that task. "Our first and foremost objective is to expand the fan's interest, enjoyment and involvement in the game, the NFL, its clubs, and its players," he said.

And to be sure, NFLP goes beyond selling souvenirs in its efforts. It funds educational programs along with its sponsors, using football cards as classroom learning tools, and computer-based programs that use players and football to teach math and science to seventh graders. It also sponsors scholarships and grants, and programs aimed at keeping students in school and off drugs.

But the heaviest concentration of the energies of NFLP's staff of 130 people goes toward developing and selling merchandise that, in one way or another, says "National Football League." You can buy bowling balls with the logo of your favorite team, and golf umbrellas and pool cues and even bags of potato chips. You can buy pewter belt buckles decorated with team symbols. You can buy Christmas tree ornaments and rhinestone jewelry, watches and inflatable helmets, briefcases and mugs and card tables, floor mats for your car and collars for your dog, pacifiers and teething rings for your kid and birdhouses for passing robins, all in designs that celebrate your favorite NFL team. And yes, they even sell bumper stickers and pennants; and clothes, all manner of clothes.

The core series of items, Pro Line, began with jerseys and warm-up jackets, and moved to sweaters and parkas. Along the way it became clear that the public really liked the look that players and coaches modeled on television during games.

"We put a sweater on Joe Walton for a Monday night game, and we got 5,000 calls about it within the next few days," John Bello told *Sports Illustrated,* describing an incident involving the former New York Jet coach. "People wanted to know where they could get one for themselves. We knew then that we had a winner."

Choices have increased since then. First came "NFL Throwbacks" for nostalgia buffs, wool caps from teams of the old days, the Canton Bulldogs and Acme Packers; 1920s-style wool jerseys and letter jackets from the 1961 Packers. Then, in 1991, came "Spirit" for women. Responding to the fact that 42 percent of NFL fans are women, NFLP began marketing fleece sweaters, rain gear, and sleepwear; and jackets in satin, fake fur, denim, and leather, priced from $125 to $800.

The men now have some pretty nice jackets, too. Team jackets in wool with leather sleeves go for $265; there's a reversible number with lambskin on one side and leather-trimmed satin on the other for $1,200. Tough guys not wanting to compromise their image can buy an authentic NFL helmet for about $200.

Of course, NFL Properties doesn't make any of these items. That's the beauty of this new merchandising. They sell the right to use the NFL's images on all of these various products. Starter and Wilson, Wells Lamont, Nutmeg Mills, and Rawlings are just some of the companies licensed to produce items. And NFLP works hard to make certain nobody else uses them. According to a 1991 article in *Newsday,* NFLP budgeted about $1.5 million for trademark protection fighting counterfeit products or knockoffs.

Coming Late to the Party

Other than baseball cards, Major League Baseball had never aggressively marketed itself to the nation's shoppers. Most of the clubs handled their own licensing in the early 1980s; Warner Communication Inc.'s Licensing Corporation of America promoted team logos. It wasn't overly successful. Teams averaged only about $30,000 in licensing revenues a year.

But in 1987, the commissioner's office passed to Peter Ueberroth, a man with a great sense of retailing, and Rick White became president of Major League Baseball Properties, Inc. Between the two men they convinced the teams to centralize their licensing efforts, and bring them in-house. They also standardized licensing policies, according to a 1991 article in *Crain's New York Business*, and insisted that each licensee produce merchandise for all teams. Royalty fees were set at 8.5 percent, and quality controls were tightened.

Licensees and profits have been growing ever since.

By 1992, Major League Baseball Properties—or MLBP—had more than 400 licensees who manufactured more than 2,500 products. Retail sales of sports-licensed products exceeded $2.3 billion, with apparel accounting for 45 to 50 percent of the business.

Items produced include mugs and cookies and even earrings that celebrate baseball teams, but nearly half of all sales come from clothing. The bulk of those sales come from the "Authentic Diamond Collection"—apparel identical to what the players wear—and the "Cooperstown Collection." Like the NFL's "Throwbacks," the "Cooperstown Collection" plays on the fascination with sports nostalgia. Logos of teams lost to history adorn shirts and jackets in styles from another age, and can sell for $150 and $500 respectively.

MLBP has also shown it can think small for big profits. In 1991 it introduced the "Rookie League," everything from crib sets to toddler wear for children from infancy to age eight. A four-color magazine was created to support sales and an animated TV series was in the works.

Then, proving that small markets were no deterrent, it dipped into the minor leagues that same year, picking up the rights to 152 teams. That's 152 more logos, and wonderful names like the Toledo Mudhens, the Chattanooga Lookouts, the Memphis Chicks, the Cedar Rapids Kernels (as in corn), and the Carolina Mud Cats. Sales started off slowly, only $3 million in 1991, but zoomed to $40 million in 1992.

The phenomenon actually changed the face of minor league baseball. Those teams that were for so long content to take the nickname of the parent club—among them the Pawtucket Red Sox, Boston's International League farm team—suddenly looked dull beside the Crawdads, Beavers, and other more individual and exotic names. More and more teams redesigned uniforms and caps to match new names that reflected their own geographic region. Knoxville's Double A team had been the Knoxville Sox when they were Chicago's farm team in the 1970s, and more recently the Blue Jays, for their affiliation with Toronto. But in 1993 they became the Smokies, and now sport a sketch of the Smoky Mountains on their uniforms.

The licensing divisions of NBA and NHL generate less in sales than do baseball and football, at least partly because they have been at it for a shorter time. Retail sales in basketball for 1992 were $1.4 billion; for hockey, $.6 billion. What they were selling, however, was remarkably similar to the other sports: team caps and beach towels; telephones sporting team logos for $70; belt buckles and ice chests and trash cans; $6 key rings shaped like little hockey players and basketball players; and pennant clocks at $30. And they both sell clothes, just like the larger divisions of the other sports: team jackets, shirts, caps, and workout suits of all kinds.

New Rules for Success

But as much as the marketing of sports-related apparel and trinkets follow similar lines, there are some new rules for success in the licensing game.

Once upon a time, winning consistently, or having a large home market, guaranteed a thriving business in licensing. The great success on the field of the Dallas Cowboys in the 1970s made them the NFL's most successful team in licensing sales well into the 1980s. And New York's Mets and Yankees were consistent leaders in the sale of licensed products.

But something strange happened in the 1990s. Sports chic struck. Consider the Colorado Rockies and the San Jose Sharks.

The Rockies, an expansion baseball team that did not begin play until 1993, sold more merchandise in 1992 than the Mets, the Dodgers, and the world champion Toronto Blue Jays. Only the Chicago White Sox, Atlanta Braves, and New York Yankees sold more.

The Sharks, an expansion team in the NHL, began its history in 1991–1992. They were abysmal, the worst team in the league, yet they sold more merchandise than any other hockey team that year. In fact, the only team in all of sports that sold more products than the Sharks that season were the Chicago Bulls, a team en route to winning its second consecutive NBA title.

The reason was style. Customers weren't devoted fans supporting their team, the way "Magnum P.I." on TV wore an old Detroit Tiger cap because he grew up rooting for the Tigers, or the way Steve Garvey wore a Brooklyn Dodgers T-shirt under his Los Angeles uniform because his dad once drove the team bus before the Dodgers moved to California.

"It's a fad," Karen Raugust of the *Licensing Letter* told *The New York Times* in 1993. "A lot of these folks are wearing T-shirts and they don't even know what sport the team plays."

In this new age of licensing, color and design make success. The Sharks selected "Pacific" teal—a hot color in 1991—to accompany their black and silver as team colors. Their logo was a shark biting a hockey stick in two. The Rockies' colors were black, silver, and purple; their logo, a baseball soaring into a mountain.

None of this happened by accident, especially in the case of the Sharks. The name was chosen after a fan sweepstakes yielded such contenders as Yodeling Yams and Screaming Squids. Sharks had a local connection—they're common in the Pacific waters off Northern California. Research revealed the name scored well with adults buying products for children, and the image wasn't so childlike to the adults themselves.

They researched team colors, rejecting turquoise, orange, black, and white because fans thought them too close to the Miami Dolphins—the same combination without the black. The NBA's Charlotte Hornets had done well with teal; San Jose's adjustment was to make their color "Pacific" teal.

"The name, the logo, the colors all add up to a sum greater than the parts," Sharks executive Matt Levine told *The Washington Post* in 1991. "The characteristics of the shark, put with the logo, and the teal lends a lot of excitement, a multidimensionality."

Levine reports that Sharks merchandise sells well even in non-hockey markets, "the Topekas, Austins and Bakersfields of the world." And the organization has helped make that happen. Their toll-free number (1-800-BE-SHARK) will get customers anywhere in the country a free catalog, which offers a wide range of shirts, Christmas cards for $1, bumper stickers for $2, and a denim jacket with a leather Sharks logo for $250.

The Rockies have no 800 number, but the team's Dugout Store in downtown Denver fields questions and orders from 10 A.M. when it opens till 6 P.M. Business is brisk on Rockies pencils at 25 cents, and even the authentic team caps at $20. Their most expensive item is a reversible jacket for $1,000—leather in purple, black, gray, and white outside; purple satin inside. Team jerseys at $109 are identical to what the players wear, except for the ceramic buttons provided by the Coors Brewery.

"We get calls from all over the country, from New York and Boston and even Hawaii," says Nino Valenti, who worked in the shop during the summer of 1993. "Somebody called all the way from Guam to get a catalogue."

It is no surprise that both these highly successful merchandising efforts selected black and silver as their basic combination. That was the combination of the hottest team in marketing, the Los Angeles Raiders. Again in 1992, eight years after their last Super Bowl appearance, the Raiders ranked ahead of the other 27 NFL teams in merchandise sales.

Other teams noticed, and figured it couldn't have been the charm of the athletes or even their prowess on the field that led to those sales. All that remained was the colors. The Los Angeles Kings switched to black, silver, and white, and instantly became hockey's leader in merchandise sales, until the Sharks arrived. The Chicago White Sox switched to silver and black, and jumped from nowhere in sales to number one in all of baseball.

"Teams are switching their colors and uniforms in order to become more appealing to the fans and to sell more merchandise, and that's something that has never happened before in the history of professional sports," Major League Baseball Production's Rick White told *The New York Times.*

"A few years ago, merchandising had little impact economically on the leagues," he added. "But now there is no owner who does not recognize that these products have a very substantial importance on their bottom line."

Selling Far from Home

Another new area of real importance is the foreign market. Retail sales from international licensing by the four major professional leagues total approximately $500 million, according to figures reported in a December 1992 article of *Licensing Letter.*

Most successful with sales overseas is the NFL, coming as part of a multifront effort to market its sport in foreign countries. This effort began as an experiment with a game in the summer of 1976 in Tokyo between the St. Louis Cardinals and the San Diego Chargers; two years later the New Orleans Saints played the Philadelphia Eagles in Mexico City. The league christened the American Bowl in 1986, a game between the Dallas Cowboys and the Chicago Bears in London's Wembley Stadium. The response was enormous, and was followed three years later by the addition of an American Bowl game played in Tokyo, and one year later by a third American Bowl played in Berlin.

These games proved to be incendiary devices, sparking interest in regions with no natural historical connection to American football. Now millions of fans watch regular-season games, highlights shows, and the Super Bowl, which is currently broadcast live to more than 35 countries around the world.

Foreign TV programming generates an additional $3 million to the NFL, but its importance was much greater when seen as part of the league's overall plan that included exhibition games, a new league, and other stimuli to help generate interest abroad. A big part of that plan, under the direction of the NFL, was the unveiling in 1991 of the World League of American Football. The league—with Barcelona, Frankfurt, London, and Montreal among its ten teams—played a ten-game schedule across Europe and North America in 1992, but its future was put in doubt when the NFL suspended operation in the wake of federal court's antitrust ruling in September of 1993.

And all of that helped stimulate international marketing. With more than 125 licensees, retail sales in 1992 were between $250 and $300 million. Japan ranked first among geographic regions that hungered for NFL goods, followed by Continental Europe, Canada, and the United Kingdom.

The National Basketball Association, with the most international of sports, has been most aggressive at exporting its game.

More than 400 million homes in 93 countries on 6 continents saw Michael Jordan and his Chicago Bulls win their second consecutive NBA title in 1992. And the men of the Dream Team were not only the stars of the 1992 Summer Olympics, also but the darlings of Europe. The league also plays regular-season games abroad, conducts clinics, and actively lures international stars to play on American teams.

And NBA commissioner David Stern has a clear view of where all this is leading. "What we're talking about is meshing with the world of international basketball, but not by establishing NBA teams overseas," he says.

He and the NBA were planting seeds for the future, a future that could include a "world cup" of basketball patterned after soccer's World Cup. For the present, the league is reaping benefits in revenue from foreign sales. *Licensing Letter* reports that the NBA had $125 million in international retail sales of licensed merchandise for the 1991–1992 season, an increase of almost $100 million from the previous season.

The league is aware of the great potential for foreign sales, and is proceeding cautiously. A 1993 article in *Agent & Manager* described the NBA's philosophy as "less is more" in terms of granting numbers of licenses: "The league is interested in prospective licensees that are financially strong and that want to make a long-term commitment."

The factors to consider when marketing abroad are many and diverse, according to *Agent & Manager.* Sometimes that means using a European designer for products intended for the European market rather than exporting American items, and sometimes it means meeting even more specialized needs. The article quotes Scott Creelman, Spalding's international vice-president:

> One large challenge is getting backboards up. People don't have driveways in other parts of the world. This is a physical difference, so where do you play? That's an issue we are addressing with the NBA and FIBRA (the international governing body of basketball).

Professional baseball has been marketing itself abroad longer than any other sport. After the 1934 season, Babe Ruth led a group of 14 American League players on a tour of Japan, playing 22 games on the long trip. They sold out Meiji Stadium in Tokyo, which held 60,000, and were even more successful in Osaka, packing 80,000 into Koshien Stadium. A team of black ball players from the Negro Leagues toured Japan that same year.

Blacks had been exporting baseball to Latin America since the turn of the century, and were greatly responsible for the popularity of the game in Cuba. (For many years before Fidel Castro came to power, and even through the 1960 season, a minor league team was based in Havana. That last franchise was the International League Havana Sugar Kings, AAA farm team of the Cincinnati Reds.)

Hockey's efforts at marketing itself internationally are consistent with its efforts at promoting itself in most other areas—late starting, but picking up momentum. The new NHL Enterprises was established in July of 1992; it has headed a rising tide of commercial activity. Over the past three years, retail sales of NHL-licensed merchandise jumped 600 percent to $600 million.

The sport does have the same advantage as basketball in that it has an international base, being widely played in Europe. In the 1991–1992 season, 70 NHL players were from outside North America. While total retail sales for licensed goods were just under $8 million, most coming from Europe, the league seemed poised for a breakthrough. League president Gary Bettman has made growth in the foreign market a priority.

"We're looking quite strong internationally, especially in Europe and the former Soviet Union," he says. "We're going to look for ways to capitalize on that popularity through licensing, sponsorship and broadcasting and beyond that, with an occasional exhibition game."

It can hardly be any other way. Hockey, like the rest of the sports, is facing greater financial challenges now than at any time in its history. No sport today can overlook any potential source of income.

Through the airways and turnstiles, selling edibles, wearables, and collectables, dealing at home and abroad—every sport must explore every marketing opportunity today to survive.

PART THREE

Where the Money Goes

11

Star Struck

The cruelest deal in the history of Canadian sports was announced midway through the summer of 1988: Wayne Gretzky was traded to the Los Angeles Kings.

Wayne Gretzky, The Great One. Wayne Gretzky, the most prolific scorer ever to lace on a pair of hockey skates. Wayne Gretzky, who had led the Edmonton Oilers to four Stanley Cup championships in the previous five seasons.

Wayne Gretzky was gone, and a nation wept.

Gretzky was more than a great hockey player; he was a national treasure. Blond and handsome, he packed more agility, strength, and quickness into his slender body than had ever been seen on ice. Oh, what magic he could perform. And it seemed as if he had been perfecting his act forever.

As an 11-year-old in 1972, skating for the sub-peewee level Brantford Steelers, he scored 378 goals in 82 games. Nine years later, playing for Edmonton, he became the first NHL player to score 50 goals in fewer than the first 50 games of a season, reaching that plateau in 39 games in 1981. That was the first year he led the league in scoring; he would repeat the feat on six more occasions while playing for Edmonton.

Now, suddenly he was gone. And not to Montreal or Toronto, or even to one of the American hockey capitals of the icy north, to snowy Boston or Detroit or Chicago. But to Los Angeles, California, where ice was created to cool drinks and snow was only seen pressed in a ball, covered with colored syrup and served in a paper cone.

The attraction for Los Angeles was not only that Gretzky was a great hockey player but also that he was a star. In the world of sports/biz, stars attract fans to arenas and ballparks, and to television sets. And in hockey in 1988, there was no greater attraction than Wayne Gretzky.

The marketing of superstars is as old as professional sports itself. Remember, in 1925 when pro football was but an imitation of the college game, it was the signing of college star Red Grange by the Chicago Bears that brought the NFL credibility and fans. And in 1965, when the AFL was struggling, the New York Jets signing University of Alabama star Joe Namath for a then-astonishing $400,000 brought the new league attention and then respect, and eventually led to its first victory over the NFL in the Super Bowl. Early pro basketball was lifted by the addition of Hank Luisetti, the scoring machine from Stanford; when the sport hit a low in the late 1970s, it was resurrected by Magic Johnson and Larry Bird, and then Michael Jordan.

Major League Baseball had no fertile college connection in its early days. When the American League was formed in 1901, many stars from the National League were lured away by higher salaries. One was Napoleon Lajoie. A solid hitter for the Philadelphia Phillies, he became a sensation with the new Philadelphia Athletics, leading the league that first season in hitting, slugging, home runs, total bases, runs batted in, hits, runs scored, and doubles. Another transfer was pitcher Denton True Young, better known as Cy Young. After going a meager 9–6 in his first National League season, Young averaged nearly 28 wins in the ten that followed. He came to Boston in the team's first American League season, and proceeded to lead the league from 1901 to 1903 with 33, 32, and 28 wins. His 511 career wins stand as the record today and are one reason the Cy Young Award goes to the best pitcher every season in each league.

Young and Lajoie anchored their new franchises, but the greatest salvage job in the history of all sports was the purchase of Babe Ruth from the Boston Red Sox by the New York Yankees during the first week *of 1920 for $125,000, more than twice the amount ever paid for a player before, plus a loan of $300,000 to the Boston owner, Harry Frazee.*

The coming of Babe Ruth to New York not only turned the Yankees into a dynasty but also excited a nation about baseball as it had never been excited before.

Ruth led the league in home runs for Boston in 1919 with 29, and went 9–5 as a pitcher, giving up less than three runs a game in 133 innings. His five years with the Red Sox kept them in or near first place, while the Yankees floundered. Only once in the nine seasons before acquiring Ruth did they rise above fourth place.

The Yankees managed to finish third in 1920, Ruth's first season in New York, then reeled off three consecutive American League championships, winning their first World Series in 1923. In his 15 years with New York, Ruth led them to seven World Series. His importance to the franchise is summed up by a line in the statement below his retired number "3" in the team media guide: "The greatest drawing card, Yankees' greatest home run hitter, an outstanding pitcher and the most colorful figure in the history of baseball."

Of these words, those that resonate most to ownership are "the greatest drawing card." Home runs and great pitching are all important elements, but the magical quality that interests all team owners and general managers is an athlete's ability to draw customers.

Ruth's charisma is what made the Yankees so eager to pay Boston all that money, not to mention the salary to the Babe himself: $20,500 in 1920, up to $52,000 for 1923, and $70,000 by 1927—just $5,000 less than President Calvin Coolidge. Charisma is what made Joe Namath's $400,000 price tag a bargain, and that is what made Wayne Gretzky the one hockey player that the Los Angeles Kings had to have.

Sure, they all had to be great athletes. But being exciting is what draws people and helps them rise above the level of stars to superstars.

No number in sports is more inflationary today than the salaries paid to athletes. Not just to superstars—they always made top dollar—but all athletes. And in no sport are the numbers more shocking than in baseball.

Forget ancient history, that period before free agency became the law of the diamond and the average major league salary was a paltry $51,500. That was 1976, when the Shah ruled Iran, Gerald Ford was president, Bowie Kuhn was commissioner of baseball, and Pete Rose played third base for the Cincinnati Reds.

By 1987 that average was up to $412,454, and the stars were all getting between $2 million and $3 million. The Mets' Gary Carter was paid $2.98 million for the season; Boston's Jim Rice, $2.22 million; Baltimore's Eddie Murray, $2.25 million. Kansas City had two players in that range, Dan Quisenberry at $2.29 million and George Brett at $2.27 million, with Willie Wilson close behind at $1.93 million.

But just five years later, the million-dollar plateau represented the *average* in the big leagues. The top stars in 1993 all made between $5 million and $8 million a season. Month after month, as teams scurried to sign free agents or lock in their own stars to long contracts, the top figure kept climbing. "Sandberg Becomes Highest-Paid Player, for Now," read the headline in *The New York Times* in March of 1992. The story told of the Cubs' second baseman signing a four-year contract bringing him $7.1 million a year. Just a few months later, Cecil Fielder signed an extension with the Detroit Tigers worth $7.2 million a year, and he became the highest-paid player.

More than 20 major leaguers were being paid at least $4 million a season as the 1993 baseball season began. Most of them were pretty good ball players, if not future Hall of Famers. Bobby Bonilla and Danny Tartabull, Doug Drabek and Barry Larkin and Andy Van Slyke; any manager would happily write their names on the lineup card.

But to understand how out of whack the system had gotten at that point, one needed to look at some of the second-tier players and what they were paid for their less than exceptional services. Bill Doran, sometime second baseman for the Reds, earned $2.83 million in 1992. Craig Lefferts, a moderately effective relief pitcher but never anybody's stopper in his nine seasons, was paid $2.07 million by Baltimore. Dan Pasqua, a outfielder/first baseman who averaged fewer than 15 home runs in his seven seasons and played in more than 129 games only once, was paid $2.50 million by the White Sox. Charlie Leibrandt, spot starter for Atlanta, was the highest-paid player on the Braves, collecting $3.18 million for the season. The list went on and on.

The biggest stars in the other sports did nearly as well as those in baseball. Larry Bird, the season before retiring from the Boston Celtics, was paid $7.4 million. Patrick Ewing was in the middle of a six-year contract with the New York Knicks in 1993 that brought him $33 million, or $5.5 million a year. Miami Dolphins quarterback Dan Marino was working on a five-year, $25-million contract. As with other areas, hockey lagged behind in top salaries. Only three players by 1993 had salaries in excess of $3 million a year. Wayne Gretzky's ten-year contract with the Los Angeles Kings was worth $31.3 million; Eric Lindros was paid $3.50 million by the Flyers. In October of 1992, Mario Lemieux signed a complicated contract with the Pittsburgh Penguins that came out to $4.25 million a year. Less than a year later, in September of 1993, the Kings gave Gretzky a new three-year contract, reported at $25.5 million, or $8.5 million a season.

The difference was the money paid to non-stars. Only in baseball did second-line players regularly earn $2 million a year and up.

While plenty of NBA players earned between $2 million and $3 million in salary, all were established starters, or older stars playing out multiyear contracts. Many younger starters earned salaries in the $500,000 to $600,000 range, and an entire list of part-time players are paid less than $200,000.

A similar pattern was reflected in the NFL. After the stars' big contracts, the numbers dropped precipitously. And in football, that upper echelon was mostly reserved for quarterbacks. Every once in a while there would be a Jerry Rice, with a three-year, $7 million contract from the 49ers; Barry Sanders earned $10 million over four years from the Lions. And a number-one draft pick might pull in $2 million.

But those players and those figures were rare. The best-paid offensive lineman in the NFL before the 1993 season was Jim Lachey, paid $3.9 million over three years by virtue of a contract signed in 1992 with the Redskins; older contracts paid celebrity linebackers—the Lawrence Taylors—from $1 million to $1.5 million. Salaries ranging from $300,000 to $500,000 were even more common for starters.

The differences in pay scale weigh heavily on a team's budget. Player costs for the Oakland Athletes, with the highest payroll in baseball in 1992, according to *Financial World,* were $39.2 million. Player costs for the football team with the highest payroll, the San Francisco 49ers, were $32.6 million. Although teams always pay for more players than they actually carry on their roster at any one time, the limit for football in 1992 was 47 (45 active plus 2 inactive) while in baseball it was only 25.

The Making of a Quagmire

Why were baseball salaries so much higher? Mostly because of the labor wars. They first created salary arbitration, in which theoretically impartial but often ill-equipped individuals decide between the player's request for a contract and the team's offer, based on the pay of other players with comparable statistics. Then they yielded free agency, viewed by players as salvation and by owners as Pandora's Box. The whole drama has taken on the look and sound of a primetime soap opera.

All sports have had their battles between players and management. Individual disputes are as old as sports itself; Oscar Robertson, when playing for an NBA team based in Cincinnati and called the Royals, often sat out the NBA's preseason while his agent haggled for more money; others have sat out entire seasons. Little NFL strikes in 1968 and 1974 cost days off during the preseason; big strikes interrupted the regular schedule in 1982 and 1988.

But no sport's history has been as littered as baseball's with conflicts over who controls the players, money, and the game. Players as far back as 1885 banded together for better conditions and compensation from owners. Their efforts resulted in 90 years of frustration, and the power remained with owners.

There was no logical reason why the owners were permitted to maintain control for so long, but it happened. From the outside, it appears that baseball simply told America that it was not like other businesses, and America agreed. "You must grant us special privileges in order that we may bring this wonderful game to you," said baseball. "Only we will decide what cities have teams, and we must have complete control over our athletes." And society said yes. Customs and even laws set baseball apart from the rest of American commerce.

Players registered some gains in those years—more money, better conditions, and especially contributions from owners toward pension funds—but the main rules never changed. Athletes remained property, to be bought and sold at the discretion of owners. They could retire if they liked, but if a player wanted to play it had to be at the owners' pleasure.

"It must be this way," said baseball, "or the game will not survive."

The first crack in that rule of servitude appeared in 1970. That year Curt Flood sued baseball in federal court, claiming that by trading him to the Philadelphia Phillies without his knowledge or approval, the St. Louis Cardinals—the team for which he had played for ten years, often as a star—had violated the antitrust law.

The Supreme Court had already ruled—in 1922 and again in 1953—that baseball was exempt from antitrust laws, and that position was affirmed by the judiciary in 1970. But a mechanism was set in motion that would eventually change baseball.

First came the 1972 dispute over the players' pension fund, resulting in baseball's first general strike. Only 13 days long, it cost 86 games at the end of the season and placed the all-important postseason in jeopardy. The play-offs and World Series were played, but ten days late. But most important, the strike showed the solidarity of the union. A 1973 strike was averted when the owners agreed on compulsory impartial arbitration of salary negotiations, an enormous concession, and one that even many players feel leads to gross inadequacies. That's saying a lot for a procedure in which players virtually always see their salaries increased, and a large part of the time increased by as much as they request.

"There needs to be a lot of modification in arbitration before it works well," says Joe Morgan, Hall of Fame second baseman, two-time Most Valuable Player, and most recently an announcer for ESPN. "You're putting numbers in front of someone who doesn't understand baseball—numbers for salary, numbers for batting average, numbers for errors. Baseball isn't a numbers game, and numbers don't tell the worth of a player."

Baseball's power continued to erode, and salaries climbed. When Jim "Catfish" Hunter charged that Oakland A's owner Charlie Finley had violated his contract, the charge was heard by a three-person arbitration panel; that panel ruled in favor of Hunter, making him a free agent.

A year later two pitchers, Dave McNally of the Montreal Expos and Andy Messersmith of the Los Angeles Dodgers, maintained that their 1975 contracts provided inadequate compensation for their skills and refused to sign them. Baseball's standard contract provided for automatic renewal for one year at the club's discretion, and that is what happened. But after playing in 1975, both pitchers declared themselves free agents, which is not how the contracts were intended to work. The matter went to arbitration, and the players won.

These arbitrators were already in place, hired with the agreement of Major League Baseball and the union. After its second setback, baseball fired the chief arbitrator—Peter Seitz, a veteran arbitrator who also worked in the Hunter case—and appealed the decision. It was upheld in federal district court and the federal circuit court of appeals.

The world was upside down. The reserve rule, written in cement since 1879, was crumbling. There would be further skirmishes in this war: Owners locked out the players from spring training in 1977; a 50-

day players' strike split the 1981 season; and a two-day strike hit 1985. Each occurred while hammering out successive Basic Agreements between baseball and the union. Details changed from contract to contract. Teams losing players to free agency were first compensated with picks in the amateur draft, then a draft pick and a player from a pool of professionals.

Bull Market in Baseball

And all along, the price of ball players went up and up. The minimum salary, which inched up from $5,000 a year in 1947 to $6,000 in 1967, had struggled to $15,000 with the help of the Baseball Players Union by 1972, the eve of baseball's labor revolution. By 1981, the minimum was $40,000; by 1990 it had shot up to $100,000. The average salary, which stood at $51,501 before the birth of free agency in 1976, jumped to $76,066 the following year, and would nearly triple by 1980, up to $143,756. By 1984 it climbed to $329,408.

Top stars in 1985 were paid between $1 million and $2 million a season, figures that tell only part of the story. Most had long-term deals, a concept that did not exist before free agency. In 1981 Dave Winfield signed a ten-year contract with the Yankees, with a base of $1.4 million, and cost-of-living adjustments every two years starting in 1982 plus various incentives. In 1985, his base salary was up to $1.7 million.

The new salary scale, and the way it was implemented, reflected a radical change in the bargaining in baseball. In their 1993 book, *Coming Apart at the Seams,* Peter Gammons and Jack Sands explained what was happening:

> Before the advent of free agency, the clubs had viewed each other as partners who, like puppeteers, pulled all the strings. After 1976, the economics of the free market began to come into play. The supply side (players) was too tempting for the demand side (owners) to pass up. Fearful that the system would work too well, clubs began to sign up their top players to long-term contracts so they wouldn't pack up their bags and move elsewhere.

As we have seen, this panic among owners was not confined to their top players but extended well below the penthouse performers. Steve Kemp, nearing the end of his less than glorious career, signed a $1.17-

million contract with Pittsburgh at the end of 1984; he played just 105 games over the next two seasons. Bill Caudill, a mid-range relief pitcher during his nine seasons, signed a five-year, $7-million contract with Toronto prior to the opening of camp in 1985, three years and 113 innings before his retirement.

It was a bizarre situation. Teams could not control themselves from spending money for one more power hitter, one more lefthanded pitcher, just in case he might be needed, or even to prevent another team from getting him. These were the years of big television money coming in, and teams acted as if the money had to be spent on players.

It had gotten out of hand, and baseball had to do something. What the owners did, according to the courts, was break the rules. Not the nation's rules—their own.

The rule was against collusion. Marvin Miller reminds us in his 1991 book, *A Whole Different Ball Game,* that baseball was given the right to collude by the courts through its antitrust exemption, at least for a time.

". . . Collusion had been an everyday part of baseball since 1876," writes Miller. "The owners controlled everything from ticket prices to the color of a ballplayer's skin." But in 1966, when Dodger pitchers Sandy Koufax and Don Drysdale combined in a joint holdout for more money, part of the settlement was an addition in the Basic Agreement preventing players from acting together in the future. The players agreed, but only if the owners made the same deal. So after 1966, neither players nor teams could "act in concert."

Which brings us to 1985, nine years after free agency, nine years during which owners had seen salaries rise astronomically while players changed clubs in a state of constant fluidity. When the new crop of free agents became available in 1985, astonishingly nobody bid. Of the 32 players who entered the free agent market after the season, a lack of options forced 28 to resign with their old clubs. The 4 who did move had been declared unwanted by their clubs.

What happened, the courts would later decide, was that baseball, under the urging of Commissioner Peter Ueberroth, got the owners together and told them that their spending sprees were killing themselves and one another. According to Gammons and Sands, Ueberroth did this through a memo written by long-time baseball man, Lee McPhail, acting for the commissioner: " 'Don't sign players to long-term guaranteed contracts' and do not 'give in to the unreasonable demands of experienced and marginal players . . . ' "

Then the authors quote the commissioner, speaking at a meeting in St. Louis during the 1985 World Series. " 'Look in the mirror and get out and spend big if you want,' the commissioner chided, 'but don't go out there whining that someone made you do it.' "

The campaign to limit the signing of free agents continued for two more years. Each year the Players Association filed a grievance, and when all was decided—the cases becoming known as Collusion I, Collusion II, and Collusion III—Major League Baseball owed the players $280 million.

Peter Ueberroth denied the charge in his first official interview after he left office. "I still have the firm opinion there was no actual collusion," Ueberroth told *The Sporting News* in July of 1991, 18 months after leaving baseball. "I don't think there was collusion involved because I don't think the owners could collude if they were forced to do so by threats on their lives."

"I think the owners operate like sheep. Sheep go in one direction or another. Right now, the owners are going in a spending direction. There'll come another time when they absolutely run out of money and, choking with losses, they'll try to go in the other direction. The problem, though, is that there will still be one or two of them who can afford to pay high prices for players."

And the owners have been spending ever since. By the beginning of the 1993 season, the latest free agent to wear the crown of highest-paid player was Barry Bonds, signed late in 1992 by the San Francisco Giants to a six-year, $43.75-million contract. At that time, it was the highest contract in sports.

A Little More Sane

The dealings in the other sports seem almost reasonable compared to baseball, at least partly because of each of their histories. None experienced the strength and economic health over the years enjoyed by baseball. In one sense or another, they all struggled toward success, and so were more receptive to the helping hand of cooperation.

The sport that today is the most healthy—basketball—was only 15 years ago in the most trouble.

The NBA's problems had been coming on for several years, but by 1980 the future looked particularly bleak. The sport had a real image problem; several players had well-publicized drug problems, and the public was turned off. Most teams were playing to half-full arenas, revenues from broadcasting were low, and player salaries were the highest in all of sports. An estimated 17 of its 23 teams were losing money, with 4 of them close to folding.

The league could not blame its financial problems on free agency; it would not be instituted for another eight years. But other factors were pushing salaries up. From 1967, when all four professional team sports paid salaries in the $19,000-to-$25,000 range, the NBA average shot up in 1972 to $90,000, more than twice any of the others. By 1977 that average was up to $143,000, an increase of 700 percent in a single decade.

Much of that was due to the bidding war between the NBA and the rival American Basketball Association. The ABA began its precarious life in 1967 and had an immediate impact on pro basketball salaries until it merged with the NBA in 1976. Along the way, there were some astonishing examples of excessive bidding. Best publicized was the Marvin Barnes case. Barnes was paid $2.1 million in 1974 to sign with the Spirits of St. Louis as the ABA's number-one pick out of Providence. He averaged 24 points a game during his two years with St. Louis but never found a place for himself in the NBA after the merger.

The merger ended the bidding war but did not bring fiscal responsibility to the league or harmony to the relationships among the owners.

"There was more unanimity in the streets of Paris during the French Revolution than there was in an NBA owner's meeting," an unnamed owner confessed to *Sports Illustrated* about that period in a 1991 article on David Stern, NBA commissioner.

"As the low point of the pre-Stern era," said the *SI* article, "many in the NBA cite the 1980 championship series between the Lakers and the 76ers, during which CBS refused to broadcast the sixth and, as it turned out, final game live. It was showed, tape-delayed, at 11:30 p.m. Eastern time. Others say the league's darkest hour was an '82 article in the *Los Angeles Times* reporting that 75% of NBA players were on drugs."

The league-wide bleeding made all the parties receptive to a little reason. The man credited with bringing that reason was Stern, who took over as commissioner in 1984. Working with NBA Players Association head Larry Fleisher, Stern forged an effective drug policy, and he instituted the salary cap. In 1988, players and league agreed on unrestricted free agency for any player who had concluded two contracts and five years in the NBA. These players may sign with any team. Their old team has the right to match that offer, but once the player is gone, the team receives no compensation for him.

Nearly as important, Stern and Fleisher agreed to shorten the draft. Ten rounds long in 1984, it was reduced to eight rounds in 1985 and by 1988 to its present length of only two rounds. This meant that any player not selected at the end of two rounds became a free agent right out of college.

The effect of these changes on the league has been dramatic. After decades of instability, only one franchise has moved since Stern took office. The nomadic Kansas City Kings—which joined the NBA in 1948 when the Rochester (New York) Royals moved to Cincinnati in 1957, became the Kansas City–Omaha Kings in 1972, and finally the Kansas City Kings in 1975—moved to Sacramento in 1984. Stern says:

> I would say that there are several key factors contributing to the growth of basketball. With respect to the NBA itself, the salary cap and the anti-drug agreement back in the early '80s let us put the game back on the court instead of focusing people's attention on events off the court. The stability that was brought by the salary cap attracted new ownership with long-term thinking which was very important to us. In order to get people to make the investment necessary to provide jobs and have teams marketed well, you've got to have something that's attractive to investors and the salary cap was important.

Important as the salary agreement was, dealing with drugs was a crucial issue. The league had gotten a great deal of negative publicity. Players' careers were being shortened by drugs, and their very lives put in jeopardy. And the health of the NBA was suffering. While he was still acting as executive vice-president, Stern got the Players' Association to agree on the stiffest drug penalty in sports history. It called for the automatic expulsion of any player convicted of a drug-related offense.

The salary cap was equally revolutionary. The NBA became the first major sports league to limit its teams' payroll while guaranteeing its players a share of the league's revenue.

Fabric of the Cap

Prior to the start of each season, the league and the Players' Association meet to determine the salary cap for the upcoming season. Roughly speaking, the cap is calculated by projecting the upcoming season's gross revenue, multiplying it by 53 percent, deducting out an amount for various player benefits, and dividing the remainder by the number of teams in the league. The previous year's gross revenue is increased by 10 percent (with the exception of national television revenue, in which case the actual revenue for the upcoming season is used) to calculate projected gross revenue.

The Players' Association and the league have agreed to implement a pre-pension benefit plan for players, which takes money that would have otherwise been paid in salary and uses it to fund the plan. This is also considered in the salary cap.

For the 1991–1992 season, the salary cap was $12.5 million. In other words, teams were required to limit the payroll for all of their players to $12.5 million. With each team carrying 12 active players, the cap resulted in an average salary of approximately $1,040,000. To ensure players will receive 53 percent of projected gross revenue, NBA teams are also subject to a minimum salary restriction. The minimum salary cap (or floor) per team was $10,120,000 for the 1991–1992 season and $11,340,000 for the 1992–1993 season. For the 1992–1993 season, the player minimum was $140,000; the team salary cap for that season was $14 million. It would rise to $15.1 million for 1993–1994, with the team minimum cap set at $12.3 million. The individual player minimum for that season was $150,000.

One of the objects behind the cap was to keep teams intact. In order to accomplish this, the league made it possible for teams to exceed the cap to sign their own free agents. So in 1991 when Miami extended John "Hot Rod" Williams a $26.5 million offer over seven years, including $5 million that season, Cleveland was allowed to match it even though it took them over the cap.

For similar reasons, a team may also extend a contract of one its players for any amount they agree on, even if it puts them over the cap during the season covered by the extension. The Portland Trailblazers used this to sign Clyde Drexler. Since his contract runs out at the end of the 1994 season, they agreed to extend it to 1995 and pay him $8 million then.

Teams that exceed the cap by re-signing their own free agents are subject to a series of rules. One example of these rules is when a player of a team that is over the limit is put on waivers, the maximum salary they can pay the player that fills his spot is 50 percent of the departing player's salary. On the other hand, if a player is lost to free agency, his entire salary can be used for a replacement. In addition, guaranteed salaries of waived or cut players must remain in the team's cap.

The Los Angeles Lakers signed Magic Johnson to a 25-year contract although they knew he could not play that long. When his salary was annualized, it kept the Lakers under the maximum. In order to address this type of contract, the league and the Players' Association agreed to treat salary paid for seasons beyond a player's 35th birthday as compensation for the seasons prior to him turning 35. For example, if Magic Johnson signed his contract on his 30th birthday and the contract was worth $25 million, the Lakers would have to divide the value of the contract by 5 rather than 25 years for cap purposes.

Another situation addressed by the league and the Players' Association were "backloaded" contracts (for example, where a team with limited cap room pays a player a relatively small amount in order to remain within the cap, then gives the player a large increase the following year). In this connection, players' salaries can now only increase or decrease by a maximum of 30 percent from year to year.

Looked at simply, without all of the exceptions that are permitted under cap rules, it seems to make sense. But the endless situations that can arise, and the equal number of responses, can make living under the salary cap a nightmare. One convoluted situation was described in a 1992 article in *The Sporting News*:

> The Nets were about $500,000 under the salary cap when it was increased to $12.5 million last summer. However, in order to get Kenny Anderson—the second pick in the 1991 draft—to sign, they figured they would have to get to about $1.8 million under the cap. Thus began a series of very difficult business decisions—not all of them good.
>
> First, they allowed Reggie Theus to leave for Italy, setting aside the 50% exception from his $960,000 salary, or $480,000. Then they added the 100% exception to which they were entitled by allowing Jack Haley and his $360,000 salary to leave for free agency, raising their reserve bankroll to $1.34 million for the Kenny Fund.
>
> Now time was running short, the season had already started and Anderson was still playing hardball by demanding a $3-million average salary for five seasons. In a move that smacked of desperation, the team waived Jud Buechler—who was part of their regular rotation—and 12th man Dave Feitl and added the combined 50% exceptions from their salaries, $167,500, to the reserve fund. That raised the balance to about $1,507,500—still not enough.

> Finally, to get to that magic figure of $1.8 million, they restructured contracts held by five players—Sam Bowie, Derrick Coleman, Roy Hinson, Tate George and Chris Morris.
>
> That $1.8-million figure, of course, was just the launching point for Anderson's $3-million-a-year aspiration. Using the 30% rule, the Nets gave him a contract that calls for a raise of $540,000 (that's 30% of $1.8 million) for each of the next four seasons. His contract, therefore, adds up to $14.5 million for five seasons—a $2.9-million average.

It wasn't exactly the $3 million Anderson wanted, but he accepted it. But in the process, one player left for Europe, another left for free agency, and two others were waived. To the casual fan, these may have looked like basketball decisions, but they weren't. They were just part of the business of sports.

It is business that not everyone involved with the NBA likes. "The purpose of the salary cap was to keep cost down, and to keep people like George Steinbrenner from thinking they could buy anybody and everything," says Ron Grinker, a Cincinnati lawyer who has been representing athletes, coaches, and even management personnel for nearly 30 years. He feels the cap has at least failed to accomplish its primary goal.

"Since the cap has been in existence, salaries have just skyrocketed," he says. "For every one of its rules, there is an exception, so it hasn't accomplished what it was intended to do."

Does the cap get in his way when negotiating for one of his clients?

"No," says Grinker, who lists Danny Manning among his clients. "With just two rounds [of the NBA draft], so much importance is placed on a team's pick that they just have to find a way to sign that player."

And despite their existing payroll, they usually do.

Out in the Cold

There is no salary cap in the National Hockey League, and the NHL has free agency. But the endless question is, how free? At least the numbers indicate that the sports market on ice is not as liberal as it is on hardwood, grass, or Astroturf.

Hockey is a sport with at least four major stars with names known around the country: Wayne Gretzky, Mario Lemieux, Mark Messier, and Eric Lindros. And all of them make good money, even by sports standards. Rising star Lindros makes $3.5 million a year; Gretzky's new deal brings him $8.5 million a season. And current league superstar Lemieux signed a seven-year, $42-million contract in 1992. (Officially, it is a base salary of $30 million—which makes it $4.28 million a year—plus $12 million in long-term marketing arrangements.) And yet the league average in 1992 was $350,000, the lowest of the four major professional team sports.

Part of the reason may be in hockey's brand of free agency, and to understand that we look at the recent case of the St. Louis Blues.

It all started in the summer of 1990 when St. Louis General Manager Ron Caron signed free agent Scott Stevens to a four-year, $4.8-million contract. That was a lot of money in the hockey world, and an unusual occasion. Several players had changed teams as free agents over the years, but most of them were aging veterans and role players. Stevens was only 26, big and strong, and in the 1987–1988 season made his first all-star appearance.

The league's compensation system had traditionally kept players of that caliber from moving. And as compensation to Stevens' old team, the Washington Capitals, St. Louis had to give up five first-round picks, a hefty price.

A 1991 article in *The New York Times* analyzed the reasoning behind the league's restrictive free agency.

> Essentially, the current system protects teams in smaller markets, particularly those in Canada. A hockey player would give his two front teeth—if he hasn't surrendered them already—rather than play in Winnipeg or Quebec. These are teams with losing traditions, in outposts with two of the highest taxation rates in the country.

Caron and St. Louis, however, were determined to build a competitive hockey team. They already had one of the league's top young stars, Brett Hull, and had twice made it to the Norris Division finals. They felt this was a chance to go further.

Stevens made a real impact. In one season he became the Blues' captain and the heart of their defense. And while the team again finished second in the 1990–1991 season, their total of 105 points was just one behind the regular-season leading Chicago Black Hawks.

The following summer, Caron stepped back into the free agent market, this time signing 23-year-old forward Brendan Shanahan from the New Jersey Devils. But when he and New Jersey General Manager Lou Lamoriello could not agree on fair compensation—reportedly Lamoriello considered demanding Hull, then demanded Stevens, a request considered by many to be only slightly less absurd—the matter went to arbitration.

And the decision, written by Edward Houston, a 72-year-old judge from Ottawa and a long-time NHL arbitrator, was to send Scott Stevens to New Jersey. So for their efforts to build a better team through free agency, St. Louis lost five first-round picks to Washington and their captain to New Jersey.

The story was widely reported throughout the league and nearly as broadly decried, as shown in a 1991 article in *The Sporting News:* "Shame on the Blues for being so naive. Double whammy on them for daring to be so different."

The comment about St. Louis "daring to be so different" points up how unusual it is for hockey teams to use free agency as a serious path to build a team worthy of winning the Stanley Cup. This is, of course, the way most of the sports world looks at free agency: It is the right of an athlete to offer his athletic ability in a "free" and open market, *and, at the same time,* the right of teams to bid "freely" for those abilities.

That is how it works in baseball and in basketball—but not in hockey.

A Brave New World for the NFL

The level of player movement within professional football remained controlled for a long time; players changed teams at the discretion of the teams. The challenge of the American Football League gave players the freedom to market themselves between two bidders for a time—mostly a boon to those coming out in the draft—but that ended with the merger of the leagues.

Compared with baseball and basketball, football compensation was relatively stable. Big contracts were there only for the big stars, which in the NFL meant quarterbacks. Dan Marino of the Dolphins was paid $4.43 million for 1992; Warren Moon, $3.56 million. But the average salary is $496,345, higher only than hockey among the four sports. And the reason was the NFL brand of free agency, which was not so free.

League control over player movement was virtually iron-clad. And when control appeared to ease, it was but an illusion. Players actually won the right to declare themselves free agents in 1972, after Baltimore Colts tight end John Mackey sued the league. But the players surrendered that right in 1977, trading it primarily for contributions to their pension fund and something called the "right-of-first-refusal."

Under this plan, a team could submit an offer sheet on any player whose contract had expired, but the player's original team had the right to match that offer and retain the player, even if he preferred to change teams. And if the old team chose not to keep him, the player's new team had to give his former team two first-round selections in the subsequent drafts.

First-round draft picks are the building blocks for a team's future in the NFL and are highly prized. Only two players were signed as free agents and changed teams under that system.

All the while, the labor situation in the NFL remained tense, with free agency being the main sticking point as league and players worked on a new collective bargaining agreement. The old agreement expired in 1987, leading to a three-week strike. The courts managed to make their feelings known while remaining somewhat distant: they would not permit such tight restrictions on player movement to continue, but neither would they arbitrarily declare total free agency. They wanted the parties to work it out.

The NFL's response in 1989 was Plan B, an arrangement under which a team could protect 37 players from its roster—usually between 45 and 48 players—leaving the others free to negotiate with other teams. There was little doubt about the quality of most of those players left unprotected. In that first year of this attempt at compromise, fewer than half the Plan B players managed to find an active roster by opening day.

In April of 1990, New York Jets running back Freeman McNeil and seven other players filed an antitrust lawsuit against the NFL. The case went to court in 1992, and the players won. Again, the court did not outline what changes were to be made; instead, it left them to the two parties. But clearly, the NFL was going to have to loosen its grip. By the end of the year, league and players had worked out their first collective bargaining agreement since 1987 and a broad-based, unrestricted free agency for the first time in the league's history.

The agreement immediately declared free agency status to 360 players who had been in the league for at least five years and who were in the final season of their contracts. They had from March 1, 1993, until the start of training camp for the following season, approximately July 15, to negotiate with any team in the NFL.

Certain restrictions remained under the new agreement. Each team had the right to select—if it wished—one man as a "franchise player" who could not negotiate with any other team. In exchange for giving up that freedom, his salary must be made one of the five best-paid players at his position. In addition, two others in the first year of contracts and one in the second year could be protected, and they must be offered a contract at the average of at least the top ten salaries of their position or 110 percent of their previous year's salary. Everybody else with five years of experience was free to peddle his services once his contract expired. The term for free agency dropped from five years to four in 1994, when football's version of the salary cap came into effect.

What would all this mean to the NFL? Would it go the route of Major League Baseball, with salaries skyrocketing ever upward?

Probably not, because part of the agreement does include a salary cap; it was designed to be triggered when player costs reached 67 percent of a team's gross revenues. The league's financial statement for 1991, released as part of the suit, placed that figure at 63.9 percent of revenues league-wide. A second cap limited the amount teams could spend on all draft choices to a total of $2 million a year, or 3.5 percent of league revenues, whichever is greater.

Still, with all these safeguards, the term "free agency" continues to strike fear in the hearts of front office personnel across the country. And if a flood of new, large contracts was their concern, that fear was justified. In the first half of 1993, the impact of the new order was felt by players at positions rarely considered in the high-price range.

Consider the following offensive linemen: Tackle Brian Habib, paid $350,000 by the Minnesota Vikings in 1992, signed by the Denver Broncos to three one-year contracts totaling approximately $4.2 million, or about $1.4 million a year; center Kirk Lowdermilk, paid $650,000 by the Vikings in 1992, signed with the Colts for $6 million over three years; tackle Will Wolford, who earned $750,000 with Buffalo in 1992, signed a three-year contract with the Colts for $7.6 million.

Then there was the Reggie White saga. White, an all-pro defensive end with Philadelphia, was the most pursued of the new free agents. He was wooed by governors and mayors and over two months visited Atlanta, Seattle, Cleveland, Detroit, Washington, New York, Phoenix, and Green Bay. Eventually White signed with the Packers, a four-year deal worth $17 million.

No Bottomless Pit

To the fan scanning the morning paper, the financial resources of sports teams appear endless. They are not, and as average salaries continued to rise in the 1990s there was evidence of that. It showed most in baseball, where the spending had been the most active for the longest time.

Several players actually took cuts in pay, a shocking occurrence in modern-day sports. First baseman/outfielder Randy Milligan, paid $1.2 million in 1992 with Baltimore, signed a one-year deal with Cincinnati worth $475,000 for the 1993 season. Longtime Los Angeles catcher Mike Scioscia, paid $2.183 million by the Dodgers in 1992, accepted the Padres' offer of $340,000 for 1993.

But even more reflective of the reality of the times were the number of veteran major league players who signed minor league contracts, just for the chance to find a place to play. Between the end of the 1991 season and spring of 1992, more than 50 former major leaguers signed Triple-A contracts, and some of them familiar names: Bert Blyleven, Pete Incaviglia, Scott Fletcher, and Doug Jones.

"This seemed like an interim step to build up some of our weak points," Houston Astros General Manager Bill Woods told *The Sporting News* in 1992. It was the Astros, last-place finishers in the National League West in 1991, that signed Jones and Incaviglia to the minor league contract before spring training. Woods continued:

> When you don't have millions available, you do what you have to do and build from there. Last year we bottomed out and spent the season answering questions we had to find out about. Now we are going in with an attitude of winning, so let's go after a Jones, an established closer coming off an off season, and an Incaviglia, who has lost 30 points and is well-known to our manager [Art Howe] and coaches, for a bargain price. Maybe they can help our won-lost record.

Incaviglia and Jones made big-league rosters in 1992, as did Fletcher and Blyleven and many others, and most of them made solid contributions to their teams. And some radically improved their own situations. Incaviglia declared himself a free agent after the season and signed a two-year, $2.2-million contract with the Phillies at the end of the year. Fletcher, who played with Milwaukee in 1992 for $350,000, signed a two-year, $1.2-million contract with Boston for 1993.

Taken individually, they were the kind of dramas that attract so many fans to sports. The stories of Fletcher and Incaviglia were of success. Others were less successful. Blyleven, who pitched for California in 1992, signed a one-year contract with Minnesota that could, with incentives, have earned him $1 million. All the elements of theater were there: He was returning for his third stint with Minnesota in 1993, where he had started his major league career in 1970. That's 24 seasons for the 42-year-old right hander, who was named Rookie of the Year by *The Sporting News* and, 19 years later, Comeback Player of the Year. But at the end of spring training, he was released.

Viewed along with all the other instances of veterans heading into spring training with nothing but a minor league contract and a prayer, they say something about the new economics of sports. Listen to Houston's Bill Woods:

> This reflects an attitude on the clubs' part that if they can't get in there for the big-money boys, it's better to take a low-key approach on a guy who is a high gamble and doesn't exactly have teams lined up around the block.

What went unspoken was that there is no risk with these players. If they pan out, the club has their services; if they fail, they can be let go with little or no compensation.

In the large picture, this effect of free agency represented little more than a shift in the pattern of salary distribution. Top players were still getting the most money, and fringe players were still struggling to hang on. That is how it always was in sports.

But what of all those dire predictions that once the owners lost control of the game—a euphemism for losing total control of the players—sports as we know it would cease to exist?

The threat was that if the players were free to sign with any team they wished, all the best ones would rush to a few rich teams in the big cities and the competitive balance would be destroyed. With the best players money could buy, those few rich teams would win all the time.

It didn't quite work out that way. In the first 16 years after free agency came to baseball, only one team won back-to-back World Championships. That team was the New York Yankees, winning in 1977 and 1978—a rich team indeed—yet the Yanks have not managed to win a single pennant since. That is very different from the days before free agency, when the "Damn Yankees" won championship after championship. (Finally in 1993, the Toronto Blue Jays matched the Yankees' feat, repeating as World Champions.)

Yes, the larger-market teams, those with money—most of it, as we have seen, coming from television—are more able to afford the top players. Little Pittsburgh lost Bobby Bonilla and Barry Bonds to New York and San Francisco, while the Chicago Cubs were able to come up with enough money to keep Ryne Sandberg from leaving.

But it has yet to be proved that buying superstars guarantees winning championships.

Their Money's Worth

Most owners of sports teams today know that buying superstar athletes is not the same as buying championships. Most probably they always did. Winning games is important, but it is only part of the prize.

Even that history-making purchase of Babe Ruth by Jacob Ruppert and the New York Yankees in 1919 was as much for Ruth's star appeal as his home runs. You might say that Ruth's 29 home runs in 1918 were his appeal, but Ruppert had expressed interest in the young sensation before that season, and he was determined to have him. Jake Ruppert was a man of vision, and he saw Babe Ruth as central to the future of his franchise.

The Yankees were a second-division team that didn't even play in their own stadium; they shared the Polo Grounds with the Giants. Sure, they needed to win ball games, but they needed credibility and an identity, and they knew the Babe would provide both.

The need was much the same when Bruce McNall went out and got Wayne Gretzky for his Los Angeles Kings. The Kings were a floundering hockey team, 1,300 miles from Canada, the only place with a reservoir of fans unconditionally committed to hockey. McNall knew he couldn't buy just a good player, he had to buy the best. And he did.

Jacob Ruppert and Bruce McNall never met; Ruppert died in 1939, before McNall was born. But they had several qualities in common. They were both wealthy, of course, but they were also strong, independent men. Ruppert's self-confidence and bearing were bred into him; the son of a millionaire New York brewer, he was prominent in society, collected show dogs and art, and served four terms in Congress. McNall, born and reared in southern California, may not have been so highborn, but he chiseled out an impressive place for himself, parlaying a childhood fascination for coins into a fortune.

Both men had clear pictures of who they were and what they needed in life to make them happy. To accomplish that, they made their own rules.

Two years after Ruppert paid $400,000 in cash and credit for the most famous baseball player in the world, he paid the Astor estate $600,000 for a plot of land on the Harlem River and then built a $2.5-million ballpark. These were all astonishing figures for the 1920s.

When McNall was 24 years old, he bought the most famous of ancient Greek coins, the Athena Decadrachm. The fact that an Aristotle Onassis and Valery Giscard D'Estaing were after the coin didn't intimidate him a bit. He blew past the highest price ever paid for a coin at auction—$100,000—laid down a bid of $420,000, and walked off with the prize. So for him to pay $15 million 14 years later for the most famous hockey player in the world was but an extension of a pattern already set.

McNall told *The Sporting News* in 1989:

> I heard that Vancouver and the New York Rangers might be in the picture. And that made me want the deal even more. I get that way. When I get something in my head, it consumes me. I get frustrated along the way and obsessive. This was not the casual thing I could walk away from.
>
> I've been pretty good over the years when I go after something—and in this case it became an obsession to get Gretzky.

Listening to McNall's words, it is clear how much of himself was in the deal. It was the right thing to do, but he needed to do it all the more because others were after the same thing. And the fact that he was after the best made the hunt all the more worthwhile, not unlike buying the Athena Decadrachm. He made that analogy himself.

McNall once said:

> The coin and the hockey business are similar in one respect. I always thought if I bought the best possible coins in the world, I'd be in good shape, even if I had to pay top dollar for them. The only time I got in trouble in the coin business was if I tried to buy things cheap, things that I thought were a good bargain because there was something wrong with them.
>
> In a funny way, that's the same as the hockey business. If you want the best team, you have to go out and get the best player.

While McNall certainly figured Wayne Gretzky was going to make his Kings a better team, it is doubtful he honestly felt becoming "the best team" was within reach. But he also knew that wasn't necessary to make his investment pay off.

Before he ever made the deal, McNall contacted Prime Ticket, the cable television station carrying Kings games, as well as the people handling the team's concessions and merchandising, and requested financial support. And he got it. It did not take long before the Kings began reaping the benefits from the trade.

The following season the per-game fee for cable rose "maybe 50 percent" according to one source, and the number of regular-season games carried rose from 37 to 60. The average ticket price jumped from $18.50 to $22, and attendance from 427,721 to 547,952, an increase in average of 3,360 a game. Instead of 5 sellouts, there were 22.

And all this was not to watch the Kings win nine more games or even move from fourth to second place in the Smythe Division. It was to see Wayne Gretzky. McNall knew that would happen. Sure, he was out to build a winner, but even if his Kings never won the Stanley Cup, his business deal would prove successful because the focus of it was a hockey player known as "the Great One," a man guaranteed to improve revenues.

Improving revenues invariably improves worth. McNall originally paid $16 million to acquire controlling interest in the Kings; by 1993 when his team fought the Montreal Canadians for the NHL championship—losing in five games—he had reportedly turned down offers of more than $90 million.

The Rose Auction

An early beneficiary of free agency in baseball was Pete Rose. Rose had a glorious career during his first tour of duty in Cincinnati, from 1963 through 1978. This was a decade before he was accused of gambling on baseball and thrown out of the game by Commissioner A. Bartlett Giamatti. During the good times, Rose collected every honor available to a player, starting with being named Rookie of the Year in 1963, player of the year in 1968, and player of the decade, 1970–1979. He was an all-star at second base, third base, first base, and all three outfield positions for the Reds, and played on their two World Series championship teams in 1975 and 1976.

So by the time he was granted free agency at the end of the 1978 season and began peddling himself around the league, he was a hot item. One of the teams on his list of possibles was the Philadelphia Phillies. Eventually Rose would sign a three-year, $2.2 million-contract with Philly.

The matching of Rose and the Phillies seemed like a perfect fit to fans around the country. Philadelphia was a team whose frustration was unmatched in all of baseball. While they had been in the World Series as late as 1950, a mere 39 years before, those Whiz Kids were swept by the Yankees. And that was their closest try since they managed one win against Boston in the Series of 1915. They had good players in the 1970s, but they seemed to lack that spark. Rose was a spark. With his drive, his hustle, his .300-lifetime batting average, surely he was the missing part of the puzzle.

But while winning their first-ever World Series would seem enough impetus to sign a $2.2-million player, it was not enough for Philadelphia. It had to be a sound business move. We learned in Benjamin Rader's *In Its Own Image* that Bill Giles, executive president of the team, went to the local television station carrying their games and asked for an additional $600,000 for the broadcasts. The station then checked with its own sales staff to find out what the addition of Pete Rose might mean to advertising sales.

The response, as told to a *Sports Illustrated* writer in 1979, was

> that Pete Rose playing for the Phillies would do two things: 1) he would certainly raise viewing levels and this could be translated into an increased demand for commercial time, and, 2) his presence would have a strong emotional effect on certain clients—people who would buy time because they could then see themselves as being instrumental in getting Pete Rose to play for the Phillies.

The deal was made. And, almost incidently, a season later in 1980, Rose led the Phillies to their first World Series championship.

Playing by Different Rules

This is not meant to imply that winning ball games and championships is not the single, all-important goal it appears to be from reading the sports section; it is only to make clear that in the real world of sports as business, winning is not everything. It is but one element in a complex collection that contributes to the overall structure of professional sports.

Knowing the relative importance of each of those elements is difficult, partly because their importance varies in different sports at different times.

In the early 1960s, the formative years of that mighty relationship between television and the National Football League, winning meant credibility to a team. As if they could see the golden years ahead, each franchise in both the NFL and the AFL needed to remain viable.

Winning was especially important for the new league. Many of the AFL teams were struggling in the early going; TV alone would not guarantee their survival. The New York entry, competing with the long-popular Giants, needed to make a statement. They needed to win games, and they needed to attract top college talent.

While Notre Dame's John Huarte won the Heisman Trophy as the nation's outstanding college football player in 1964, Joe Namath was the fans' darling, the man who led Alabama to a national championship. Just to make certain, the New York Jets drafted both of them. But they paid Namath nearly $400,000, a staggering amount of money at the time. The decision was immediately popular. Within four months, season ticket sales jumped to 28,000, compared to 9,000 at the same point the season before; that was an increase in revenues of nearly $1 million.

Signing Namath also paid off on the field. Proclaimed in headlines as "Short Cut to AFL Title," he went one better when, after winning the title in 1968, he led the Jets and the AFL to their first win over the NFL in the game later to be christened Super Bowl III.

The Jets have never approached those heights since, but they didn't have to. Because with the AFL/NFL merger and the introduction of the sharing of national television revenues among all teams, winning does not mean to professional football what it once did. Quoting from the Houlihan Lokey Howard & Zukin report on "The Changing Structre of Professional Sports," issued in 1992:

> As a result of the NFL's revenue sharing principles, there is little difference in revenue between the best and worst performing teams. For example, in 1990 the average NFL team generated about $45 million in annual revenue. The most successful teams in terms of revenue averaged about $46–$47 million in comparison with $43–$44 million in annual revenue for the least successful teams.

How do these numbers affect the internal drive of a franchise to put a winning team on the field? It's a question that is hard to answer; no one can look inside an owner and know his goals for the season. Easier to see is the effect that revenue-sharing and an absence of free agency have had on the valuing of athletic talent. Up until the new agreement granting free agency to the NFL, only the marquee names earned the big salaries, and all of them were quarterbacks.

Suddenly all those other positions are being evaluated for their true worth. Now, for the first time in football, "support players" capable of impacting games are free to change teams; we have already seen many quality offensive linemen and defensive players move for record salaries. This mobility should add a new element of competitiveness in the NFL. The actual impact on the game remains to be seen.

Endless Debate

Deciding the value of star athletes addresses the oldest question in sports: Is this entertainment or competition? It is a question that permeates every aspect of every game.

Putting on a good show is not always the same as putting winning first. We saw this in the early days of professional basketball, when the need to survive drove the Harlem Globe Trotters in one direction and teams like the Original Celtics in another. We see it today, when coaches and managers must decide to bench an under-performing superstar for the good of the team or let him play because the fans have paid to see him.

The correct line lies somewhere in the middle. And right with it is the value each team places on its superstars. As we have seen, that decision is very individual, depending not only on the sport but also on the team, the wealth and attitude of the owner, and even the location of the franchise. A hockey franchise in California probably needs a Wayne Gretzky to prosper, where a star of that magnitude would be less important in Montreal or Toronto. A basketball franchise in central Florida probably needs a Shaquille O'Neal more than a Boston or New York.

At least that's the logic.

"It's true," says Red Auerbach, former coach and 1993 president of the Boston Celtics, a man noted for being able to spot and sign athletes who became superstars. Bob Cousy and Bill Russell were two of his best players. Another was Larry Bird.

"It's especially important for teams outside the major markets to have one of these marquee players," says Auerbach. "A good example is Charlotte. They've come up with Larry Johnson, and he's become a household name. In some of these markets, the NBA is the only thing going. Look at what Charles Barkley has done for Phoenix."

But the need for that special kind of celebrity is not limited to small markets, Auerbach points out. All franchises desire it, for athletes who possess it change the chemistry between spectators and team. Without them, people attend games because of their interest in the sport, as part of the process of spending recreational time. This is casual motivation, rarely compelling, and can even be somewhat clinical, as when individuals are drawn to basketball for the athleticism of the players or to hockey for the brutality. What owners want is a passionate appeal. Passion comes with true fans, built over years, but it can be developed more quickly with a star the magnitude of a Charles Barkley or a Shaquille O'Neal.

"Some players have a natural charisma, and those players sell tickets," says Auerbach, explaining that while winning is part of the attraction, it goes beyond that.

"Michael Jordan sells tickets. Magic Johnson sold tickets. Dr. J [Julius Erving] sold tickets. Olajuwon, as great as he is, doesn't sell tickets. Shaquille O'Neal sells lots of tickets. But look at a great player like Karl Malone—he doesn't sell tickets.

"It's either there or it's not. If you could explain it, you'd be a genius."

Part of this mysterious chemistry is matching the right player and the right place, which is different from matching the right player on the right team. That's just sports; the guard who fits with the flow of a basketball team or a quick infielder playing on a baseball team housed in an artificial-surface field. Chemistry is harder. Joe Namath, a bachelor who loved the nightlife, was the right player for New York; that was why they called him Broadway Joe. Magic Johnson was the right player for Los Angeles.

Maybe the best match of all was Larry Bird and Boston. Bird, with extraordinary ability as a shooter and passer, became an instant success in Boston. A private person from French Lick, Indiana, he had the confidence even as a teenager enrolled at mighty Indiana University to know that he would be better off at little Indiana State. He led Indiana State to the NCAA finals and led the Celtics to three NBA championships in his 13 seasons.

And when back problems forced him to retire in 1992, the citizens of Boston wept. "The Bird Era Is Over," read the front-page headline in *The Boston Globe* on Wednesday, August 19. And beneath it, these words began a long commentary by staff sportswriter Bob Ryan:

> Larry Bird is gone and we are again reminded that at the upper level there is God, Great, Superstar and Truly Irreplaceable. And inside Truly Irreplaceable there is one further subsection, wherein reside the athletes whose ultimate gift to the sports fan is a vision, a feel, an actual inspiration that is so rare and so highly developed that when these individuals cease playing, they leave a spiritual void that threatens the True Believer's subsequent appreciation of the game.

With the distance of time, the words seem excessive. Yet so beloved was Larry Bird that they seem to describe the feelings of many of the Celtic faithful. And these are not fans who give of themselves lightly.

Bill Russell joined the Celtics in 1956. In the following 13 seasons, the great center led the team to 11 NBA championships compared to Bird's 3, yet Russell was never the darling of Boston. Only twice in those 13 seasons did the team average more than 10,000 at games, compared to an endless succession of sellouts in the Bird years. Nearly every season, the average was the same—14,890, the Garden capacity.

Some observers of the Boston scene said the difference was that Russell was a black man and Bird a white man. Red Auerbach is not one of them.

"It was a different time, and Russell had a different personality," says Auerbach. "Great a player as Russell was, he wasn't their darling. He wouldn't sign autographs; had his own personality. But no one could deny how great he was as a performer."

Auerbach paused.

"Charisma. You can't measure it and you can't develop it, but it's so important to a franchise.

"Winning's important, but sometimes you win and you still can't sell tickets."

12

Building Blocks of Dreams

It is well past midnight, someplace east of Asheville, North Carolina, along Route 74. Our bus once belonged to the Trailways Bus Company, but that had been many years ago, before Continental was added to its proud name. This venerable if obsolete version of the logo is now barely visible on the outside, faded by the sun and washed by rain and wind. The inside, too, has been changed by time and use; institutional plastic covers the seats, and the floor is dented and scarred.

Instead of passengers traveling from town to town to visit friends and family, 25 young ball players ride from ballpark to ballpark, playing one of the more than 200 minor league baseball teams scattered across this country, Mexico, and Canada.

Tall, lanky pitchers are crammed into the double seats. A lightweight infielder is stretched out in the luggage rack on the driver's side, and an outfielder of similar size in the rack across the aisle. Two players have brought slabs of uncovered foam rubber and sleep end-to-end on the floor. Only one player is still awake. At the very back of the bus, the club's veteran catcher leans against the glass of the window, trying to get decent reception on his little transistor radio, listening to the final inning of a West Coast game that fades in and out as the bus climbs in and out of the mountains.

Who these players are or what uniform they wear on the field is of no importance. They are presented here as a point of reference, to continue that bond with all the minor league players who came before them and all who will follow. For this bus is as much a part of baseball as bats and balls, just as the hopes and dreams of athletes struggling on the fringe of their games are a part of all sports.

They are here to remind us that as much as sports is a business—entertainment exchanged for money—it is still played by men who came to their calling in the first place because of their love of sport. All too soon they get to the point where every dollar must be fought for and sitting out an entire season in a contract dispute—as quarterback Bobby Herbert did for the entire 1990 season with New Orleans in the NFL—is an option. But in the beginning, the game is too important.

We see this most easily in baseball's minor leagues: in Toledo, Ohio, where the Mud Hens play; in Columbus, Georgia, home of the Mudcats; in Buffalo, where the Bisons play; and up in Portland, Oregon, home to the Beavers. These are where the seeds are planted for the major leagues of tomorrow.

The growing process is simple along the back roads of America. Players sleep late, then head to the ballpark to work with their coaches and managers on the fundamentals of baseball, the bunt and the pickoff and the double play. They play in ballparks that seat 4,000 and 5,000 fans, dress in clubhouses with two or three showers and enough towels and hot water only for those who get in and out fast. Then they get back on the bus, stop at Burger King or Pizza Hut for dinner, and drive all night to their next game.

What time is free they spend in their motel rooms, watching soap operas on television and running up huge phone bills calling former teammates who were traded along the way, getting the latest word on hits and homers and runs given up, consoling players who have been hurt or released, getting the news on who has been sent up to the majors, the place they call "The Show."

The process predates bonuses, free agency, and even television as a force in sports. Yet it continues to be baseball's most reliable means of providing for its own future.

And while only two or three out of a hundred minor leaguers ever make it to the majors for more than that proverbial cup of coffee, this is where they come from.

Organizations with good farm systems put contending teams on the field season after season, generation after generation. The others rely on luck and money.

Baseball's minor leagues have been around nearly as long as the majors. The official starting date for the International League is 1877, one year after the start of the National League. By 1883, the National League accepted that the International League "owned" its own players and could only obtain one by "purchase." Drafting players began as early as the 1890s, which was about the time major league owners began buying minor league teams.

According to the information in Andrew Zimbalist's *Baseball and Billions*, the prices for the purchase of minor league players rose steadily, from $750 for a top-classification draft pick in 1903 to $1,000 in 1905, $2,500 in 1911, and $5,000 in 1913. When it became clear that the draft was the major league's way of controlling prices, the top three minor leagues soon separated themselves from the system, pushing their profits on players even higher. In 1922, the White Sox paid San Francisco of the Western League $100,000 for Willie Kamm.

The concept of a farm system was begun by Branch Rickey when he was with the St. Louis Cardinals. By 1928 the Cardinals owned five farm teams outright and had working arrangements with several others. In 1937, St. Louis controlled more than 600 players in the 33 farm clubs. One of the better teams in the National League, the Cardinals, won the World Series in 1934 and again in 1942, 1944, and 1946.

By then the rest of baseball had caught on. At their zenith, in 1949, the minors consisted of 59 leagues divided into eight classifications, with 464 teams located in over 450 cities and towns. Long before then Rickey had taken his ideas to Brooklyn, and in 1949 the Dodgers had the largest minor league system and more than 600 players under contract.

Unfortunately, what was a good idea had grown too much for its own good or for baseball's. Zimbalist reports that from 1945 to 1950, the Chicago Cubs spent an average of $113,637 per player on player development and that counts only players remaining on the major league roster for two or more years; Yankees' per-player development costs were $201,118. They and a lot of other clubs were getting the impression that buying players was cheaper than developing them. By 1950, two-thirds of all minor league teams operated at a loss.

Those numbers, along with the loss of players to the Korean War and the loss of fans to television, cost the minor leagues dearly. Attendance fell from 42 million in 1949 to 24 million in 1952. Over the same period, leagues dropped from 59 to 43 and teams from 464 to 324. By 1975 the leagues were down to 18, the clubs to 137, and the attendance to 11 million.

Revival in the Bushes

But the minor leagues fought back from that low point. While the number of leagues rose to only 19 by 1991, the teams were up to 207 and the attendance to 26.5 million. For 1993, the leagues remained at 19, but teams were up to 214, and attendance topped 30 million.

The renewed popularity probably has a lot to do with the nation's rediscovered interest in its simpler past, its craving for plain-colored cotton shirts and wood-grained furniture, for maple syrup from Vermont, and revivals of musicals from the 1950s.

"For a while in the 60s and 70s, we were being hurt badly by the televising of big-league games," Class AA Eastern League President Charlie Eshbach told *The New York Times,* covering the boom in progress in 1989. "But now we feel that television benefits us by advertising baseball and getting people out to the ballpark, particularly in areas far from major league cities. What also helps is the fact that baseball is more popular than ever."

Fan interest has been building for the last decade. After hitting its modern-day low of 9.77 million in 1961, minor league attendance has been increasing each year, and those fans have been spread over fewer and fewer clubs. Those 41.9 million fans in 1949 were cheering on 464 teams, for a season average of 90,301 per team; the average draw for the 189 teams in 1991 was 140,741.

These figures don't include the millions who attended all the high school and college games in the country that year or those who carried picnic baskets to the Cape Cod League, the Alaska League, or any of the other summer leagues around the country for college players.

The minor leagues offer baseball in its purest form. Players come and go so quickly in some of these leagues that fans hardly get to know their names. And stars are hard to come by. The game's the thing. For those turned off by multimillion dollar contracts, strikes, and lockouts, minor league ball is a chance to watch young athletes running out every ground ball, chasing every pop foul, all in an effort to catch a lifelong dream to make it to the major leagues.

Baseball learned from its earlier experience with the minors, and it has approached the project differently. Today only a fraction of the teams in the minor leagues are actually owned by the parent clubs. Individuals or groups own and operate the clubs under an arrangement called Player Development Contract (PDC), which is part of the Professional Baseball Agreement (PBA). The PBA is the agreement between the National and American Leagues and the National Association of Professional Baseball Leagues—or the minor leagues—regarding all matters that involve the minors. The PBA delineates the responsibilities of the parent club and the minor league owner.

Under the PBA, the parent club provides the ball players, manager, trainer, and coach or coaches and pays their salaries and all other baseball expenses, including equipment. The local club provides and maintains a home field and clubhouse of a certain quality and pays for travel and expenses on the road other than meal money.

These arrangements, coupled with the recent popularity of minor league baseball have made ownership very attractive. North Carolina's Kingston Indians in the Class A Carolina League sold for $100,000 after the 1983 season and then for $225,000 in 1985. By the time the team was sold in 1989, the price was $750,000, and its estimated value in 1992 was $1.5 million. And that's no fluke.

In October of 1992, former Mets shortstop and later manager Bud Harrelson paid $2.5 million for the Peninsula Pilots, the Virginia-based Class A farm team of the Seattle Mariners in the Carolina League. About that time, Daniel Burke—then chief executive of Capital Cities/ABC but looking toward his retirement in 1994—purchased an expansion franchise in the Eastern League for $3.5 million; the Class AA farm team of the new Florida Marlins was dubbed the Portland (Maine) Sea Dogs. That same fall the New York Mets sold their top farm team, the Triple A Tidewater Tides in the International League, for a sum reported to be in the neighborhood of $7 million. While that is an unusually high figure, Triple A teams were changing hands in 1992 and 1993 for $4 and $5 million.

One man who paid considerably less for a team in 1992 was Bill Gladstone, who retired the previous year as co-CEO of Ernst & Young. In April of 1992, Gladstone and four friends purchased the Pittsfield Mets, a New York–Pennsylvania League team located in the Berkshire Mountains of Massachusetts. Still, they paid what Gladstone terms "a premium price."

This Class A league had not shown the appreciation in value of minor leagues elsewhere, and the Pittsfield franchise had weathered the economic strife of having one of its owners lose his share of the team to his personal creditors. (Gladstone and his partners purchased the team after what he calls "a long and distasteful process involving creditors and bankruptcy court.") The high $850,000 price—a record for a team in that league, according to Gladstone—was paid to become part of the New York Mets organization. The new owners put in another $140,000 of working capital, bringing the price close to $1 million.

It was, he says, a purchase made less with his business mind than with his heart. "From the time I retired, I had in the back of my mind the thought of acquiring a team," says Gladstone, a Brooklyn native who nurtured his love of baseball in the stands of Ebbets Field. "I looked at a Double A team in New York State, but they were in the $3.5 to $4 million range, more capital than I wanted to put in or raise. Then I heard about Pittsfield."

Pittsfield offered a team closer to his New York State home than some of the other Class A teams he had been considering and gave him a situation with a touch of history. The team's vintage home, Wahconah Park, built in 1919, had seen nearly steady occupancy by one minor league team or another, from the Pittsfield Hillies to the Pittsfield Ponies to the Mets.

Such factors are a consideration to people who purchase minor league teams. Baseball seems to be a sport that forces old connections to the surface. For writer Roger Kahn, author of *The Boys of Summer*, it was his relationship with his father that drove him to purchase the Class A Utica Blue Sox in 1983; no doubt Bud Harrelson's frustrations as manager of the Mets influenced his purchase. Gladstone had a connection with baseball through work—Ernst & Young does accounting work for many teams—and developed an appreciation for the aesthetic images of the game. He has one of the world's major collections of baseball art; it began with the works of Willard Mullin, the cartoonist whose "Brooklyn Bum" was the symbol of the Dodgers.

"Baseball has a fascination that is deep-rooted in the American culture," says Gladstone and then admits that his interest in the game preceded his professional involvement and his art collection.

"I had always hoped I could put together a group to buy a major league team, but the prices got out of line, and the nature of that business changed dramatically," he says. "Then I began thinking about a minor league club. That was a new thought; for a long time, people didn't realize that you could be the owner of a minor league team."

He starts talking about the people attending Pittsfield games, about the $5.75 box seats that come with cushions and waitress service and the bleacher seats that go for $2.75—$1 for fans over 60. The owner's box? "That's wherever I sit," he says, and then adds he saw almost all the Pittsfield Mets 39 home games in 1993. Suddenly he stops and reflects on the group he once dreamed of joining, those who own the major league teams today, and on the economic difficulties that surround the game. "Somehow I don't think those owners are having much fun today, and we're having a lot of fun."

Baseball's new regulations toward its minor leagues has cut into some of that fun. The latest version of the PBA, issued at the end of 1990, includes a section detailing the requirements for a minor league ballpark. No area was overlooked. Not only were standards set for the field and clubhouses but also covered were the number, type, and arrangement of seating in the stands; the number of toilets; the amount of counter space at concession stands; and even the height of the foul poles.

The standards were tougher for new facilities than those already built and slightly more relaxed for Class A franchises than the higher classifications, but many of the old parks would not take easily to renovation, especially in a Northeast still struggling out of the recession as the Major League Baseball's 1994 deadline approached.

"Our biggest thing is the visitor's clubhouse—it's short by 130 square feet of space," says Gladstone. "It will be a real challenge to build out the clubhouse right now, but the park and the franchise are important to Pittsfield, and they're going to make every effort to come up with the money."

The new agreement also had a lot to say about finances, Major League Baseball's effort to cut their expenditures in their farm systems at a time of prosperity for the minors. The majors continued to pay salaries, equipment, and meal money for players. But the minors had to join in a revenue-sharing system that called for a payment to the

Major League central fund of $750,000 in 1991. Thereafter, the minors would pay a percentage of net income from ticket sales, resulting in minimum payments of $1.5 million in 1992, $1.75 million in 1993, and $2 million in 1994, along with complete financial records to support those payments.

"Baseball has been accustomed to helping the minor leagues," says Bill Gladstone, who says they may start helping a little less. "If they think the minors are making too much money, they're just going to say, 'Well, we used to pay for the bats and balls, now you guys are going to have to pay for them.' "

It is the new economy of sports—higher players' salaries and projected lower revenues from television—that drives baseball to examine its minor leagues more closely. With more people wanting to own teams, baseball can set higher standards for the facilities that house the teams. And if the majors can also cut some expenses, that's all the better.

Growing Players, Not Money

But the primary importance of the farms was always to grow talent, and in the early 1990s that was more important than it had been in years.

Today's escalating player salaries drive home a point to every general manager of every franchise: the longer your talented ball players remain with your team, the better the chance they'll be making more than a million dollars a season. And as we've seen, this isn't only the stars. Everyday players regularly signed for $2 million and $3 million in 1993; even reserves were paid $1 million and up.

The only answer—after signing one or two top stars for whatever the market demands—was to continually develop good, young ball players and to get those three years of service out of them at the major league level before they are eligible to enter the arbitration sweepstakes and free-agent heaven beyond, becoming part of the ever-ascending spiral of player costs.

Says Astros General Manager Bill Woods:

> As soon as a guy takes his position on the field for the first time, you need to be developing someone to take his place. The only way up in this era is to have the capability within your own system to fill the gaps when a Ruben Sierra, Barry Bonds or Greg Maddux leaves you after only six years in your major league system.

As the minors became more and more important—economically as well as athletically—the signing of quality ball players became more important.

Traditionally that was the province of baseball scouts, men burdened with the responsibility of deciding who best fits their organization's needs.

Through the 1940s and 1950s, they were baseball's lonely prospectors, mining for talent. Staffs of men driving cars badly in need of washing along the back roads of the country, piling on thousands of miles between spring and fall, checking out high schools and junior colleges, universities and summer leagues. They were bound by their notepads, carried to jot down the skills and weaknesses of young hopefuls, and by their small brimmed hats worn to ward off the effects of too many afternoons in the sun.

The question they confronted was the universal question of sports: Not so much how good is the player they are watching on the field, but how good will he be when playing in the majors? By the mid-1960s, each major league team employed a staff of at least 25 full-time scouts and an assemblage of part-time and free-lance contacts. They all funneled information into the front office, which had the decision on whom to sign and how much to offer. Signing meant bonus, as little as a few thousand dollars and a convertible, or as much as $100,000.

The rules of pursuing amateur talent changed in 1965, when baseball's first draft was instituted. Similar to the drafts in basketball and football, the intent was economic—to cut down on the amount of money going in bonuses. It also altered the job of scouting. Now the scout was advising his team instead of making the decision himself, and since any "find" was still subject to the draft, competition among scouts was lessened. Our rugged old prospector became part of a complex machine, with regional scouts checking and cross-checking information before the draft.

Baseball's Joint Effort

Another money-saving measure was proposed by Branch Rickey. He envisioned a program of "pooled scouting" that would save baseball millions of dollars. In 1974—eight years after Rickey's death—the Major League Scouting Bureau was established, pushed by long-time baseball men Lee McPhail, Joe Brown, and Jim Campbell. Teams subscribed by choice; 17 signed up initially, paying $120,000 each. For many teams, it was one step down a path of fiscal conservatism.

"The econo-scout approach was epitomized by the Seattle Mariners, Texas Rangers, and Houston Astros," wrote Kevin Kerrane in his thorough study of scouting, *Dollar Sign on the Muscle.* "Besides subscribing to the Bureau, these three teams had formed a 'combine' to pool scouting information, enabling them to make even further staff cutbacks. In 1981 the Mariners were operating with six full-time and two part-time scouts, the Rangers with eight and two. Each organization stayed within a yearly scouting budget of $900,000 or less," Kerrane writes.

It should be noted that the "$900,000 or less" figures covered the years 1981–1983, lean years on the field for the Mariners, Rangers, and Astros. In fact, with the exception of Houston's division title in 1986, that was a decade of losses for all three clubs. Teams that were building in that same period—most notably Oakland—used the Bureau to supplement their own scouting operations, which cost them an average of $1 million to $1.5 million, according to Kerrane. Scouting for the non-Bureau teams in 1981 ranged from $1.4 million to $1.8 million.

To join or not join ceased to be a decision after 1983, when Bureau membership became mandatory; payment from each of the 26 teams for the 1984 season was $85,000. By 1991, the total allotment to the Bureau was $3.3 million, or about $126,900 from each team.

But by then the importance of scouting talent for a healthy and productive farm system was so widely accepted in baseball that nearly every team maintained a large scouting staff of its own. Thirty or 35 scouts was a normal number in 1991; the Yankees had more than 50. After the frugality of previous owners, Seattle's Jeff Smulyan invested heavily in future talent while he still was in charge. For 1992 the Mariners listed five men at the top of the scouting system, three supervisors, 39 area scouts, and 41 associate scouts, all in addition to their involvement with the Bureau.

"We are a supplement to the staffs of the teams, and do other things that they do not do," says Don Pries, head of the Major League Scouting Bureau, housed in El Toro, California. The Bureau's staff of 71 men covers the United States, Canada, and Puerto Rico, evaluating high school, junior college, and college players.

"The most innovative part of our operation is that we videotape the top prospects around the country," says Pries, former director of player development for Baltimore who has been with the Bureau since its inception. "We provide the teams with video on some 250 players each year."

The Bureau's basic method of scouting does not differ very much from that followed by the clubs it serves. Don Pries explains:

> We grade individual skills—running, throwing, fielding, hitting and power—rating them from 2 to 8, and give each player an overall number from 20 to 80 which evaluates him as a prospect. Five is an average major leaguer on the individual skills, and 50 on the overall.
>
> Pitchers are rated on their fastball, their curveball and their slider. Then all this is fed into the computers of the different teams.
>
> We use a three-man evaluating system, using a territorial supervisor and a national cross-checker, with all of these reports going into the computer, which generates an average number in qualifying a player.
>
> Every year we tell you the best prospects, one through 700, across the country.

Their scouts are mostly former major and minor league players, recommended by the teams and then trained for their assignment. The Bureau's assignment also includes operating 55 tryout camps in the United States, Canada, and Puerto Rico, and running high school coaches' clinics.

Mining the Ice

The only sport other than baseball with an established farm system is hockey. This is only natural, since hockey has such a long history of minor but professional leagues, dating back to the 1920s, some ten years after the NHL got its start.

First on the scene were the Canadian Professional and the Canadian-American Leagues. The Canadian Professional League lasted only three seasons, replaced by the International League. The Can-Am was replaced for the 1936–1937 season by the International-American League, which later became known as the American Hockey League, the lone survivor of those early hockey confederations and today the premier minor league in the world.

It was during World War II, when manpower was thin, that the American Hockey League began supplying players to the NHL. Others followed: the Pacific Coast Hockey League, which became the Western League; the United States Hockey League, which spawned the Central League.

Today they are all part of the network that forms minor league hockey in North America. That network consists of professional and amateur teams. The NHL's closest association is with the two leagues at the top—the American Hockey League and the International Hockey League; they are the heart of the hockey's farm system. Also active in that system is the East Coast Hockey League, but a step below. Further below are the Central League and the Colonial League. The other leagues—among them the Canadian Hockey League and the National Collegiate Athletic Association—feature amateur hockey, and form the pool of players from which the NHL drafts its future players.

In the AHL and IHL, the parent club pays the salaries of the players, the coaches, and the managers; the minor league owner picks up most other bills. The NHL also uses the top three minor leagues in their development program for referees and pays a part of their salaries.

The specific financial arrangement between the major league and minor league clubs depends on the exact nature of their relationship. Where the NHL team owns its farm team outright, it is simply responsible for the economics of that team, a situation that is becoming increasingly rare in baseball but more common in hockey. The Detroit Red Wings own their farm team in the AHL, the Adirondack team from Glens Falls, New York; the Montreal Canadians own their AHL team, Fredericton from New Brunswick; Edmonton owns the Cape Breton Oilers in the AHL.

Those teams with working arrangements have more complicated finances. One such relationship was described in a 1992 article in the *Providence Journal-Bulletin:*

> Take the AHL's Maine Mariners, for example, the Boston Bruins top affiliate in Portland. The Bruins pay all player salaries, the coach's salary, insurance and taxes, such as Social Security and workers' compensation. In return, Ed Anderson, the Mariners' president, CEO and general manager, said he pays Boston $15,000 per player. But because of the explosion in NHL salaries, the Bruins are pressuring Anderson for more money to help defray their end of the operating costs.

In some of the other leagues, the parent clubs pay only a percentage of the athlete's salaries. Those salaries cover a wide range. The average in the AHL in 1992 was about $35,000; in the International Hockey League, about $10,000 less. The ECHL has a salary cap of $4,650.50 per week, or about $270 per player.

While profits are good at the budget ECHL, the upper levels of minor league hockey lose a lot of money. Much of that loss is translated to the major league clubs, even those that don't own their farm teams.

"This year the team is in last place and has scant hope of making the playoffs," the *Journal-Bulletin* wrote of the Mariners late in the 1992 season. "If it doesn't Anderson estimated his loss will range between $150,000 and $175,000. The Bruins, he said, would probably lose about $800,000. Last year, he said, he lost $200,000."

Minor league hockey in the early 1990s was where minor league baseball was in the 1950s, losing money but fulfilling its obligation to develop players for the major leagues, all of which made it vital that those players receiving all this attention were the players with the best possible chance to make it with the big clubs.

That gets down to signing the right men in the first place, which is a matter of scouting. Compared to professional baseball, hockey scouting staffs are small. Seven or eight is usual; ten or twelve is a lot. And yet their geographic responsibilities are great, forcing them to cover high schools, colleges, and junior hockey clubs all throughout Canada.

And when the scouts get to the ice and see their prospects, judging what is actually before them has proved to be a difficult task. Listen to Larry Wigge, who has covered hockey for *The Sporting News* since 1969:

"Why don't you be a scout for a moment?" he posed in an article in 1992. "Do you notice that Brett Hull of the Blues can't skate as well as some players in the NHL? Or that he is a little lazy? Of course not. You see a player who works extremely hard to get into scoring position and then fires shots so hard that even the best goaltenders can't stop them.

"When you see Los Angeles' Wayne Gretzky, do you notice a player who is too small and too slow? What's wrong with Luc Robitaille or the Kings? Or Pittsburgh's Kevin Stevens? Or Boston's Adam Oates?

"All are among the NHL's top stars, but they have much more in common. None of them received the Grade-A seal of approval by the league's scouting experts," Wigge writes.

One of the problems is that NHL scouts are evaluating very young athletes, often 17 and 18 years old. It is extremely hard to see great physical ability at that age, much less evaluate the kind of heart and commitment—what baseball scouts call those lower-level qualities—that go into making up a great player.

As a result, a lot of mistakes are made in the draft. Boston had three of its draft choices from the previous six years on the 1992–1993 team that was preparing for the playoffs, but Buffalo had only one, and St. Louis and the New York Islanders didn't have any. Neither did the Rangers or Calgary, both failing to qualify for the playoffs that season.

That represents a lot of wasted investment, and just one more reason why hockey teams don't make more money.

The Natural Farm Systems

The ideal farm system would cost the professional teams no money and permit them to delay selecting which players they wanted to sign until those athletes were full grown, say 21 or 22 years old, thereby eliminating some of the guesswork.

Dream no more. Such a farm system exists, and it's called collegiate sports.

While all the major team sports exist in college as well as at the professional level, collegiate football and basketball programs have the most impact on the pros. Most NHL players still come from Canada, from high school and junior hockey leagues. More and more baseball players enter the pros after successful college careers, but many more sign right out of high school. And given a choice, most baseball executives prefer to see their prospects develop in their own systems rather than even those universities considered baseball powerhouses—Miami or Arizona, USC or Florida State or Texas.

With basketball and especially football, there is little choice. College ball is the accepted route. Players do their growing in college and learn their sport. Some do leave early; "hardship" financial considerations can lead to a player's turning professional before his eligibility is used up. But it is a shortcut taken by comparatively few. Most basketball and football players become pros by going through the draft with their graduating class. Some are drafted, and others sign as free agents.

Either way, the decisions by the pro scouts are most important. In basketball and football, first-round draft picks are blocks on which professional teams are built. Look down the rosters of the top pro teams of the 1990s and find the athletes who lead them: Dallas Cowboys with quarterback Troy Aikman and running back Emmitt Smith, both first-round picks; Buffalo Bills with quarterback Jim Kelly and defensive end Bruce Smith, both first-round picks; Chicago Bulls and Michael Jordan, first-round pick; Detroit Pistons with Isiah Thomas, first-round pick.

For the players, going high in the draft brings big money. Especially going first. Here are some of the signing arrangements in 1992 for first-round picks in football: number one pick, Steve Emtman by the Indianapolis Colts, four years for $9.16 million; number two pick, Quentin Coryatt by the Colts, four years for $8.86 million; number three pick, Sean Gilbert by the Los Angeles Rams, five years for $7.5 million.

The Record Rookie Signing Award of 1992 went to basketball. Number one pick, Shaquille O'Neal, hammered out a deal on the signing deadline with the Orlando Magic, estimated at $40 million over seven years. Only $3.5 million went to O'Neal for the 1992–1993 season, permitting the team to remain below the salary cap. Some other first-round signings: number eight pick, Todd Day by the Milwaukee Bucks, five years for $10.5 million; number ten pick, Adam Keefe by the Atlanta Hawks, five years for $7 million.

But that money means even more as insurance on the young athlete's professional career than it buys in cars, houses, and stocks. Big money invested on a high draft pick means the team has made a commitment to him, will give him more attention in camp, more playing time during the season, and more seasons to prove himself. There is little investment in a free agent. A poor training camp and he's likely gone. But no team is going to quickly cut a first-round draft pick, especially one signed for several million dollars. It's embarrassing; first-round picks draw a lot of attention. And it's also expensive; most of those contracts are guaranteed.

All of which makes picking the right man all the more important.

The Gridiron Search

The NFL has always invested in scouting. But in earlier days, most of that investment came from the dedicated individuals who covered the country looking for talent. The following account from William Wallace in a 1964 *New York Times* article talks of Emlen Tunnell, a coach for the New York Giants, and one of four scouts they had covering the country:

> An intrasquad game finished spring football practice at Penn State yesterday and it also finished Emlen Tunnel. The coach and scout for the New York Giants last night left State College, Pennsylvania, ending three months of almost uninterrupted travel during which he visited 51 campuses.

> The travel-worn scout had been in pursuit of elusive game—young men good enough to be the Giants of the future. He saw thousands of collegians labor in spring practice and soon he will turn in elaborate reports on 300 of them to Jim Lee Howell, the Giants director of player personnel.

By the 1990s, the Giants scouting department included 11 full-time scouts, a full-time coordinator, and 2 part-time scouts. From time to time, the general manager and assistant general manger also traveled to see a player. Between the first summer practice and the last game of winter, the scouts visit up to 360 schools, view videos of games, and compile files on 700 players. The operation was budgeted at slightly more than $1 million.

That represented a somewhat better than average commitment to preparing for the annual draft. But no team in the NFL stops there. Most of them employ the services of free-lance scouts, men who file independent reports. And all of them belong to one of two scouting services: the National Scouting Combine, based in Tulsa, or Blesto, working out of Pittsburgh. They are the NFL's *Consumer's Union*—the testing laboratory for football players—only more expensive. Subscriptions here cost about $50,000 a year.

The 28 teams that signed up with one of the two services for the 1992 season received detailed reports on more than 700 college players eligible for the draft. Then, in the middle of winter, those most highly rated of the young athletes were invited to be examined. The yearly ritual has been referred to as a cattle call, a meat market, and worse.

The Combine, which began operating in 1981, moved around a lot in its early years, but has used the Hoosier Dome in Indianapolis as its testing facility since 1987. In the beginning the schedule mostly included medical tests in preparation for the draft. That first year 150 players were tested.

But the Combine's list of services expanded, as did the number of men tested. In 1991 and 1992, when the draft was 12 rounds long, about 450 athletes were invited. For the 1993 draft, cut to seven rounds by the new agreement, the guest list was cut to approximately 350. But there was no stinting on what they were put through.

During the three-day ordeal, every possible measurement of the young men was taken. Height and weight were measured, as were their biceps and triceps and everything down to their feet. Technicians X-rayed them and analyzed their urine and measured their strength by counting how many times they could bench press a standard weight of 225 pounds.

The final day—the one considered most important by most in attendance—was devoted to workouts. Vertical jumps and long jumps were tested, and the 40-yard-dash. Standards were different for different positions. Acceptable times in the 40 for offensive linemen were 5.1 to 5.2 seconds; for defensive linemen, 5.0 to 5.1 seconds; for linebackers and tight ends, 4.8 to 4.9 seconds; for quarterbacks, 4.8 to 5.0 seconds. Those playing the "skill positions" of wide receivers and cornerbacks needed to run the 40 in under 4.5 seconds. Receivers and cornerbacks also had to jump 34 inches straight up, compared to only 26 to 30 for linemen.

"It's really turned into a mammoth event since it moved to Indianapolis," Washington Redskin General Manager Charley Casserly told *The Washington Post* at the 1993 combine tests. "It gives teams a good chance to see exactly what's out there. For the most part, you've seen all of these players before, either at all-star games or on film, so you know what they can do. But there are some advantages of having them all here together."

Since professional teams are often attracted to a player for his athleticism and not simply those talents demanded by a specific football program, the workouts afford the opportunity to see skills that were not required during a prospect's college career.

"It may be something as simple as a running back catching a pass out of the backfield, but for some of these guys they weren't required to do that in college," said Casserly. "The same is true with a linebacker who may have been primarily a pass rusher in college, but in this setting you can see how he is in pass defense. It's that kind of thing, along with being able to stack them up against all the best people at their particular position at one time, that makes the scouting combine particularly worthwhile."

Not all athletes view these invitation-only performances as important to their careers. Top prospects often skip the on-field workouts. University of Washington defensive tackle Steve Emtman didn't even show up in 1992. He was the first pick in the draft that spring, the guy who signed a four-year, $9.16-million contract with the Colts. A year later, Notre Dame's Rick Mirer skipped the Hoosier Dome party. The quarterback instead held his own audition, a private gathering three weeks before the draft for some 50 NFL scouts and coaches at South Bend. Mirer would go second in the 1993 draft, be selected by the Seattle

Seahawks, and sign one of the year's most lucrative rookie contracts, one that could earn him $15.7 million over three seasons.

But for the lesser lights, and especially for those players from smaller schools, the combine workouts are an opportunity to gain attention.

Decisions on the Hardwood

Basketball does not approach its evaluation of talent with quite the same organizational zeal that football brings to the hunt. Every team has a small staff of scouts, and that staff puts in a lot of hours over many miles over the year. As with the NFL, NBA teams also subscribe to the services of free-lance scouts. But the style is different from what goes on in pro football.

One reason may be the importance of team personality in basketball. Teams are different, and what they need to make them a better team is highly individual. More than in any other sport, scouting in basketball is a matter of building a team based on the individual taste of the coach or the personality of the talent he has.

Certainly a talent as dominating as Shaquille O'Neal is worth adjusting the men on your team, but players of his size and talent are very unusual.

What scouts do need is an opportunity to view the talent available. Fortunately, basketball players are always playing basketball somewhere, all year long. They play all summer, in city leagues around the country. New York City's Halcombe Rucker League has drawn such future legends as Kareem Abdul-Jabbar and Julius Erving. Basketball season runs from fall till spring, and that is when scouts do their traveling, viewing, and keeping records on the top prospects they might draft.

At season's end comes the biggest parade of collegiate talent in the country, the NCAA tournament, 64 teams worth of basketball players from what the Selection Committee considered the most successful teams for that season. Those teams left out are picked up by the National Invitation Tournament, another 32 schools.

Of course not even the NIT is played wholly in New York anymore, only the last two rounds. As for the NCAA, it's spread all over the nation, from Syracuse to Orlando to Salt Lake City in 1993. This is a problem for scouts; few like doing their job in front of a television set.

Fortunately for them, there are the other tournaments, the ones that never get on television. The Phoenix Classic is one, and the Portsmouth

Invitational another. They don't get much press outside local coverage, but no NBA team would fail to send a scout.

The best-established is the Portsmouth Invitational Tournament in Virginia. Run by the Department of Parks and Recreation of the city of Portsmouth, the PIT was in its 41st year in 1993.

The avowed goal of the tournament is to gather "the most exciting basketball players in the country" for four nights of basketball. Talent is important, but not the size of the player's school. Junior colleges, community colleges, and Division II colleges are represented, along with those from the major conferences. There are sixty-four players, divided into eight teams.

It's quite a show, and the fans who pay to watch love it. But they may not appreciate it quite as much as the NBA scouts in attendance.

"There's no connection between the tournament and the NBA," said Rudolph Freeman, who ran the tournament in 1993. "The scouts just come because they know the talent is here."

Among those collegiate players who helped enhance their stock in the eyes of NBA teams by performing well in Portsmouth Invitationals of the past were Rick Barry, Larry Nance, Tim Hardaway, John Stockton and Scottie Pippen. All went on to productive professional careers.

But the most specialized event—and the one that most resembles the NFL's Combine—is the Chicago Pre-Draft Camp. This one is run by the NBA, strictly for the information of scouts. No tickets sold, and no fans permitted. Just 30 or so of the best players about to enter the draft, invited to showcase their talents. Physical measurements are taken, and skills demonstrated, all to help the scouts decide whom to select on draft day.

As exacting as all this sounds, it is still people and talents being judged in these camps, and that is far from a science. Basketball and football scouts will tell you this, over and over. Fortunately, basketball enjoys the advantage of having a couple safety nets.

Players who do not find a home in the NBA—or whose careers have run their course—have many more options than those deemed unwanted by the NFL. Professional basketball has become truly international in the last 20 years; today teams flourish not only in Europe but in the Middle East. Teams such as Aris in Greece, Real Madrid in Spain, and the powerful Il Messaggero in Italy now compete for NBA players with big money.

For those with a little less marquee value, there is the Continental Basketball Association. The CBA is the old Eastern Basketball League that in the 1970s had teams in Cherry Hill, New Jersey; Scranton, Pennsylvania; and Hartford, Connecticut. By the 1990s it had 16 teams in cities as broadly spaced as Albany, New York; Fort Wayne, Indiana; Oklahoma City; and Yakima, Washington.

The CBA has a successful working relationship with the NBA that involves money for support of development programs for players, coaches, and officials. The $2.7-million agreement already in place was renewed for an additional three years in September of 1992, and the amount of support was expanded to $4 million. The NBA bought the right to call up players from the CBA, to place former NBA players in coaching positions with the CBA, and to work with the league to develop officials.

Without being part of an official farm system, CBA teams have served that function for years to the NBA. Players made the giant step all the time—New York's fiery guard John Starks came to the Knicks via the CBA—as well as coaches. The Chicago Bulls' Phil Jackson started his coaching career in the CBA, as did Seattle's George Karl and Indiana's Bob Hill. During the 1993 season, former pro star Rick Berry—the only player ever to lead the NCAA, NBA, and ABA in scoring—worked as the coach of the Fort Wayne Fury.

"The NBA is proud of its long-standing ties with the CBA," NBA Commissioner David Stern said when the new contract was signed. "We are pleased that the CBA will continue to be our official development league as we expand our relationship both on and off the court."

13

The Nuts and Bolts of Sports

At the core of every sports franchise is a separate little business, which is more like any other business than the big business of sports. Far from the television cameras and the headlines, it is occupied with plumbing in the clubhouse, with the insurance on the field, and which long distance phone company to use. And while the numbers may be different from the biggest franchise to the smallest, many of the problems are identical.

"It's relatively simple at our level," says Bill Gladstone, principal partner of baseball's Class A Pittsfield Mets. "The major league team pays the players, the manager, coach, and a trainer, supplies the bats and balls, and pays the meal money. All we have to do is run the business side.

"The city of Pittsfield owns the park; we maintain the field. We sell tickets, have promotions, do advertising and hope to generate enough money to make a profit."

Class A baseball lies at one end of a broad spectrum. Profit is generated from concessions and souvenirs—they make up about half the operating revenues—with the other half coming from tickets and advertising. Expenses include the club's office staff, promotions, and advertising, and purchasing those items that are sold at concession and souvenir stands. Park deals vary. The Pittsfield Mets' arrangement is to pay no rent but in exchange to maintain the field and pay utilities—mostly the light bill, which Gladstone calls "considerable" for a team playing nearly all night games.

According to a 1992 article in *The Atlanta Constitution* on minor league baseball, a typical operating budget for Class A teams that year was $600,000. Anything they made over that figure was profit. No escalating player costs; no million-dollar scoreboards. At that level, it is a relatively simple operation.

Making a profit at the other end of the spectrum—in the big leagues—is anything but simple. And this applies to every aspect of every sport. Certainly player compensation amounts to an awesome amount of money, and those are the figures that make news. Published reports out of Major League Baseball's 1992 winter meetings tell us that the total figure for major league player costs in 1991 came to more than $728 million, or about half the total operating expenses for the game.

As for the other half, those same reports indicated that the 26 teams in 1991 spent more than $187 million on scouting and player development, nearly $141 million on stadium operations, and almost $180 million on general and administrative costs. These are numbers and headings, but what do they mean in terms of actual amounts spent on specific expenses?

"One of our big expenses is player development," says Bob Graziano, vice-president of finance for the Los Angeles Dodgers. "The Dodgers have between 50 and 55 scouts, and a lot of those live here [in California] and travel all over the world, to South America and Australia and even Europe. Before we used to scout mostly in the U.S., but today scouting is much more of an international operation, and much more costly."

While the Dodgers and other teams scout and sign players from all over, the central place where all those athletes eventually meet is Vero Beach, Florida, home of Dodgertown, the team's spring training facility. During the six weeks from late February till early April, it is a mass of activity, of testing and evaluating the young talent recently signed and already in the farm system as well as non-roster players invited to camp, veteran Dodgers, and free agents signed over the winter.

With its clean streets, dormitories, and apartments, athletic fields and dining halls, Dodgertown resembles less a training facility and more a baseball city.

"At any particular point in time, we'll have about 210 players in camp, with a support group of up to 350 people," says Graziano. "Even though we own the facility, we have enormous staffing costs and food costs, and all the incidental charges that go with that.

"The cost for the spring is about $2 million, including travel. And travel is a big part of it. We pick up people from all over the country and fly them to Florida. In fact, we've got a good number of people traveling for six weeks straight."

Another big expense is insurance. Because the Dodgers own their own stadium, they carry high liability insurance on the stadium, just in case someone is injured at a game. But the larger part of their insurance is consistent with every athletic team—worker's compensation.

"If a Dodger pitcher needs arm surgery—as Orel Hershiser did in 1991—that's covered by workman's compensation, because it's work-related," says Graziano, who estimates the organization's insurance at more than $4 million for 1992.

And there are many other business expenses that each club incurs in the course of the year, all adding up to the $16 million to $20 million average that teams spend on items other than selecting, acquiring, training, and paying players. Even the little costs add up; the Dodgers spent between $200,000 and $300,000 on bats and balls in 1992. "The players order the bats they want, made to their specifications, from the manufacturer, but we pay the bill," says Graziano.

Some of those business costs come directly from the teams and go to the league; they're called league assessments. From every ticket sold at Dodger Stadium, 30 cents go to the National League to cover such things as umpire development; in 1991 the 26 teams spent almost $4 million on that particular expense.

Just what some of these other costs are is rarely released. Sometimes, however, events conspire to free that information. Much information on the NFL came out as part of evidence presented in the *Freeman McNeil vs. the NFL* antitrust suit in 1992.

The evidence in that case, which was decided on behalf of the players and led to the league's first taste of true free agency, offered a revealing insight into salaries paid in the NFL. Here are a few examples:

- Buffalo Bills owner Ralph Wilson paid himself a salary of $3.486 million in 1990; Philadelphia Eagles owner Norman Braman paid himself $7.5 million in 1990; New York Giants owners Tim and Wellington Mara each got $150,000 in 1990.

- Giants general manager George Young earned $441,000 for the 1990 season. The highest-paid NFL coach in 1990 was Dallas' Jimmy Johnson, $1.4 million; followed by Don Shula, nearly $1.1 million. Joe Gibbs, who won his third Super Bowl with the Washington Redskins at the end of the 1990 season, earned $927,000.

The dramatic rise in all expenses in professional sports over the last two decades has seriously affected the kinds of people able or willing to own teams. As we have seen, the old-time sports impresarios—the Bill Veecks—found they could no longer keep pace. This new environment has driven out all but the wealthiest individuals—or groups of individuals.

Since the beginning of the great inflation of costs that first hit baseball, starting with the arrival of free agency, a passing of the old guard has taken place. Gone are the Carpenters from Philadelphia, the Wrigleys from Chicago, the Galbreaths from Pittsburgh.

But while it appears that all owners today must come from the list of America's Wealthiest People, there is another option, another way for communities to have a professional team in their city. Consider the concept of public ownership.

Public Ownership in Baseball

The idea of public ownership of baseball teams is nearly as old as the game itself. In 1869, the first professional club, the Cincinnati Red Stockings, were financed through a joint stock association which raised $15,000 in capital. The team was a good investment—it finished with a 57–0 record that first season—as crowds as large as 10,000 paid as much as 50 cents a ticket. The club earned a profit of $1,700 that first year, though *The Baseball Encyclopedia* tells us "the Reds returned no profits to their joint-stock company investors."

Still, a germ of an idea was planted. And it grew. Investors over the next three years put their money into at least 11 more professional ball clubs that organized as stock companies. But over-capitalized ballparks and high ticket prices combined with rising players' salaries led to the demise of several clubs in the 1870s. Cincinnati's player payroll for the 1869 season totalled $9,000, but by 1875 the Boston entry in the National Association had a payroll that reached $20,685.

These rising costs ultimately led to losses for many investors. In 1869, investors put up $20,000 to finance the new Chicago White Stockings in the National Association, only to see them fail in 1871. In 1873, the Philadelphia Whites in the same league offered its shares to the public for a price of $50, but the team went bankrupt and never completed the 1876 season. Similarly the Washington Olympics issued shares to investors in 1870 but did not survive through 1872. The St. Louis Brown Stockings and Providence Grays—both in the National League—crashed in 1877 and 1886.

Investors in baseball experienced increased profits at the end of the nineteenth century due to the game's increasing popularity combined with low players' salaries. The decline in salaries at this time was most attributable to the formation of the National League in 1876, its introduction of the now-famous reserve clause, and its success in discouraging rival leagues. However, as investment in the sport became more lucrative, small groups of investors gained controlling interests in teams and shares rarely changed hands.

Baseball's economy experienced a temporary setback late in 1889 when the National Player's League of Baseball Clubs was formed. The Player's League, as it was known, featured clubs owned jointly by players and outside investors. Competition between the two leagues resulted in losses for both. It was said the National League lost more than $200,000 and the Player's League twice that in 1890, the one year the new league existed.

Several teams in the early 1900s were owned by the public, among them the Washington Senators and St. Louis Cardinals. Neither of these teams was very successful on the field, and the Cardinals had the added burden of serious money trouble. In an effort to raise $500,000 from a public offering, an advertisement in the March 15, 1917 *Sporting News* presented the investment as a "cardinal" idea. Few were swayed. By 1922 Branch Rickey and Sam Breadon were able to gain a controlling interest in the team, a disappointment for stockholders but a boon to baseball. Rickey took advantage of his situation in St. Louis to develop his theory for the farm system.

The last public offering for a major-league baseball team was made in 1936—the St. Louis Browns. The Browns were traded openly until the 1950s, when Bill Veeck gained controlling interest and then sold the team to a group of Baltimore investors. The team has prospered as the Baltimore Orioles since and is probably one of the reasons there is no baseball team in Washington, D.C.

Today three major league baseball teams are owned by publicly held companies, but none is traded publicly on its own. The Atlanta Braves are owned by Turner Broadcasting, the St. Louis Cardinals by Anheuser–Busch, and the Chicago Cubs by the Tribune Company. Financial reports are available on Turner Broadcasting, Anheuser–Busch, and the Tribune Company, but because the ball clubs are only parts of those corporations, information regarding the teams is not separately disclosed.

Public Ownership Outside Baseball

Professional hockey and basketball have at least one team that is owned by the public. Oddly, so does professional football, even though the league has a rule forbidding it.

Green Bay is unique among NFL franchises because it is the only community-owned team. The team was originally sold to team supporters in 1950 for $25 per share. There were 4,627 shares owned by 1,856 stockholders in 1993, but the team has been set up as a nonprofit corporation and no dividends are paid on the initial investment. The Packers are governed by 45 directors and a seven-member executive committee. That arrangement predates the NFL's rule forbidding public ownership.

A 1931 public offering by Maple Leaf Gardens presented Toronto hockey fans with the opportunity to back their local team financially. The offering was the solution to Toronto's need for a new arena for the Maple Leaf hockey team. As a shareholder in Maple Leaf Gardens, investors would be owners of the Maple Leaf franchise as well as the Garden. Many years and several stock splits later, Maple Leaf Gardens is still publicly traded on the Toronto Stock Exchange. As of the end of 1991, each share was worth $27. Dividends paid in 1991 totalled 80 cents per share.

In 1986, the Boston Celtics became publicly owned as its majority owners raised $48 million by selling 40 percent of the team in an offering that is now listed on the New York Stock Exchange. Smith Barney handled the underwriting. The stock appears in the newspaper stock listing under the symbol Bcelts and, at present, there are approximately 6,435,000 partnership units outstanding. Upon its initial offering, the stock sold for $18.50 per share. The September 30, 1993 closing price of Celtics' stock was $20. Dividends paid in the past year amounted to $1.25 per share.

Those who follow the stock closely say it rarely fluctuates with team performance, though one analyst said that each home play-off game can add two cents per share to the dividend.

All of these teams have found stability in public ownership, and the obvious questions is, why don't others try it? A public offering would seem particularly appealing in the case of an expansion team. Coming up with $95 or $100 million for a new team would be easier with a public offering, and that would certainly demonstrate the community's support for the new team, even more than season ticket sales.

But the awarding of new franchises is a delicate procedure, especially with so many cities in the running. Leagues would probably be more comfortable with private ownership, people they can examine closely, interview, and ultimately hold responsible.

This does not, however, explain why more existing teams in other sports don't consider it appealing. We have seen that sports teams are a good investment. While they may not appear to make a lot of money from year to year, few owners lose money when they sell.

One possibility for the dearth of publicly owned teams is the personality of sports owners. Private ownership seems more consistent with their psyche; it permits a greater degree of control. Public ownership means stockholders, who might well make demands on how the team is run. At the very least, public ownership means public disclosure of expenses.

Teams that are privately owned can control information about the details of their inner workings and the salaries of their employees or officers. Players' salaries are news today and end up in headlines; those listings are usually made public by the players' unions, or sometimes by the leagues. The NFL antitrust case is a highly unusual situation, which made teams' financial records public.

But when a team is a publicly held company, its financial transactions could be made public so that anyone interested in investing may learn enough to make an informed decision about purchasing stock, which brings us back to the Boston Celtics.

A Detailed Peek Inside

The annual report for the Boston Celtics Limited Partnership, filed in September of 1993 with the Securities and Exchange Commission in Washington, D.C., tells us that for the year ending in June of 1993, the company recorded revenues from ticket sales for exhibition games and the regular season totaling $20.20 million, and an additional $1.35 million from the play-offs, from which the team was eliminated in the opening round.

These revenues reflect the following conditions, stated in the report:

> Under the NBA Constitution and By-laws, the Boston Celtics receive all revenues from the sale of tickets to regular season home games (subject to the NBA gate assessment) and no revenue from the sale of tickets to regular season away games. Generally, the Boston Celtics retain all revenues from the sale of tickets to home exhibition games played in Boston and Hartford (less appearance fees paid to the visiting team), and receive appearance fees for exhibition games played elsewhere.

The other major source of revenue, according to the report, was from broadcast television, cable television, and radio. The national television contract, delivering $162 million to the league for the 1992–1993 season, contributed $5.97 million to the Celtics, with another $2.73 million coming from the TNT contract. But the largest factor was local broadcasting fees, totaling $13.57 million for the season from radio and television. Altogether, they gave the Celtics more than $22 million for the regular season and the play-offs.

The final source of revenue, totaling $3.60 million for the season, came mostly from NBA Properties, the entity to which each NBA team has assigned exclusive rights to merchandise team names, insignias, and other licensing ventures. The 1993 revenue came to $47.56 million, an increase of nearly $5 million over the previous year.

As with every other big-league sports franchise, the biggest expense for the Celtics was payment to its players. For the fiscal year 1993, current payments came to $17.794 million, with another $3.12 million in deferred payments. Quoting from the report:

> Substantially all of the payments shown above are guaranteed and must be paid during the balance of the term of the player's contract, even if the player is released or, in some cases, injured.

The Celtics paid salaries totaling $1.04 million to their head coach and two assistants during the 1992–1993 season; $200,000 of that went to former coach Jimmy Rodgers. For the 1993–1994 season, payments to its coaches totaled $1.1 million.

The Boston Celtics Limited Partnership paid its General Partner—

the corporation that runs the Celtics—a total exceeding $750,000 in 1993. Out of that the three directors—Don Gaston, chairman of the board; Alan Cohen, vice-chairman and treasurer; and Paul Dupee, Jr., vice-chairman and secretary—must run the corporation and pay themselves. Compensation for the Celtics' four "most highly compensated executive officers"— chief operating officer David Gavitt, president of the basketball subsidiary partnership "Red" Auerbach, executive manager Jan Volk, and president of communications Gerald Walsh—came to $1.49 million for the year.

There was a time when the Celtics, the Boston Bruins, and Boston Garden were one big family, but now their arrangement is strictly business.

By 1993 Boston Garden was owned by the New Boston Garden Corporation (NBGC), which is not affiliated with the Celtics but is a division of Delaware North, the holding company that also owns the Boston Bruins hockey team, and Sportservice, the concessionaires. The Garden Corporation handles all ticket sales, then remits the proceeds to the Celtics. The Celtics are not as fortunate when it comes to concessions; all of that goes to the Garden.

"The Boston Celtics do not share in revenue from food and beverage concessions or parking rights at the Boston Garden," reads the annual report. "The Boston Celtics may sell programs at each game subject to the payment of a commission to NBGC's concessionaires."

The Garden has 36 skyboxes, containing 469 seats, all along the inside upper balcony. These also belong to the Garden Corporation and lease for $75,000 a year. All that revenue belongs to NBGC, except for a fixed annual amount it must pay to the Celtics as compensation for use during regular season games and an additional amount for playoff games. The new Boston Garden, scheduled to open in September of 1995, will have 104 of those luxury boxes, available for least at an average of $150,000, but for as much as $211,000. The Celtics also earn no percentage of that revenue, receiving instead a fixed amount for each game.

The Celtics paid $1.265 million in rent for the year ending June 30, 1993, covering use of the Boston Garden and the Hartford Civic Center, and for use of office space in the Garden.

The House We Play in

The Boston Celtics was not the only team paying rent to play in a facility and being shut out of revenue from skyboxes and concessions. In recent years, this has been one of the main reasons for building new stadiums and arenas and for much of the mobility of franchises.

Most stadiums and arenas were privately owned until the 1950s. That meant the expense of building and upkeep fell to the owner—often the home team—but so did revenues from concessions. All the great arenas—Boston Garden and Madison Square Garden—and the great ballparks—Yankee Stadium, Wrigley Field, and Ebbets Field—were built with private funds, and most of them by the club owners. This meant that whatever revenues were generated by parking, food, and souvenir concessions came to the club.

But the expense of maintenance was also the responsibility of the clubs. And by the 1950s, there were a lot of old sports facilities around the country. The newer ones were built in the 1920s, the older generation before World War I. Most of them were small. Many seated under 35,000 for baseball, especially in the National League, where the parks were smaller and older, and fewer than 15,000 for basketball and hockey. (NFL teams generally played in baseball stadiums where available.) And being old, they required an active and costly program of upkeep.

One owner unhappy with the state of ballparks was Walter O'Malley of the Brooklyn Dodgers. Famous Ebbets Field in Flatbush opened in 1913 and even with improvements seated only about 32,000 people in 1950; it was the third smallest in the National League. Its 700 parking spaces, hardly a serious consideration in 1913, became more of a problem with each succeeding decade.

O'Malley began bargaining with the city of New York for land for a new stadium as early as 1952, but nothing they offered was agreeable. At that point it is impossible to know whether he had decided to move his team, but before long he found himself being courted as no owner had been before.

New York State offered to buy the team to take the problem off his hands, but O'Malley refused. Then the city of Los Angeles, hungry for major league baseball, made its move. It offered him 300 choice acres of land in 1957 in exchange for Wrigley Field, a minor league ballpark near downtown. In a deal with the Chicago Cubs earlier that year, O'Malley had purchased the park and its tenants, the Los Angeles

Angels, a charter member of the Pacific Coast League. Los Angeles then agreed to spend $2.74 million in access roads and other improvements. Estimates on what the city and county actually spent in preparation for the new stadium range as high as $5 million. Total cost of the stadium itself, which opened for the 1962 season, was $18 million.

It proved to be an enormous success. Dodger Stadium celebrated its 30th anniversary in 1992, having averaged more than 2.6 million fans per year. In 1978 it became the first ballpark to top the 3-million mark in attendance and went on to accomplish that seven more times by its 30th year.

Because it is wholly owned by the Dodgers, all the profit from concessions, souvenirs, and the 24,000 parking spaces goes to the organization. So does income from the events held at the stadium: religious conventions and special occasions, musical shows featuring the Beatles, the Bee Gees, Elton John, Michael Jackson, and Simon and Garfunkel. The stadium also served as the home field for the then–Los Angeles Angels from 1962 through 1965, before the team became the California Angels and moved to suburban Anaheim.

But as the Dodgers reaped the profits from those renters, so was the team responsible for the expenses. "The expenses of maintaining the stadium throughout the year are incredibly high," says the Dodgers' Bob Graziano, explaining that even with the other events, the fact that it's a baseball-only stadium creates a lot of downtime throughout the year. "We don't have a lot of debt, so no payments on a note, but it's expensive keeping it up. You can't just close up something like Dodger Stadium and come back for the season and play.

"We probably spend $7 million to $8 million a year, and that doesn't include game operations, but it does include depreciation and property tax."

And then there is the problem of keeping a 30-year-old stadium modern. "For 1991 we did a lot," says Graziano, pointing out that was the year the Dodgers ended their relationship with Arthur Foods, a local concessionaire, and began a new and more ambitious venture with Marriott. "They put in a lot of money. Between the two of us, about $18 million. A lot of that was the renovation of concession stands, but we also added rest rooms and more office space for the Dodgers."

The Dodgers also installed a new television screen—called a "video display system"—on the stadium scoreboard.

"The old Diamond Vision board had been leased for ten years from Mitsubishi, and was out of date," says Graziano. "We had to decide what to do. We installed a new Mitsubishi; now we own it. The cost, with controls, came to about $4 million."

A Renters' World

There are more modern examples of privately financed and owned stadiums. The Miami Dolphins left the city-owned Orange Bowl for the team-financed Joe Robbie Stadium; the St. Louis Cardinals purchased the title to the city-owned Busch Stadium. And there are even more examples with arenas. The Detroit Pistons, Minnesota Timberwolves, and Sacramento Kings—all in the NBA—built privately owned facilities.

But these are not the usual, and with good reason. That $18 million to build Dodger Stadium in 1962 would not go very far by the 1990s. Basketball arenas in Phoenix and Minneapolis for the Suns and Timberwolves cost $85 million and $93 million; the open-air Camden Yards in Baltimore cost $275 million; the Georgia Dome, $210 million.

More common arrangements in the 1980s and 1990s were publicly financed and owned sports complexes. This leaves the team as a renter. The financial arrangements in these situations differ greatly and have a profound affect on how much money a team makes or loses at the end of the year.

Over and over in the 1992 *Financial World* report on the value of sports franchises, the arrangement with the facility where a team plays is listed as one of the "main factors" for its strength or weakness. For the second-ranked Los Angeles Dodgers, "owner controls stadium and team." For the sixth-ranked Los Angeles Lakers, the report comments "owner controls team and arena." For the Philadelphia Eagles, Baltimore Orioles, Chicago White Sox, and Chicago Bears, all in the top ten in their sports, the phrase "great lease" is repeated over and over. The report is not only talking about high attendance—and certainly that adds to the value of the franchise—but also who gets the money generated from all those fans.

How the money is divided is complicated, but there are some guides. From the 1992 book *Pay Dirt: The Business of Professional Team Sports*, we get the following generalities:

> The typical pattern of stadium contracts in baseball is one in which the stadium gets most or all of the revenue from parking, teams get most or all of the revenue from the sale of programs and novelties, and food and drink revenues are split, with between one-third and one-half going

to the stadium and the rest to the team. There are a few cases in which luxury box revenues are captured by the stadium, but generally such revenues go mainly to the team, which often incurs the expense of building the boxes.

These guidelines are tricky. Teams that play in privately owned stadiums—such as the Dodgers, Cubs, and Red Sox—make their own deals. Several other teams—among them the Mets, Royals, and Yankees—manage the publicly owned stadiums where they play.

But for those teams that rent, they must negotiate every item. Look at the deal hammered out between the Atlanta Falcons of the NFL and the Georgia Dome, which opened in the summer of 1992. The Falcons had shared Atlanta-Fulton County Stadium with the Braves, an open-air field that seated 59,643 for football. A new baseball stadium was scheduled to open in 1997.

The Georgia Dome, owned by the State of Georgia, was to finance its $210 million cost through private financing (70 percent) and public funding (30 percent). That plan failed, and the project was taken over by the state, which issued $200 million in industrial revenue bonds.

Many features were included in the Dome plan to make it profitable. The 183 skyboxes available ranged in price from $20,000 to $120,000 per year. An additional 5,618 club seats cost from $1,000 to $1,800 per year. Seating capacity for football is 71,500, but the Dome floor seats up to 8,600 theater-style, up to 6,000 in a classroom setting, and up to 8,000 for banquets and 10,000 for receptions. Four meeting rooms accommodate from 50 to 150 people. Parking for 3,260 cars is available on site, and nearly 14,000 more spaces are within blocks.

Events already scheduled when the Dome opened were the Super Bowl in 1994, basketball and gymnastics during the 1996 Olympics, and the Peach Bowl. Weather would not be a problem since the stadium was enclosed in the largest cable-supported dome in the world.

In this great scenario, the Falcons were renters. They shared in no revenue from parking, none from concessions, none from skyboxes or any advertising within the stadium. In addition, they paid rent—10 percent of net receipts. In 1992 that came to $1.8 million. But in exchange for surrendering the concession and skybox rights, the Dome paid the Falcons $6 million up front.

The team doesn't even have to be very successful to share in the wealth. The Indianapolis Colts showed little of the championship form of their Baltimore past after moving west, yet the franchise remained a profitable entity during most of that time. The reason, despite a poor record on the field and low gate receipts, was their lease in the Hoosier Dome, which was part of the lure to move. The Colts pay only $25,000 per game for the stadium, which works out to less than 2 percent of admission receipts, according to *Pay Dirt.*

And a bad situation can turn in a flash. The Boston Celtics have been a profitable NBA franchise for years, despite their terrible lease at Boston Garden, one of the worst in the league. It was those high local media revenues that kept the franchise riding high. But the builders of the new Boston Garden decided to throw them a lucrative bone: No, they still won't get a share of concessions or luxury boxes, but when the new facility opens in 1995, that year will be the first of ten years in which the Celtics will pay no rent. That's nearly $1.5 million saved a year.

Putting a winning team on the field or the court is a crucial part of being successful in sports. But in the big picture—coming out with a profit at the end of the year—it is only one element of many.

PART FOUR

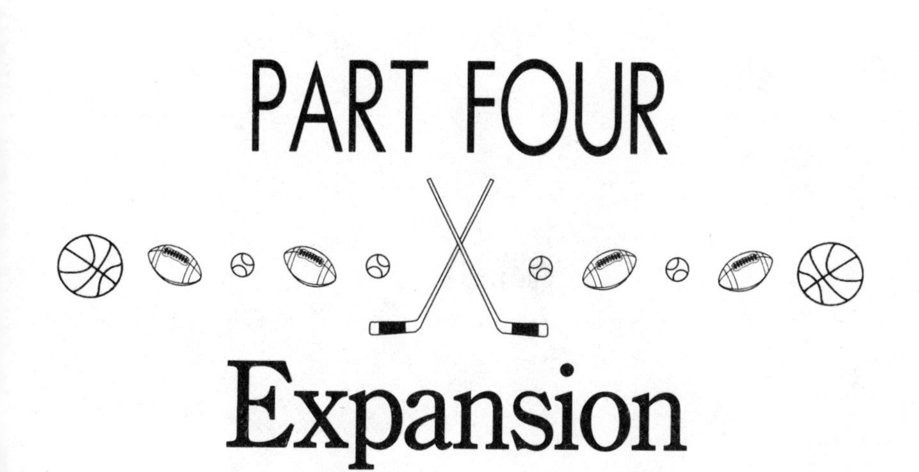

Expansion

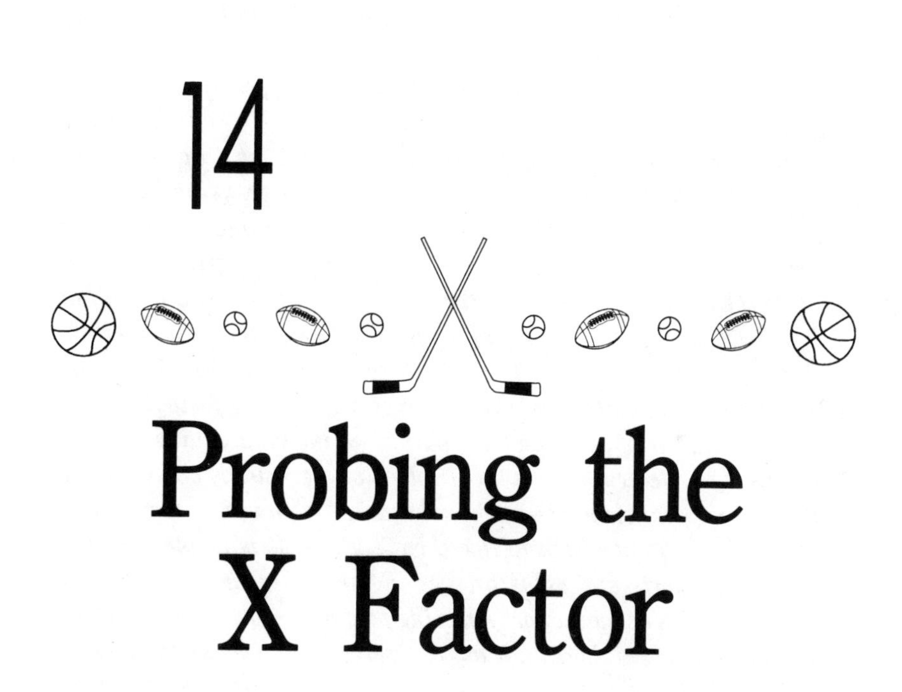

14

Probing the X Factor

The place is Tampa, Florida, known for its cigars and the frequency of its thunderstorms. Storm clouds gather quickly here. A single wisp of haze, floating lazily across a clear blue sky, will suddenly grow, darken, and spread until it blocks out all evidence of the sun. Thunder will shake the earth, and jagged rips of lightning will stagger across the blackened sky. And then rain, hard rain, will gush down in torrents. It is the way here, at almost any time during the summer. Yet on this particular day, only hot, glaring sunlight drenches the cities and towns around Tampa Bay. The long July Fourth weekend has ended. Natives are back in air-conditioned offices and air-conditioned homes or are traveling from one to the other in air-conditioned automobiles. Tourists are staked out by their pools or lie greased and prostrate at the beaches here, or in neighboring Clearwater, Dunedin, and St. Petersburg.

And on a large patch of ground just to the southwest, a professional football team is about to be born. The day is July 6, 1976. For the Tampa Bay Buccaneers, newest entry in the National Football League, this is their first day of practice.

From the outside, the five-acre complex has the appearance of a painting. There is no visible movement, no audible sound. The parallel practice fields, grass freshly sprigged and bright green, still await the first imprint of a cleat. The goalposts, straight and silver, shine in the sun. Off to the left are the new blocking sleds, one blue and white and the other red and black, and neither has been hit in anger. The 38-foot photography tower at the rear of the lot has never been used. No fan has yet pressed against the encircling fence, peering at the drama within.

It is perfect, without a flaw, the product of scientific design and efficient planning culled from 80 years of professional football. But all of this is frill. Strip away the fresh paint and the landscaping and what remains is an element that is the lifeblood of every newly created professional team. That element—worn and scarred from use, gray with age—is the desire of grown men to live a boy's game. It is at the core of all professional sports and is as present in the locker room of the Super Bowl champions as on the rocky playing field of the lowest semipro team. But it is most evident here and easy to observe. At a time when superstars and their million-dollar contracts dominate the sports pages, expansion brings together athletes delighted to be offered any contract to sign and any uniform to wear. Winning and stardom and championship rings are goals, but for now belonging is enough. It is the crucial ingredient, that necessary first step. A player must be on a team before he can play; he must get into the game before he can play brilliantly.

Look for no unassailed egos here. Of the 80 veterans reporting to camp, almost every one has been dropped at least once. Released. Cut. Dumped. Fired. For most, it has happened more than once. Now they focus on survival. Their dreams, tilted toward pure glory as rookies, are now edged in desperation. They know if they cannot make it here, they are not likely to get another chance. In the great mandala of sports, this is the final stop.

It is nearly two o'clock. Players have been coming in the locker room and training room since noon, preparing for the opening practice an hour away. While the mind of this sophisticated organization whirs in the other side of the building—coaching staff and ticket people, public relations department and business section, carrying on their various functions—the arms and legs are being attended to by Dave Kendall and his staff of trainers. Men of all sizes and ages, from the 5-feet-7-inch kick returner to the 6-feet-8-inch tackle, from the youngest rookie to the ten-year veterans, wait to have their ankles taped and special attention given to whatever physical problems have accumulated during their careers in football. As each finishes he takes up a position in front of his locker or stretches out on the floor or in the corridor that leads to the field, and he waits.

Even in the filtered cool of the air conditioning there is the unmistakable scent of fear. And with reason. Ninety-six men have reported to today's practice; 43 will be carried on the active roster during the season. That is the normal formula of an opening camp, but the uncertainty is more pronounced here. No one's future is guaranteed here. One or two high-priced veterans seem reasonably safe, as do the club's top draft choices, but they are the only ones with even that modest level of assurance. For most of these men their continued presence here is moment-to-moment, and they know it. A look along the rows of new, wood-grained lockers reveals a study in frustrated ambition: Charlie Evans sits on the floor and looks down at his hands. They are broad and strong, like the man himself, and abused from four hard years of clinging to professional football. Originally a 14th-round draft pick from the University of Southern California, he had been released by the New York Giants and Washington Redskins before signing with Tampa Bay. Nearby is Steve Chomyszak, a huge tackle who had played on five different teams in three leagues before being cut by the Cincinnati Bengals and coming here.

There are others who have made the rounds, playing on different teams in different leagues, paid as much as $100,000 a season and as little as $10 a game. Endless names on an ever-changing roster. Most of the men have come here as free agents, which means they were not on any other NFL roster when Tampa Bay signed them. But they are football players, not salesmen or businessmen or teachers or anything else. That is why they are here, hoping for "a shot," as the players put it, a fair chance to show what they can do. They walk around in the neatly carpeted rooms in their stockinged feet—no cleats are permitted inside—and drink soda from the large, lighted dispensers. There is little conversation. Those who talk do so quietly, as if this were a hospital. No one laughs. They just sit, listening to the recorded music that seeps in through the acoustical ceiling, and wait for three o'clock and the beginning of practice.

So very much is at stake. The pattern and quality of each man's future—where and how well he will live, what he will be doing, how well he will provide for his wife and children—will be determined by what happens in the following days and weeks.

And it has all happened before, over and over since the beginning of professional athletics. In the relatively brief history of professional football, this drama has even been played out before in central Florida. It opened first across the bay from here in St. Petersburg in 1966, when the Miami Dolphins began as an expansion team in the young and struggling AFL; it moved next to Deland in 1974, where the Jacksonville Sharks opened camp as the Florida entry in the World Football League; and now it has come to Tampa. And everywhere it plays, the plot is the same: Men from all over the country, traveling wherever necessary to practice their trade, which happens to be football. Names, more names than anyone can remember. Men fresh out of college who would never have been in uniform if it were not for expansion, and others, veterans cut from other clubs, given one more chance because of the additional jobs.

Names. Endless names. Billy Joe and Ross O'Hanley; Frank Laskey and Tom Moore and Frank Cornish and Ernie Park, all men who came to one camp or the other with the thought that they could make it, all now long out of football. By the time this summer is over, that is what will happen to most of the names on the Tampa Bay roster. It has already begun; two men failed their physicals and have left camp. Of the men here and dressed today, fewer than 25 will make it to the season's first game.

These men know that, and it is one reason they are so quiet.

It is now 20 minutes to three, and the first players are beginning to walk through the big, brown double door at the end of the corridor. All carry their shoes and helmets, and some their pads and jerseys. One by one, hesitantly, they come out, squinting against the bright, strong sun. It is not only anxiety that kept them inside so long but also the heat outside. The official temperature is 89 degrees, but official measurements are taken in the shade. There is no shade out here, just sun, intensified as it reflects off the building and the silver fence.

As three o'clock approaches, the players begin to spill out onto the field and go through whatever exercises they use to prepare themselves mentally and physically. Some stand with their legs spread apart and bend the top half of their bodies first toward one foot and then the other. Some sit on the ground, one leg stuck straight out to the front and the other to the rear, and then lean forward, stretching to touch the tips of their toes. Others run laps around the field or sprints back and forth between the line markers. Over on the sidelines, one large tackle, a free agent, slams his arms violently against the pads of a blocking sled, over and over.

It is a strange sight. Men with helmets on their heads and numbers on their backs, going though ceremonial routines.

Spectators have begun assembling on the other side of the chain-link fence for the past few minutes. They are another part of this drama, the fans who have been waiting for a pro team since late in 1974 when the WFL's Florida Blazers vanished into the night from their home just up I-4 in Orlando. Now they have a new stadium and a new team in the NFL—The Big League—and they have come to share their dreams for a championship with their heroes on the field.

A few minutes before three, the last of the players makes his way down the little grade in the lawn and onto the practice field. They gather around John McKay, the new coach of this new team, who speaks to them in a quiet, normal voice so they must be very quiet to hear. On the other side of the fence, the new Buccaneer fans strain their ears, hoping for some fragment of this historic moment.

And all the while, high overhead, the bright Florida sky begins to turn gray. How long before it is black, before the earth begins to shake with thunder and the rain comes gushing down to wash away the dreams of athletes and fans alike? How long?

The birth of an expansion team is a powerful event in sports. It represents the dreams and fantasies of players and fans and even owners. Each group has its own emotional investment in the team.

For the players, an expansion team is one more chance to fulfill the potential that carried them through childhood and high school and often college. At each level, they were one of the best, but like those men in the scene above, now they face what is probably their last opportunity. The arrival of an expansion team places the fans alongside residents of the first-class cities around the country, those that already have teams. If it does not elevate them to the status of a New York or a Chicago and a Los Angeles, at least it puts them in the neighborhood of Pittsburgh and San Diego and Cincinnati.

Expansion is more complicated for the owner. An expansion team can be an opportunity for the owner to place himself among that elite group of men and women that have included the likes of George Halas,

John Galbreath, Joan Payson, and George Preston Marshall. The impetus could be service to the community; after the Dodgers and Giants fled to California, Joan Payson felt a responsibility to return a National League team to New York. Or it could be as simple as making a financial investment.

Regardless of what draws these people to the team, their personal investment is great. They all expect so much, and not all will be rewarded. Owners generally do pretty well; rarely is a loss incurred when selling a team. But fate and history have not always treated kindly the others who cast their fate with young franchises.

Fans need to be very patient. Winning does not come easily to expansion teams, and sometimes they don't get much of a chance. In baseball, the 1961 expansion Washington Senators moved to Texas in 1972; the 1969 expansion Seattle Pilots were moved to Milwaukee the very next year. Expansion basketball teams have left Chicago—before the Bulls existed—Buffalo, and New Orleans, and expansion hockey teams have moved so often that any history of current NHL franchises should include a map of where they've been.

But expansion life is hardest on those with the greatest emotional investment, the ever-hopeful players. Original roster members of expansion teams rarely last long, and their limited tenures rarely include much winning. Of the 96 men at that first camp of the Tampa Bay Buccaneers, only 22 made it through the season. And it was a painful season; no wins, 14 losses.

The Forces at Work

While writers often describe with eloquence the opening days of new teams, and while these events do embody the hopes and prayers of hundreds of athletes and thousands of fans, it is valuable to remember how they came about.

The forces creating new sports teams are neither poetic nor inspiring. They are, alas, a matter of economics. And in that respect, expansion becomes the X Factor in sports: X for unknown. Are they good economics or bad economics? Are they money into the sport or money out?

Teams are a commodity, a rare commodity. And as with other rare commodities—like gold or silver—the most popular thinking about franchises by those who own them has historically been that scarcity increases value. The fewer the major league teams, the more money those teams will make, and the more they are worth when sold. That is why, until recently, leagues expanded so infrequently. Keep the fraternity of owners small, has been the attitude; limit growth, especially within geographic regions.

It was no surprise that the first time baseball expanded in modern times, in 1961, the American League put a team in California, that league's first venture on the West Coast. They also put a team in the nation's capital, appeasing the lawmakers who lost their old Washington Senators that same year to far-off Minnesota. When the National League expanded a year later, it was to Houston—the first major-league team in the Southwest—and to New York, a team to replace the Dodgers and Giants.

The NFL was just as cautious. Its first expansion of the modern era came with the creation of the Dallas Cowboys for the 1960 season and the Minnesota Vikings for 1961. So many teams moved from city to city in the NBA that it's hard to keep track, but their first real expansion came in 1961, with the forming of the Chicago Packers. A season later the Packers became the Chicago Zephyrs, and they moved to Baltimore as the Bullets in 1963. After much debate, the NHL expanded for the 1967–1968 season, creating a division of new teams: Philadelphia, Minnesota, Los Angeles, Oakland, Pittsburgh, and St. Louis. (Oakland would become California, then move to Cleveland, and eventually merge with Minnesota; Minnesota moved to Dallas for the 1993–1994 season.)

Ambitious as the hockey growth was—from 6 teams to 12 in one jump—the expansion of the 1960s did not constitute a broad-based professional sports explosion. Major League Baseball went from 16 to 20 teams in two stages, the NBA from 9 to 14 teams, and the NFL from 12 to 14. Control was still tight.

The problem with that degree of control is that the civilians—those not part of the owners' fraternity—get restless. All this was going on in the 1960s, a period of calm on the labor front in sports, and of a growing interest in sports. Attendance was up in all sports, and the impact of television was just beginning to make itself felt. Joan Payson, who paid only $1.8 million for the expansion New York Mets in 1961, made more than that from broadcast revenues in their first season, even with the worst team in the majors.

The owners' secret was out—sports was good business.

Those close to the workings of major league teams, and even those who kept an eye on business, already knew it. And if the major leagues weren't going to expand any quicker than they were indicating, these astute observers of the forces of economics knew what to do about it. This was America; they could compete.

It was hardly a revolutionary idea. The early success of the National League led to the challenge of the American Association in 1882, the Union Association in 1884, the Players League in 1890, and the American League in 1901. Only the American League survived. But the idea lived on. The Federal League surfaced in 1914, and while it survived only two seasons, its presence was not without impact. Authors Quirk and Fort report in *Pay Dirt* the following effects: 96 players from the American or National League signed with the Federal League, and attendance in the two major leagues dropped by nearly two million from 1913 to 1914. Philadelphia owner Connie Mack was so panicked that he sold off his best players to other American League teams in 1915, causing his Athletics to fall from first place in 1914 to last in 1915.

But the threat to baseball was not over. The formation of the Mexican League after World War II offered American major leaguers an optional place to play. Baseball's response was for Commissioner Happy Chandler to impose a five-year ban in 1946 on any player who jumped leagues, but the blacklist was dropped after Giants outfielder Danny Gardella sued. It was about the same time that a group of franchise owners in the Pacific Coast League, top level of the minor league system, began talking about creating a new major league. Their contention was that Major League Baseball had ignored the national move of population west.

The pressure on baseball surfaced in Washington, D.C., where Brooklyn Congressman Emanuel Celler chaired a House Subcommittee on monopoly power. In the summer of 1951 his subcommittee investigated baseball's antitrust immunity. A year later, while he recommended no legislation, he made the observation that "the baseball map needs realignment."

Within six years the Dodgers and Giants would move to California, and another rival league would struggle toward existence to prompt more changing of the map. That league—a paper creation called The Continental League—began to take shape as a direct result of the moving of the Dodgers and Giants. Once it was clear the teams were leaving his city, New York Mayor Robert Wagner tried to attract an existing team to take their place. After New York was rejected by the Cincinnati Reds and Pittsburgh Pirates—teams representing two of the smaller markets in the National League—Wagner proposed a third major league to William Shea, a New York lawyer with money and political connections.

In his book, *The Baseball Business,* James Miller writes:

> The idea of a third league startled organized baseball into action to protect its monopoly. Commissioner [Ford] Frick had broached the idea before, primarily to pacify Congress without any apparent intention of taking action. After the Giants' and Dodgers' moves, Frick again talked about bringing more teams to New York, either through a third league or by expanding the two existing leagues.

Miller makes it clear that Shea was savvy enough to keep the pressure on; Shea knew the owners would not welcome competition on their own. He hired Branch Rickey—then 77 years old—to proceed with plans toward making the Continental League a reality. Meanwhile, support around the country and in Washington, D.C., swelled. Joan Payson, one of those on the board of the Giants who voted against the move to San Francisco, signed on for 30 percent of the New York entry. Congressmen Celler supported the idea, as did Senator Estes Kefauver, chairman of the Senate Antitrust Subcommittee. Miller reports the following progression:

> While Shea and Rickey pressed forward with plans for the third league, major league owners continued to employ delaying tactics that they hoped would kill the Continental League but permit them to avoid shouldering responsibility before Congress, the press, and the public. Although reluctant to authorize an expansion of the existing leagues, the owners were equally unwilling to let anyone else control the process. Major league tactics failed to foil Rickey or Shea, who appealed to Kefauver for support. Guided by Rickey, Kefauver's staff drafted a bill that would put an end to major league control of the minor leagues and, in short order, permit the third league to compete on an equal footing with the two older circuits in talent recruitment.

The new legislation that grew out of the hearings was defeated in Congress in June of 1960, but Major League Baseball realized that by continuing to avoid expansion it was putting itself and its precious antitrust exemption at risk. In July the National League voted to expand to ten teams, and a month later the American League made the same commitment. Joan Payson purchased the New York entry—the Mets—which began playing in the Polo Grounds, former home of the Giants, but in 1964 moved into their new home, Shea Stadium.

New Version of an Old Story

That same combination of pressures was present for baseball's latest expansion. Again there was action in Washington, a Congressional Baseball Task Force, 17 senators looking into baseball and the law.

"Why," asked an obviously hostile Ohio Senator Howard Metzenbaum, "should the business of baseball be granted advantages available to no other sport or business?"

And again there was the pressure of a rival league. Rumors surfaced earlier, but in the summer of 1989 came the first confirmation of plans for a new eight-team league to rival the majors and begin operation within two years.

"I have agreed to become a part of it, to work with them and make this league a great success," developer Donald Trump told *The New York Times* in August of 1989, who identified himself as an owner of one of the teams. "I see it as a very viable league; otherwise I would not do it."

The league would play a 154-game schedule, then have three rounds of play-offs involving three teams in each of two, four-team divisions. The founders were David LeFevre, formerly a part-owner of the Houston Astros and an investor in the Cleveland Indians, and agent Dick Moss. In addition to Trump, Edward J. DeBartolo, Sr., was to be a team owner, as well as Portland timber tycoon Bruce Engle.

Timing for a new league was good. Baseball had not expanded since Toronto and Seattle began play in the American League in 1977; the most recent National League teams added were Montreal and San Diego in 1969. And back in 1989, no further expansion was in the immediate plans. Acrimony between players and owners was also high. The major league clubs denounced the players' high pay scale and pushed for a salary cap in negotiations for the new contract. Eventually, 1990's spring training would be lost to an owners' lockout.

"We plan to open The Baseball League in 1991 with eight cities," LeFevre was quoted in November of 1989 in *Coming Apart at the Seams.* "ABC has made a proposal to us to broadcast our games. Their proposal is close to eighty percent of what we are looking for."

But by 1991 the atmosphere had changed. The owners and players signed a new agreement, salaries were up again, and the National League had granted expansion to Denver and Miami. Their bargaining chips gone, the new league was dead before taking its first breath.

Not all of the other sports have gone through such painful contortions to expand, but the process has rarely been graceful. And in nearly every instance, outside pressure was involved.

The NFL, under aggressive attack from the AFL, added Atlanta for the 1966 season and New Orleans for 1967; it showed its greatest growth through absorption in 1970 when it merged with the AFL to form one big 26-team league. Then in 1974, the year the World Football League began play, the NFL granted franchises to Tampa Bay and Seattle for the 1976 season, its last expansion to date. (The league voted in October of 1993 to expand to Charlotte, North Carolina, deferring the decision on a second franchise for the 1995 season.

Basketball has shown the most growth in the last 25 years. Adding teams on a regular basis from 1967, the league stood at 17 in 1971. The hard times of the 1970s were ill-suited to expansion; the one new team, New Orleans, lasted only four seasons before moving to Utah. Growth came through absorbing four surviving teams from the crippled American Basketball Association for the 1976–1977 season. The NBA's recent health led to new franchises in Miami and Charlotte in 1988 and Orlando and Minnesota in 1989, with Toronto added for the 1995–1996 season.

The process never seemed to be easy. Owners have behaved as if their leagues exist in a state of perfect balance and they are charged with the responsibility of protecting that condition. Fans without teams in their cities have responded as if they were being denied an essential element of life. Look at what happened in the closing days of the World Hockey Association (WHA).

Created in 1972, the WHA showed real strength in its early years, raiding NHL teams of such stars as Bobby Hull, Gerry Cheevers, and Derek Sanderson. Gordie Howe made an incredible comeback at the age of 45, skating with his sons Mark and Marty for the Houston Aeros and leading the team to the WHA championship in 1974. Attendance rose steadily, as did league credibility. The WHA even had its own stars, most notably the Edmonton Oilers' Wayne Gretzky.

The NHL was hurting. It had lost star players, attendance was down, and salaries had jumped in the heat of competitive bidding. But the expense was taking a toll on the new league as well. Teams folded but were immediately replaced. The Los Angeles Sharks became the Michigan Stags, died, and were reborn as the Baltimore Blades. Exit the Birmingham Bulls; enter the Phoenix Roadrunners. In the beginning both leagues said a merger would never happen, but by the start of the 1978–1979 season there were serious talks. It looked as if three strong franchises—Winnipeg, Quebec, and Edmonton—would be admitted into the NHL. Then in March of 1979, the NHL backed out of the deal. For what happened, we turn to the pages of Quirk and Fort's *Pay Dirt:*

> Outraged fans in Winnipeg, Quebec, and Edmonton announced a boycott of Molson beer after the Montreal Canadiens, owned by Molson, voted against admitting those teams. In Quebec City, there was a bomb threat against the local Molson brewery, and in Winnipeg, someone fired a bullet through the front door of the Molson brewery. One week later, the NHL reconsidered its vote, agreeing to admit the Winnipeg Jets, Quebec Nordiques, Edmonton Oilers, and Hartford Whalers as NHL members, and also agreeing to allow Edmonton to retain title to Wayne Gretzky, something that had been a major stumbling block in the earlier discussions. Each of the WHA teams going into the NHL had to pay a $6 million entrance fee; in addition, the teams paid $1.5 million each (a total of $6 million) as compensation to the Cincinnati and Birmingham teams, which had survived the 1978/79 season, but which did not move into the NHL.

The High Price of Belonging

It has been the pattern in sports since the earliest years: The existing leagues are elite clubs with huge "Members Only" signs on the door. The price for admittance is always high, and it keeps getting higher.

But back in 1961 when the expansion Los Angeles Angels and Washington Senators were created, the price for entering the league was $2.1 million. (Oddly, the teams entering the National League a year later—in Houston and New York—got a bargain at $1.8 million.) Three decades later, when the Colorado Rockies and Florida Marlins joined the National League, their entrance fee was $95 million.

But those amounts were only enough to get in the door and play in the league, though they did include the fees for drafting 36 players from existing teams. While they were used as the "official" expansion price tag—just as $2.1 million was used in 1961—they reflected only part of the actual expense. A 1991 article in *The Washington Post* went into greater detail and estimated the actual cost:

Player salaries, beginning opening day, 1993 .... $6–$15 million
Minor leagues and player development .... $6–$10 million

Interest, assuming half expansion fee is borrowed .... $5 million
Stadium operating cost, including rent .... $4 million
Administrative expenses, including front office .... $3 million
Sales and marketing .... $1.6 million
Team equipment $700,000
Amateur signing bonuses .... $.5–$1 million
Office equipment, including computers and such $500,000
Legal and other professional services $300,000

That was an actual start-up price of $140 million. And while we do not have such complete figures for the other sports, it is not too difficult to see how the prices might add to the figures for expansion teams that are released. Clearly, the $32.5 million for the expansion Minnesota and Orlando teams in the NBA, the $50 million for the five latest hockey teams, and the projected $140 million for the NFL expansion planned for 1995 are far from complete figures. And complete numbers are hard to project; there are always hidden factors.

Pro teams are given territories that are considered their own, not so different from national boundaries in terms of trade, or even local turfs for gangs. If an outsider wants to do business there, a penalty must be paid. The fee in 1976 for the ABA New York Nets to share New York with the NBA Knicks was $4 million; the fee paid 17 years later to the Los Angeles Kings by the new Anaheim Ducks for infringing on that turf was $25 million.

The two new baseball teams in Florida and Colorado had no territorial conflicts to increase their first-year operating costs, but they were denied the revenue from the major league television deal, negotiated before they existed but running through that maiden season. That is a loss per team of more than $10 million.

There are some who look at the pattern of new leagues and charge that they are nothing but an expression of greed—by players, levers to gain more money by creating bidding wars, and by the new league, hoping to win money in antitrust suits. We have seen both happen when new leagues come on the scene, and rarely does peaceful coexistence result. In all of sports, the only example of the challenge by a rival group of teams surviving, intact, alongside the established league was baseball's American League, and that was in 1901.

Others say it is just a ploy to force expansion, that all along the founders of the new league assume their strong teams will be merged and the weaker teams sacrificed. And there is plenty of historical evidence that this is the best a rival league can expect.

But all these individual factors may be true, and it still does not mean that new leagues must have greed and merger as their motivations. It can simply be a genuine desire for more teams . . . more teams for fans and more teams for players. If the slow pace of expansion is enough to get Congress to investigate, it can easily be enough to get fans and businesspeople around the country to create their own league if the big boys won't let them play.

That these leagues rarely survive may simply be the price of being on the outside wanting to get in. Competition with any existing entity is a risky business. Small companies are constantly swallowed up by larger ones, their products added to a huge list. The fate of independent political parties is classically to be absorbed by the Democrats or the Republicans, the platforms on which they were formed adopted, stripping them of their primary reason for existing.

Looking at sports today, we see nearly half the professional teams coming directly from rival leagues that were absorbed or from expansion teams formed under threat from a rival league. There is also a smattering of ideas lifted from those rival leagues; the NBA took the three-point shot from the ABA, and major league baseball is extending its play-offs to another tier, one selling point of the stillborn league proposed by David LeFevre.

Expansion: Good Business or Bad?

The passions that surround the existence of a major league team in any sport are so strong, they often cloud other, more practical considerations. One of these is the financial soundness of such a move.

From the standpoint of the community, there is little question that having a professional sports team is good for the local and regional economy. This argument was used in 1984, when Baltimore's mayor at the time, William Schaefer, spoke before a U.S. Senate Committee considering restricting the movement of teams.

"The Colts were a vital economic resource. Experts agree that the presence of the Colts generated between $25 to $30 million in economic activity," said Schaefer about the NFL team that earlier in the year had moved to Indianapolis, a loss that affected more than just the restaurants and hotels serving people coming to games.

"There is a direct relationship of the loss of patronage and harm to the community," he said. "Suppliers and concessions, and the intangible but important factor that contributes to local and metropolitan economic development, and of course taxes. . . . It is the equivalent, quite frankly, of losing a major industry."

This kind of impact is no secret. Municipalities know what the presence of a team means to their economy, and they want one to be added to their list of "industries." It is one of the reasons they fight so hard to win expansion franchises. Few cities have tried harder—and been more successful—than Miami. Only the 15th largest market in the country, it was the smallest to enter 1994 with a team in each of the four major pro sports. All began as expansion teams, three of the four having arrived since 1988.

South Florida has a long tradition in sports. Professional baseball teams began training in the Tampa–St. Petersburg area and farther south in the spring of 1911. The Orange Bowl game has been drawing people since the 1930s, and the University of Miami has been a power in football since the 1980s. A study by the Florida Department of Commerce indicated that in 1991, spring training produced $121 million in revenues for the state's host cities. This study added that non-Florida residents alone spent about $10 million in Palm Beach County in 1991 as a direct result of spring training.

Miami joined the professional sports family in 1966 with the arrival of the Miami Dolphins, the first expansion franchise awarded in the American Football League. While specific figures on the economic impact of the Dolphins are not available, Miami General Manager Eddie Jones notes that a 1992 study done by the University of North Florida estimated that a typical NFL team adds 3,000 full-time and part-time jobs and produces an annual impact of $130 million.

The local NBA team, the Miami Heat, started in the 1988–1989 season and regularly runs well over 90 percent of capacity at its 15,008-seat Miami Arena. The Sports and Exhibition Authority reports that each of the Heat's 41 home games has an economic impact of about $1 million.

The Florida Panthers did not begin NHL play in Miami until the 1993–1994 season, but the newly arrived Florida Marlins baseball team has already made its presence felt. The estimated impact on South Florida economy is $100 million a year, with the addition of 900 new jobs.

All of these teams contribute to making a community more desirable, more appealing to vacationers and industry alike. Companies are more interested in relocating, and family members more likely to visit for a vacation. And in the case of Miami, the attraction is not only to "snow birds" looking for relief from the harsh northern winter.

"In the Caribbean, we can package weekend trips," says Miami vice-mayor Victor DeYurre. "Come to Miami for the weekend and go to the ball game. In Puerto Rico, Venezuela, Nicaragua, some of these other countries that are baseball-loving countries, you can promote Miami in that sense and bring the people in."

The question of economic impact on the sports themselves is less clear. All that is certain is the initial flood of money, the fee paid by the expansion team for joining the league. In some cases, that instant infusion of money appears to be a major reason for expansion. Hockey has been accused of such motivation.

When the NHL and NBA expanded in 1967, the fee for each new team was about $2 million. They both expanded in 1974; the fee for the entering New Orleans Jazz—which later moved to Utah—was $6.15 million, and for the Washington Capitals and Kansas City Scouts, the fee was $6 million. (The Scouts later moved to Denver, were renamed the Colorado Rockies, and in 1976 went to New Jersey as the Devils.) The NBA expanded again in 1980, accepting the Dallas Mavericks for the price of $12 million.

The 1980s were years of strong growth for professional basketball, on the court and at the bank. Profits rose through television, marketing, and attendance. When the league expanded again, in 1988, to Miami and Charlotte, and again in 1989, to Orlando and Minnesota, the entrance fee was $32.5 million. But the decade was not so successful for the NHL, and there was no expansion. Yet when the league began an explosion of growth—expanding for 1991–1992 to San Jose, again to Ottawa and Tampa Bay for 1992–1993, and surprisingly again for the 1993–1994 season to Miami and Anaheim—the fee was a whopping $50 million.

"Hockey is struggling to gain popularity in this country and thinks expansion is the answer," read a 1991 editorial in *The Sporting News.* "But at $50 million a pop—the fee was set so high because hockey simply needs the money—the risk for new teams will be great."

Part of that risk is what happens after teams pay their entrance dues and join the league. Suddenly there are more pieces to the pie being cut up, and those pieces are smaller than before. All shared revenue becomes less. National television contracts are split to include the new teams, as well as money from licensing and whatever other marketing funds are generated by the league.

Expansion: Good Sport or Bad?

It is even less certain what expansion means for the games themselves. The issue is clouded by the strong, personal positions held by advocates of both sides. Just as many owners want to keep down the number of teams to make their own positions and properties more valuable, many players want more teams because it affords more places to play and prolongs careers.

"The whole expansion process has to be brought out of the closet," Major League Baseball Players Association head Don Fehr told *The New York Times* back in 1988. At that point the American League had not added a team in 11 years, and the National League in 19.

"If a city can support a team, it ought to have a chance to have one," said Fehr. "We ought not to be telling American citizens you can't go watch baseball games because we want to maintain a vacant market. That's nuts, but that's what they do."

So the only people who don't like expansion are those owners who view their positions as if they were divinely granted and wish to keep the residents of Olympus down to the fewest possible and the purists in sports who believe expansion dilutes the quality of the game.

The purists do have the laws of logic on their side: The more teams competing for players, the fewer top-flight athletes to go around. And some numbers support that thesis. Baseball, that most statistical of all the sports, informs us that home runs increase each season in which expansion forces teams to use more pitchers who would otherwise still be in the minor leagues.

But the number of top-quality players is reduced daily even without expansion. More sports are paying big money today, giving multi-sport athletes such as John Elway and Deion Sanders (both played baseball and football) and Danny Ainge (basketball and baseball) a choice as to where they want to make their millions. And a more enlightened society offers better education to minorities; young men who once saw sports as their only professional path now have greater options.

To suggest that there is a finite number of good athletes for any sport is naive. The number of athletes of professional quality is determined by the level of priority any population places on succeeding in that sport. If distance running were suddenly a celebrity event in America, with millions of dollars in prizes and endorsements, marathon records would start falling in rapid succession, and other sports would start losing some talented athletes.

One thing is certain—there will always be bad teams, just as there have always been bad teams. Remember the St. Louis Browns, frequent cellar-dwellers in the American League, and that Philadelphia 76er team that won only nine games all season. Back then it was more random; sometimes the Washington Senators beat the Browns out of last place. But since expansion, the odds are good the worst team in any league will be the newest.

And maybe even more important in this age of fans' needing instant gratification, expansion teams generally take a long time to become consistent winners.

The Tampa Bay Buccaneers—expansion class of 1976—lost all 14 games their first season and entered the 1990s as a still-struggling team. The New Orleans Saints—class of 1967—took 13 seasons to reach the .500 mark and began play in the 1993 season still looking for their first play-off victory. But then there is the Dallas Cowboys—class of 1961—a team that rose from a 0–12 start its first season to become a winner by the end of the decade, a powerhouse with two Super Bowl victories in the 1970s that fell toward the end of the 1980s only to rise again and claim its third Super Bowl in 1993. And the Miami Dolphins—class of 1966—was a team never far from contention once Don Shula signed on as coach.

And while it is true the expansion California Angels and Texas Rangers, the Houston Astros, Montreal Expos, and Seattle Mariners never made it to a World Series, three other expansion teams have Series trophies in their display cases. And the worst new team of them all—those hopeless Mets of 1962—have two championships to show for their three trips to the fall classic.

That's one of the great things about sports: You can examine and analyze and come up with all kinds of tendencies based on good sound logic, then sit back and watch some rookie or aging veteran get hot and blow all that logic away.

This rule of unpredictability was well demonstrated during the 1993 baseball season, when neither the expansion Florida Marlins or Colorado Rockies finished last in their divisions, and those awesome Atlanta Braves were sidetracked from going to their third consecutive World Series when they lost in the National League Championship Series to the Philadelphia Phillies, last-place finishers in 1992.

PART FIVE

Fan Equity

15

A Business Lesson

An ordinary-looking sedan speeds along the straight, flat surface of Interstate 80, west of Chicago. It is nearly midnight, yet the August heat rises off the pavement in waves that are caught in the glare of oncoming headlights and distort the images of the other vehicles on the road.

Hours before, the highway was filled with motorists, driving all manner of cars bearing the unmistakable signs of vacation. Some pulled trailers. Others sported bikes stacked on racks affixed to rear bumpers and trunk hoods, their back windows stuffed with soft suitcases and plastic grocery bags filled with clothes. But most of those travelers have stopped for the night, at the Holiday Inns and Howard Johnsons and Slumber Lodges that beckon at every exit, leaving the highway to the semis that race relentlessly across the country and the occasional car needing to make time.

Our sedan is one of those, driven by a man trying to cram a week-long trip into a weekend. Inside, his teenage son fiddles with the manual control of the radio, searching for music he considers acceptable. He wants rock; what he gets is country-and-western and oldies. Three, four times he has run the length of the FM dial, never staying on any station longer than a few seconds.

"I wish you'd find something you like," says his father.

"I wish you'd left me home," says the boy.

"It's your grandmother's 80th birthday. She misses you."

The boy does not respond but goes back to his search. He stumbles onto Elvis Presley's "Jailhouse Rock" and pauses for an instant before twirling on.

"Hey," says his father. "That's good." The boy shoots his father an expression, a cross between pity and impatience, but it is lost in the dark.

"You could go to a concert with me," says the boy. "There is music written within the last 30 years you might like. We could see the Grateful Dead. Lots of old people like them."

His father says nothing, but gestures for his son to move away and give him a chance at the radio. That was their bargain; every two hours he gets to choose. He flips to AM. Instantly, the crackle of interference breaks onto the speakers. Without watching the dial, he passes a syndicated talk show airing the advisability of using Series E Bonds to save for your children's college education, a doctor stressing the importance of beta carotene in the diet, and a farm report. Finally he stops when he picks up the faint sound of a familiar voice. He listens to make sure. There, a name he recognizes—Strawberry—and another—Davis; he increases the volume and carefully adjusts the tuning until the crackling subsides. Now the voice comes through clearly. But before he can enjoy the fruits of his labor, the boy breaks in.

"Not baseball. You're not going to make me listen to baseball!"

"It's my turn. And this is Vin Scully—the Dodgers. The Reds are on the Coast this week."

"Bor-ing," says his son, and sinks into his seat. The man turns up the volume a little more. Within minutes he has confirmation that this is the game between the Los Angeles Dodgers and the Cincinnati Reds, from Dodger Stadium. Vin Scully, the long-time Dodger and by then network television broadcaster tells him the Reds lead by a run with a man out in the Dodger fourth inning, Eric Davis on first base and Daryl Strawberry at the plate. His son forces a dramatic yawn; he hates baseball. But the ride is long, and the night so dark and quiet. He begins

to listen casually to the words from the radio. Then, quite suddenly, he is caught by the action.

"Davis has his lead off first. The pitch to Strawberry is lined deep to right center. Roberts and O'Neill are racing back, racing, racing, and it's O'Neill who makes a stumbling, incredible catch, falling to the warning track as he does but holding the ball. Davis, already around second, is in trouble. O'Neill is up and throws a strike to Barry Larkin who spins and fires a bullet to first to double up Davis by a wide and humiliating four feet! Daryl Strawberry hit the ball as wide and as deep as the August sky and has come away with only the dust of a double play to show for it!"

There is silence from the crowd at Dodger Stadium, and silence from inside the sedan. For a few seconds, only the whir of the tires speeding along I-80 can be heard.

"I used to listen to the Reds games all the time when I was a kid. Your Uncle Bill and I would have our radio in bed, under the sheet. We'd keep it down low, so nobody would know we were still up. The Cincinnati announcer was Waite Hoyt; he was a pitcher on those great Yankee teams with Ruth and Gehrig.

"He was a terrible announcer. He'd get so excited he'd forget to tell you what was happening. But the stories he told about the old days were like seeing history in your head."

"About Babe Ruth?" asked the boy.

"Yes, about Babe Ruth," said the father; the boy reacts with the sound of air being sucked in amazement.

"Every time there was a rain delay, Hoyt would break into another story about old-time baseball, a lot of it about Babe and the Yankees. He talked about the parties, about how much beer Ruth could drink and remain on his feet, stuff you never read in the sports pages back then.

"He used to talk about the Babe's funeral. Ruth died in August, and Hoyt was one of the pallbearers, along with some other old Yankees. Ruth was a big man, 6–2, and the coffin was heavy. Walking out of church, Joe Dugan, the man in front of Hoyt, groaned in the heat. 'I'd sure love a beer,' he whispered back. Hoyt told us he had to smile. 'So would the Babe,' he told Dugan."

Something about the simple story catches the boy, and he just sits there, listening with his father as the game proceeds on the radio. Even when the signal weakens, and they must fight to hear, he listens.

Finally it is lost in the night. Another station, broadcasting a local call-in show, takes over the air. The father flips the radio back to FM, turning the selection over to his son. But the boy does not touch the dial.

"Maybe," he says, "when we get back home, we can go to a game."
"Maybe," says the father, smiling in the dark.

We have explored the many ways in which sports is a business. Because of the huge amounts of money generated and spent, because of the way it acts on the marketplace and is in turn acted upon by that marketplace, sports is a business.

But in one important respect, sports resembles no other business. That is in the way it interacts with its fans.

In business terms, fans are the customers of sports. But what customers! Surely every car manufacturer in the world would want customers so devoted they continued to purchase automobiles that ran well only occasionally. Oh, to operate a restaurant that is always popular even though the meals are edible only half the time, or to be the prominent doctor who cures patients only now and then.

This is exactly what sports fans ask of their teams: occasional success; satisfaction every few tries. Fans spend their money on games—easily a hundred dollars to take the family, pay for parking, buy tickets and food; often thousands for season tickets alone—and ask only that their team try hard. Success, or winning, is always the goal, but it is not crucial to ensure the support of true fans.

These aren't the terms of the business world, where everyone wants guarantees. They are the elements of love, the kind of love that exists among members of a family.

To demand consistent winning is boorish; winning at any cost, the antithesis of sportsmanship. Fans of all-winning teams are always suspected of being front-runners. Not only were the Yankees hated outside New York during their heyday—remember, "*Damn Yankees*"!—but their fans were despised as well. And the season after Magic Johnson retired, America mocked the famous movie stars who no longer populated the Great Western Forum. In Boston, *The Globe's* headline told this sad story soon after Larry Bird retired: "Minus Bird, Celtics No Longer Hot Ticket."

It is the fans who prove their devotion in bad times that we venerate. And the very best fans in sports, the ones held up as the model, are those who have suffered the longest without being rewarded with a championship.

Those other New Yorkers, New York Ranger fans, who keep coming to Madison Square Garden, season after season, even though their team has not won the Stanley Cup since 1940, are revered. They stand in the Fans Hall of Fame right behind those great Chicago Cubs fans, packing Wrigley Field, game after game, hoping and praying that their team will finally repeat its success of 1908; next are the White Sox faithful, whose last championship season came in 1917. Their devotion is praised by fans and sportswriters alike; their understanding of the true meaning of being a fan is legend.

Sometimes the closer the team gets to that ultimate glory, the higher the praise. Boston Red Sox fans are renowned throughout sports. Not only do they watch their team play in one of the great old stadiums—Fenway Park—but they also stuff the place every season, good team or lousy. And on those occasions when they have fielded a good enough team to challenge for the championship, the results of their efforts—all failures since the franchise traded Babe Ruth—made history. The 1975 World Series against the Cincinnati Reds, its famous sixth game won in the 12th inning by Carlton Fisk's home run, is still called one of the greatest ever played. Eleven years later, the Sox seemed surely to have the Series won, only to let destiny roll through the legs of their aging and infirm first baseman: another heart-breaking classic.

Yet the Boston fans never blinked, and a nation applauded. "Boston Enfolds Its Heroes," proclaimed the 1986 headline in *The New York Times* when 750,000 fans honored their beloved losers. And in *Sports Illustrated:* "The Hub Hails Its Hobbling Hero," referring to the man committing the fatal error. The subhead said it all: "Even though Bill Buckner let Game 6 slip through his injured legs, the fans in Boston showed last week how much they admired his courageous play in the World Series." (Although, to be historically complete, we must add that seven years after that event, fans were still reminding Buckner. And after yet one more painful confrontation, he swore he was moving his family from their home near Boston, offering the following explanation: "At least once a week during the baseball season, I hear something said. I'm definitely out of here. I don't want to hear it anymore.")

When the Buffalo Bills lost their third consecutive Super Bowl, while the team received harsh reviews, the fans got a standing ovation. "Super Fans Go Up and Down with Their Team," read the headline over one story in the *Albany Times Union.* And over a story in *USA Today*: "Even After Third Loss, Buffalo Is Home to True Believers." But perhaps the hometown *Buffalo News* said it best: "Buffalo Fans Don't Quit."

Really great fans don't even give up when their teams do. Surely the greatest statement of devotion is made by fans of teams that no longer exist. We have already noted the pain felt by the abandoned fans of Baltimore, who woke on the morning of March 29, 1984, to find that their beloved Colts had been spirited away in the middle of the night. Fan clubs still meet to mourn the moving of the Giants from New York, and the Athletics from Philadelphia, and even an occasional glass is raised in anguish over the A's moving from Kansas City to Oakland.

The loudest and longest wailing is for the Dodgers, yanked out of Brooklyn after the 1957 season. Although that happened 37 years ago, the torch of rejected love is still carried by Brooklynites who continue to miss their Bums. They have never forgotten what happened to their Dodgers or forgiven who did it to them.

In 1993, when the Brooklyn Dodger Sports Bar and Restaurant—a Flatbush establishment of relatively recent vintage—was sued by the Los Angeles Dodgers over use of the Dodger name, the decision against the ball team made headlines. "L.A. given Bum's rush," said the *Daily News* in New York. And *The New York Times*, in a boxed story on the front page of the local section: "Historic Day at Bar: Dodger Stays in Brooklyn." The suit was part of Major League Baseball's effort to keep a tight control over the unauthorized use of team names and logos for profit. But in Brooklyn, there was nothing routine about the case. The bar was defending its name and the memory of the home team.

"We were hurt when they moved," customer Frank Baratta told *The Times*; the 55-year-old chauffeur contributed $50 to fight the case. "The name of this bar is very special." The judge agreed that the name belonged as much to the people of Brooklyn as it did to the team that left.

"Defendants testified that many of the patrons who frequent the Brooklyn Dodger are well aware of Los Angeles's now-infamous abandonment of the borough of Brooklyn and—to the third generation since then—remain bitter about it," the judge wrote in the ruling. She added that the club's contention that the bar was trying to profit from the good name of the Los Angeles club was ludicrous.

"Trading upon Los Angeles 'good will' in Brooklyn would have been fatal to defendants because many Brooklynites despise the Los Angeles Dodgers," the judge wrote.

Losing plays an important part in this drama. Those long-suffering Dodgers fans proved their worth through endless seasons of "Wait Till Next Year." Before the Colts forged their tradition of winning in Baltimore, there were long seasons of frustration. Their football team was first the New York Yanks, shipped in disgrace to Dallas in 1952, where it lasted only four games before being turned into gypsies, playing home games in Hershey, Pennsylvania, and Akron, Ohio. Baltimore gave a home to the team nobody wanted, only to have that team stolen away.

Take those pathetic St. Louis Browns, a baseball team that finished last or next to last 22 times; in its eight worst seasons, it lost 100 or more games. What fame it enjoyed was for its one-armed outfielder, Pete Gray, and its midget pinch-hitter, Eddie Gaedel. The only pennant came in 1944, the year that World War II distorted the face of baseball.

The team was purchased in 1954, moved to Baltimore, and re-christened the Orioles. Yet the memory and spirit of the Browns live on. As late as 1987, *The Los Angeles Times* chronicled some of those still celebrating the 52-year history of the Browns: a baseball collector's shop in St. Louis dealing exclusively in Browns memorabilia; a California branch of the St. Louis Browns Fan Club of Chicago, meeting weekly for lunch; a St. Louis branch of the club with more than 500 members; a rock 'n' roll band called Brian Clarke and the St. Louis Browns.

But of course St. Louis residents have had lots of practice suffering the loss of teams. In 1968 they lost their NBA team, the Hawks, to Atlanta. In 1988 they lost their NFL team, the Cardinals, to Phoenix. An ABA team, the Spirits, also played there briefly, as did an early NHL team, the Eagles.

Power of the Fans

Obviously, the subject here is not support for winning; everybody supports winning. The subject here is the value to a franchise of fans who remain faithful, even when their team is not winning.

We call it fan equity. Equity in a business is made up of assets minus liabilities; it is the part of the assets that is derived from the owner's investment. Fan equity is never listed in the annual report of a franchise but at the same time has a profound effect on how well that franchise does at the end of the financial year. It is any team's most important asset.

Fan equity is the relentless emotional and physical investment that certain fans make in their teams; it gives those teams an added measure of strength to prosper and survive. Examples are the Washington Redskins and their fans, the Boston Bruins and their fans, the Chicago Cubs and their fans, the New York Knicks and their fans. In each case, fans support their teams through good seasons and bad, while winning or losing.

That support may end when the franchise moves, but real fans do not lose interest when they leave town. More casual supporters check television schedules for dates when the home team is on network or cable; serious fans search the radio dial at night, hoping for the combination of atmospheric conditions that permit their team to be transmitted across the miles. In either case, they connect with not only the team but also products that sponsor the game and are subjected to the promotions that sell other programming. For team and fan, the connection goes on.

The loyalties of years show up on T-shirts and caps bearing the team logo, in coffee cups and glasses, on golf bags and bumper stickers and bibs for babies, all of which communicate to the world that this is a family of true believers.

Don't be confused. These are not fashion statements, the wearing of a San Jose Sharks cap because of the appealing logo or a Colorado Rockies shirt because the colors are in. It is not the supporting of the Dallas Cowboys because they won the Super Bowl or wearing a copy of Michael Jordan's jersey because he repeatedly led the Chicago Bulls to the NBA championship. Years later, acts of winning could prove to be the beginning of a greater commitment, but they could never be the whole story.

One is a fad, a testimony to the popularity of the moment. Fan equity is etched in stone, often passed down through generations. It does not always start with a parent taking a son or daughter to a ball game or listening together to a broadcast over the radio on the porch on a hot summer night. But a surprising number of serious fans trace their adult dedication to some early exposure, often with a parent, a brother or sister, or sometimes to a special friend now long gone.

Those incidents are as varied as the people who carry them in their memories: on what appears to be a casual trip to Crosley Field to watch the Cincinnati Reds, the older brother buys a pennant that hangs over his little brother's bed, and then his desk, for 40 years; on a Thanksgiving afternoon, after the table has been cleared, the Lions-Packers game on television is shared with the uncle just returned from the war; a July 4th car ride that happens upon the radio broadcast of Dave Righetti's no-hitter spurs the emotional telling by a normally stoic father of the day he saw Bob Feller no-hit the Yankees.

There is in these moments a sense of sharing and well-being that stays with us long after the event has passed. And while they can happen around all types of events, a surprising number involve sports. The sport then becomes the conduit of that good feeling, a connection to a time worth preserving. Earlier we heard Jeff Smulyan recall his childhood introduction to baseball by his father and tell of listening late into the night to games broadcast over radio from across the country. He grew to know the stations, their place on the dial, and how each brought him the call of another team, an experience that hooked him on radio and baseball and led him into both businesses.

Even in this age of television, radio plays an important role in this phenomenon. Radio broadcasts help draw fans to their teams, and hold them. Radios go with us everywhere and permit us to absorb what is being broadcast while still allowing the mind to place that action within the larger context of our lives. The game becomes interwoven with ourselves, a transformation that does not occur when watching the same game on television. The radio announcer is part of this chemistry of inclusion. As his personality imprints on the scene he is creating, a bonding is fostered between the announcer and the listener and, in turn, with the team.

What this connection does for the fan becomes a major part of his or her investment and goes a long way toward solidifying a relationship that can last for years. For some the relationship is more casual, the means to a pleasant diversion. But for others, it is profound. Several recent studies have explored what goes on between fans and their teams and come up with evidence that is far from casual. "Fans see their teams as an extension of themselves," says Edward Hirt, assistant professor of psychology at Indiana University and chief investigator of one of the studies. "Team success is personal success, and team failure is personal failure."

The game—whatever game it is—is surely central to this process. But today each game is part of a huge structure that includes thousands and thousands of people who neither play nor cheer the players. And it is a big business, one of our most influential. Sports may have begun more simply, as recreation, mostly for those who participated, with spectators being an afterthought, but that is history. Fans and their devotion have been the primary cause of this great evolution, and an entire industry has been created because of them.

Rocking the Boat

This element we call fan equity, strong and resilient and far-reaching as it is, can be destroyed. The mechanism for that destruction is already in place.

Television, on whose money every professional sports team has become so dependent, has exacted a high fee for its contribution. Because of television, the celebrity events are mostly played at night. All the play-offs in basketball and hockey, except the occasional Sunday afternoon contest, are at night. The Super Bowl starts after 6 P.M. in the East. Baseball's All-Star Game, most of its League Championship Series, and every game of the World Series are all at night. Many of them don't start until 8 P.M. on the East Coast, often making them last until 11 P.M., and occasionally later.

The reason is simple: Prime-time programming is worth more to the networks on the basis of dollar-per-advertising units than programming during the day.

While getting the most out of the celebrity events of sports, the networks have sacrificed anybody who cannot stay up till 11 P.M. in the East to watch a game. The leagues may have gained in today's revenues, but that gain may cost them tomorrow.

Consider baseball. Baseball is a sport with a pattern of attracting its fans young and holding onto them despite the lure of faster and flashier sports. It has not been as hard for those young fans to watch baseball on television since the network's earliest days of broadcasting. "What they have done is write off an entire generation of Americans," according to Curt Smith in *Voices in the Game.*

Not only has that generation been denied access to the big-ticket events of baseball, but young fans have also been locked out of many everyday events they had long enjoyed and probably taken for granted. The much-publicized 1989 contract between CBS and Major League baseball marked the end of the "Game of the Week," which had run in one form or another since 1957.

Begun on NBC with Dizzy Dean, the show became an institution. Part of that was Dean, a direct and folksy character who brought his history as an all-star pitcher and his down-home humor to the broadcast booth. He was in many ways more radio than television; Dean talked viewers through the games, mixing in stories of his days with the Gas House Gang of the St. Louis Cardinals.

But Saturday afternoon games during the regular season were not why CBS paid $1.1 billion for baseball. The network wanted the All-Star Game, the League Championship Series, and the World Series. It got them all and cut what had been 40 regular season games—32 Saturdays on NBC and eight night games on ABC—down to 12.

Cries from newspaper and magazine columnists across the country tried to save some version of the show. "The 'Game of the Week' must be saved. Your move, Commish," wrote Curt Smith in *Sports Illustrated,* trying to raise then-Commissioner Bart Giamatti to action. But to no avail.

Television and baseball continued the trend when they signed their new six-year contract in the spring of 1993. Not only will all nationally broadcast games be at night—during the season and for the play-offs and World Series—but only the Series will be seen by all viewers in the nation. Regular season and league championship games will be shown regionally, to those areas deemed to have the greatest interest; it is the networks' attempt to boost ratings. This means games of the two League Championship Series will be played simultaneously, with National League games going to National League cities and American League games going to cities considered to have mostly American League fans. Only games six and seven of the Championship Series would be staggered and shown to everyone.

Regional broadcasting proved economically successful in the National Football League and with college basketball and football, but all NFL postseason games go to the entire country. The baseball contract—with ABC and NBC—could black out those Boston residents who happen to be National League fans and Cincinnatians with an interest in the American League, further separating fans from the teams. Whether it also drives them from interest in their sport remains to be seen.

Even the games themselves have been affected by television. Every televised game in every sport is subjected to the control of the medium. Commercial breaks are more frequent and longer. By 1993 the networks were allowed to sell 56 units of advertising per NFL game, or 28 minutes of commercial time. And in baseball, while critics suggested putting a stopwatch on the pitcher to speed up the game, many said the culprit was television. "The advertising time between half-innings of a ball game has already been expanded from one minute to two minutes and ten seconds, in consequence, the average length of games has increased from just over two hours to close to three hours," said Andrew Zimblast in *Baseball and Billions* in 1992.

As we have seen, the actual length of the football season was changed for television. The changes began in 1990 with the signing of the new $3.6 billion contract. The original plan called for the regular season to expand to 17 weeks in 1990 and then move to 18 weeks in 1992 and 1993, giving each team first one week off and then two weeks off during their 16-game schedule. The plan for extension was to sell more advertising over a longer period, that space filled not by more games but by more televised games; Turner Broadcasting and ESPN would broadcast Sunday night games, earning the league about $900 million. The ploy simply didn't help the network's losses during the period of the contract. The NFL announced scrapping the plan after the 1992 season, but the 1993 season remained at 18 weeks.

The play-off format was altered the same year, adding two wild-card games. This brought ABC into the NFL's play-off plans and increased the league's broadcast revenues even further. The four-year ABC deal, which included "Monday Night Football," the Super Bowl for January of 1991, and the two play-off games, was worth about $900 million to the NFL. That nearly doubled the network's payments from $120 million a year to about $225 million.

It all amounted to a serious strain on the trust and devotion of the fans: More and more games pushed from the afternoon into the prime-time schedule for higher advertising rates and better ratings; games in all sports lengthened because of more and longer breaks for advertising; the football season artificially spread out by two weeks, all for the benefit of television. There was even some talk in 1993 of the NFL's pushing back the Super Bowl to February so that it would fall in a "sweeps" month.

Perhaps these kinds of maneuvers have always gone on in professional athletics; decisions that were presented as sports-driven but were really money-driven, and the public just didn't know. But the rules of reporting are different now; it's hard to cover up anything.

Fans and Stadiums

Television was not the only culprit conspiring to make more distance between the fans and their games. In the 1950s, baseball teams began moving out of cities with which they had long been associated and out of stadiums that had been their homes for nearly as long. Those "modern" stadiums were mostly built between 1909 and 1914.

The first victim was Braves Field in Boston, last of that series of stadiums to be built. Finished in 1914, it was the largest, seating 40,000 people. It was home to the Boston Braves until 1954, when the team moved to Milwaukee. No major league franchise had moved since 1903, but the flight of the Braves launched a major migration and tolled the death knell for some of the game's proudest parks.

When the Dodgers moved to Los Angeles in 1957, it spelled the end of Ebbets Field, replaced by a high-rise apartment complex in 1960. When the Giants moved to San Francisco, their home in the Polo Grounds was also doomed to destruction; that came in 1964. The moving of the Washington Senators to Minnesota in 1961 meant the end of Griffith Stadium; it was one of baseball's oldest, built in 1899.

In the late 1960s and early 1970s came the new generation of stadiums, replacing those judged too small and decrepit to meet the needs of the new economy of sports. The industry was changing. Airplane travel had replaced trains, free agency was coming to baseball, and a rival league had pushed up salaries in football. Sports needed more revenue, and new stadiums were an obvious source.

Busch Memorial Stadium replaced old Busch Stadium in St. Louis in 1966. Riverfront Stadium in Cincinnati replaced Crosley Field, and Three Rivers Stadium replaced Forbes Field in Pittsburgh, both in 1970. The Philadelphia A's moved to Kansas City in 1954, but Shibe Park remained active; the National League Phillies had shared the park since 1938. But Philadelphia got brand-new Veterans Stadium in 1971, and old Shibe was history.

There was a sameness to all of these new facilities. Big, round structures, they reminded some observers of flying saucers, especially at night, all aglow with lights. They seated between 52,000 and 62,000 people, and most were designed for football and baseball for business reasons. To facilitate the concept of multiuse, most also had artificial surfaces instead of grass, AstroTurf or some other kind of artificial carpet.

Even before the increased crowds began streaming into the new stadiums, there were indications that fans had formed sentimental attachments for the old parks that would not easily be transferred. Some clubs dealt with the matter openly and with sensitivity. Before the Pirates moved into Three Rivers, the management encouraged fans to begin the dismantling of the Forbes Field. Thousands accepted the offer. Right beside them was Roberto Clemente, the Bucs' all-star outfielder who was later killed in a plane crash; he removed his number "21" from the scoreboard and took it home to Puerto Rico.

Many expressions of devotion were less public. For years around baseball, clubs have quietly granted the final requests of fans who wished their ashes to be scattered after their cremation in the stadium. The Chicago White Sox reported some 12 requests were so honored during the last ten years of old Comiskey Park, according to a story in *The New York Times* in 1990. Other teams have admitted to the same practice.

The New York Times wrote,

> Roger O'Connor, the grounds foreman at Wrigley Field, said he has not only assisted several families who asked if they could scatter the ashes of relatives on the field, but has watched a few others do it alone, after sneaking through a gate and furtively dumping the urn on the closest piece of turf.

There were some accounts of services unsanctioned by any ball club and unnoticed by most of the world. The following report appears in Lawrence Ritter's book, *Lost Ballparks*:

> Ebbets Field was razed in 1960. When demolition was about to begin—on a wintry day in February—Lucy Monroe sang the National Anthem, as she had at the start of many Dodger ball games. A number of ex-Brooklyn players were also present for the pre-demolition ceremonies.

Everywhere, people find ways to honor ballparks past and present. A Cincinnati Reds fan bought up parts of Crosley Field when the team moved to Riverfront and reconstructed a small version in his backyard; a Pirates fan made the same gesture when Pittsburgh tore down Forbes Field. A Minnesota entrepreneur sells refurbished seats from Forbes Field, Yankee Stadium, the Polo Grounds, and Comiskey Park, $250 for a single and $550 for a set of three. For less-devoted fans, there is William Hartel. In 1991, this baseball-loving dentist scrounged up pieces of seats from old Comiskey Field, Crosley Field, and some that had been replaced in Wrigley Field. He cut them into two-inch sections, affixed flat magnets to them, and sold them for $10 apiece. "A little bit of old-time baseball stuck on your refrigerator can brighten any day," says Hartel.

Taken individually, these items could be seen as the extreme behavior of a few fanatics. But viewed together, they constitute a strong expression of fan equity. These old parks held strong meaning for many people who had followed their teams for years. To want to be buried there in the field is a powerful statement of commitment.

And for some, the new stadiums were not all that satisfying.

They opened to general approval. From Atlanta-Fulton County Stadium to Busch Memorial Stadium to the stadiums in Cincinnati and Pittsburgh, they were shiny clean, equipped with escalators and plenty of washrooms. They boasted comfortable seats, and no posts to block the action; 100 percent unobstructed views was a big selling point.

They were also very big. Not just big in the number of seats, big as in "Gee, look how far away the field is!" It wasn't so bad for those sitting in ground-level box seats, but the picture was different from the upper deck. The distance from the front row of the upper stands to home plate in old Comiskey Park was 100 feet, while that same seat at Riverfront Stadium was more than 200 feet away. Sitting in the back row of the top deck at old Comiskey put a fan 150 feet from the action; the back row at Riverfront is 295 feet away.

The most common reason for the greater distances was that for these new and very expensive parks to be profitable they had to accommodate two sports—football and baseball. Football action is traditionally viewed from a greater distance and is well served by a large stadium. Baseball—often referred to as "a game of inches"—is better suited to a smaller, more intimate setting.

The other concession to multiuse stadiums is the decision to install synthetic surfaces instead of grass. There are many arguments against what has become known as "the rug," most by baseball purists who cite the high bounces taken by balls or the way they accelerate as they skip off the surface. It has also been charged that artificial surfaces increase injuries: leg problems caused by the lack of shock absorption in the asphalt foundation; abrasions from sliding on the nylon; ligament damage when cleats and spikes catch in the fabric, causing knees and ankles to surrender to the force.

Most serious injuries have been in football. While still Orange Bowl tenants, the Miami Dolphins had the surface changed from turf to grass for that reason. Chicago eventually came to the same conclusion about Soldier Field. "We felt that playing on a grass field will help us decrease some injuries that might otherwise occur," said Bears president Michael McCaskey in 1988, when the change was made.

Strong feelings have also arisen in baseball. Some players have made major decisions based on playing surfaces. In 1987, Andre Dawson rejuvenated his career by taking his tender knees from Montreal's artificial turf to the grass of Wrigley Field; after six years in Chicago, he signed with Boston to play on the grass of Fenway Park.

But artificial turf is cheaper to maintain than grass and makes stadiums easier to lease, generating more money. And the official NFL line is there is "no great difference" in injuries on grass and turf. More than half the NFL teams play on artificial surfaces, as do 10 of 28 major league baseball teams.

The problem for fans, in addition to the way "the rug" changes the game, is the perception that clubs are making decisions based more on money than the health of their players. With so many players so certain that the artificial surface poses a threat, they argue, why not be safe and play on grass? Any perception of callousness can intensify as a fan sits for hours in a rain delay in Cincinnati, St. Louis, or Pittsburgh, all parks where baseball rarely gets called because the field never gets saturated. Once over with the Zamboni—even at midnight—and the game can resume, saving the home team the expense of replaying the date.

Equity at Risk

All of this threatens that personal connection between fans and their teams. Seasons of subpar performances don't seem to do it, but enough examples that fans are not valued can. For many, that sense begins to sink in when they try to purchase a ticket to a game.

The stated prices for a four-person outing at a game—over $100 in many baseball stadiums, over $200 for a game of hockey, basketball, or football—are only valid if the party in question can get the tickets they want. And that is getting harder to do within the normal channels.

Even in baseball, where sellouts are rare, more and more of the preferred seats are sold long before the season starts. Season ticket-holders snatch up the lower level box, mezzanine, and even upper decks, and the majority of these are purchased not by individual fans but corporations. What remains are bleacher seats, where available, and less desirable locations in the grandstands.

The NFL average of about 62,000 fans per game per team represents sellouts or near-sellouts for many teams, making it virtually impossible to get a decent seat during the season. A 1989 article in *The New York Times*, under the headline "Getting a Good Seat: A Shutout Before the Game," described the Denver Broncos official who often had to go to "secondary sources" to buy tickets for visiting officials and friends. And the situation is at least as bad in basketball.

The New York Times said:

> For each of their NBA playoff games, the Knicks had only 4,300 tickets remaining after taking care of season ticket-holders, the news media and other very-important-people in 19,591-seat Madison Square Garden. And brokers and scalpers were selling many of those 4,300 for prices from $25 for a ticket of $15 face value to up to $500 for $40 courtside seats.
>
> In Portland, Ore., the Trail Blazers have sold out every NBA game since 1977, prompting the creation of a regular newspaper exchange column in which people trade tickets.

The situation is made even worse by the proliferation of luxury boxes. The more luxury boxes, the fewer seats for the average fan. Add on the number of other specialized seats—from the restaurant-service courtside seats at Madison Square Garden to Fenway Park's 600 Club of air-conditioned theater seating behind home plate—and the space for the average fan continues to shrink. For those who manage to purchase the equivalent of a general admission seat, that once-great democratic sports experience of banker cheering beside butcher is lost. A 1987 article in *The Washington Post* expressed a concern about the effect of elite seating.

> Critics say it could lead to a virtual caste system, in which ordinary ticket-holders on bleachers cheer in the rain while thousands of upper-crust attendees sip champagne (it costs $6.75 in the Miami Dolphins' new stadium) and watch instant replays in climate-controlled cubicles.

Support of the corporate community—which pays for an estimated 90 percent of all elite seating—is essential for any franchise. But so is developing fans for the future. That is the source of fan equity. And as young fans are priced out of the stadiums and arenas, as games are taken off the free airways and put on cable television, more and more fans are denied access to professional sports, and a fan base that would serve those sports well into the future is never built.

Some franchises worry about this. The Boston Celtics, a team that began selling out regularly with the beginning of the Larry Bird era, cut off the season ticket sales at 12,000, guaranteeing 2,800 seats for the general public. The new Florida Marlins of the National League charges $24, $27, and $30 to sit in its Club Seats at Joe Robbie Stadium, an elevated, protected section, cooled by air conditioning and serviced by food and drink attendants. Club Seats help keep down the prices in the cheap sections—$3.50 for adults and $1.50 for kids.

"There should be no deterrent to a father taking his son at the last minute to a ball game," says Marlins owner Wayne Huizenga. "If you can get him in there for $1 or $1.50, that's a good price."

Some other teams that have acted on their concern for access to games are the Texas Rangers, charging $4 for general admission tickets and $2 for children; the Atlanta Braves and Houston Astros, $4 for general admission and $1 for children; and New York's Mets and Yankees, charging senior citizens $1 for game-day tickets.

And the Los Angeles Dodgers have made a similar statement, which might come as news to a lot of people.

One reason the Dodgers were such a successful baseball franchise in the 1940s and early 1950s was the fans of Brooklyn, surely among the best examples of fan equity in all of sports. The Dodgers and the fans; it was a marriage. Listen to what Bill Veeck wrote in 1965 about that relationship in his book *The Hustler's Handbook,* and about how it ended:

> Brooklyn fans had become the symbol of the baseball fanatic. They were recognized by ballplayers throughout the league as the most knowledgeable in the country. The Dodgers were a part of the city's identification, a part of its pulse beat. The loyal rooters never doubted for a moment that their beloved Bums were as much a part of their heritage as Prospect Park. They discovered they were wrong. The Dodgers were only a piece of merchandise that passed from hand to hand.

One incentive to move to Los Angeles was the city's generosity in dealing for land and access roads for a new ballpark. The stadium the Dodgers built remains one of the finest in the big leagues and was widely praised when it opened in 1962. But there was one indication that fan comfort had not entered every stage of the planning. When Dodger Stadium opened, there were only three drinking fountains—one in owner Walter O'Malley's private office and two in the players' dugouts. A local uproar ensued, followed by the installation of 13 water fountains in the stands within a week.

But in this current environment of the average fan as a threatened species, the Dodgers have stood firm on their behalf. Dodger Stadium is one of the few with no luxury boxes. And it's no oversight. While the addition of the suites would surely increase the revenues of the already profitable stadium, their construction would force the eviction of some long-time fans from the club level, four rows of particularly desirable seating, high up, adjacent to the stadium club.

"It was a cut and dry decision; no ifs, ands or buts," says Walter Nash, vice-president in charge of ticket operations who has been with the Dodgers since 1962. "Walter and Peter (O'Malley) had talked about it. Walter didn't want to move them and Peter didn't want to move anybody.

"People in this area that we looked at, most of them have been there since 1962 when the park opened. If you tried to move them, it would be like asking your mother to move. It's possible that we might do it one of these years, when the sales decline on the level. Anything's possible. But not now."

The Heart of the Matter

There seems to be little doubt that at least part of the breakdown in the relationship between fans and their sports is a product of the new economy. But the impact is even deeper than who gets to attend games or watch them on TV.

As free agency creates a more fluid structure within leagues, the stability that fans once enjoyed vanishes. The core of Cincinnati's Big Red Machine was in place for six years, with many of those players together for a decade. The Dodgers infield of Steve Garvey, Ron Cey, Bill Russell, and Davey Lopes played together for eight seasons. The same Pittsburgh Steelers took that team to four Super Bowl wins over six years: Terry Bradshaw, Franco Harris, Lynn Swann, and Dave Stallworth on offense; Jack Lambert, Jack Ham, and Joe Green on defense. The Los Angeles Lakers won their four championships in the 1980s with Kareem and Magic in charge; those 11 Celtics crowns in 13 years were keyed by Bill Russell at center, but the scene on the Boston Garden's parquet floor included Bob Cousy, Sam Jones, K.C. Jones, Tom Sanders, and John Havlicek in one combination or another.

There is little chance that the future of professional sports will feature such consistency. We have already seen what lies ahead; baseball has given us a peek into the future. When the Mets decided they could not sign David Cone during the 1992 season, they traded him for the best deal they could get instead of losing him to free agency at the end of the season. Toronto offered that deal, giving up some of their young and untested talent for a pitcher who would help them win their first World Series.

The fact that Cone could be gone after the post-season play—as he was—was just part of the new economics. The teams involved understood it, and so did the players.

But it is doubtful that the fans did. And if they come to understand the new rules of the game, will they come to accept them? Fans are a special breed of consumer. They become attached to their favorite players, and they are not shy in letting team owners know exactly how they feel.

A season-and-a-half after the Minnesota Twins won the 1987 World Series, the new economy of baseball led them to trade their star pitcher, Frank Viola. But that very winter, when hometown product Kent Hrbek became a free agent, hometown urging helped the Twins decide to re-sign him to a $3-million contract. And in 1992, when Kirby Puckett—perhaps the most popular player in Twins history—offered himself around baseball as a free agent, the uproar of the local fans was deafening. Minnesota is considered a small-market city; only 10 of baseball's 28 teams play in smaller markets. But at least partly as a result of fan pressure, the Twins management felt compelled to sign Puckett to a $5.20 million contract.

Not every owner views his responsibility toward the fans in the same light. The San Diego Padres began trading some of their high-salaried players in 1992 to cut the team's payroll, reported to be $29 million at the start of the season. They unloaded regulars Tony Fernandez, Benito Santiago, Darrin Jackson, and Randy Myers, reducing their contenders of 1992 to a club that in 1993 would successfully beat out the expansion Rockies for last place in the National League West. When in June they traded Gary Sheffield—defending league batting champ—fans protested, and 62 season ticket-holders demanded refunds. One especially angry pair filed a class-action suit, charging the team with failure to comply with its preseason promise to retain the core of its team.

The suit was settled in July, the fans accepting the promise of a more liberal refund policy for season ticket holders as well as those with individual game tickets. Four days later, the team traded star Fred McGriff, baseball's most consistent home-run hitter. By the end of the month, the Padres had unloaded two more top players—pitchers Bruce Hurst and Greg Harris—and that 1992 payroll of $29 million was cut to under $10 million. *USA Today* covered the story in early August; its count on ticket refunds was up to 400.

That these examples have occurred in baseball is a statement of that game's precarious position in the early 1990s. It can happen in any sport. The new free agency coming to the NFL is already showing that. And as the Joe Montanas and Reggie Whites begin to move from the teams where they earned fame and adoration to the teams that offer the pay and situation they want, football fans, too, may make themselves heard: "These are our players," they may well say; "pay them what the market demands but keep them home."

There is no question that the staggering salaries paid to the athletes annoy and even offend many fans, but not as much as losing the men who play for their teams.

This constant changing of rosters—and teams and stadiums—threatens to further destroy the bond that holds fans to their sports. Whatever they get out of that connection—be it casual entertainment or some investment far more personal—it only works so long as their teams are familiar enough to recognize. But neither can they be expected to pay these new salaries out of their pockets. The average fan is simply not able to ante up $50 for a seat in baseball, or $200 in football or hockey or basketball, in order to maintain the stability of the home teams. At the same time, sports cannot afford to totally sacrifice its average fans to the big corporations that lease the luxury boxes today.

It is a quandary. Sports is a business, no question about it. But it is a very special business, one that survives and prospers because of the relentless attachment—even love—of fans.

If sports loses its fans, it becomes just another product being sold on the open market, and no sport can afford to abandon its unique status and join the soap merchants and car salesmen. Soaps and cars come and go; sports must provide something more lasting.

This was the essence of the last official message of Major League Baseball's ousted commissioner, Fay Vincent, as expressed in his letter of resignation. The final paragraph of that letter follows:

> I bear no personal ill will toward any of the owners and I wish them well. At the same time I remind all that ownership of a baseball team is more than ownership of an ordinary business. Owners have a duty to take into consideration that they own a part of America's national pastime—in trust. This trust sometimes requires putting self-interest second.

He could have been talking to owners in any of the other major team sports, and to the commissioners who represent them and the heads of the players' unions, as well.

It is time for all of them to begin thinking of protecting sports' place in our society, not only of improving their own high standard of living.

Fans already do their part by pledging their devotion through good seasons and bad. But the labor wars have for too long set owners and players against one another.

Players and owners alike must make the survival of their games their top priority, and they must act immediately. Options already exist; several forms of cooperation are already factors in negotiations. Now they must be embraced by labor and by management.

If cooperation does not become the prime order of the day, our sports will become just another product in the American mercantile system. In that environment, every entity is at risk. After *at risk* comes *in jeopardy;* the next step is extinction. Once there were Nash automobiles, Philco radios, Burger beer, and *The Saturday Evening Post.* All are now history. This is a warning! Our sports could be next.

We must protect sports' place in our society. Let us hope that the force of fan equity can coexist with the forces of economics and keep sports as the favorite pastime for the American public for generations to come.

Bibliography

American Sports, Benjamin G. Rader, Prentice Hall, Englewood Cliffs, N.J., 1983.

Babe, Robert W. Creamer, Simon and Schuster, New York, 1974.

Baseball America, Donald Honig, Macmillan, New York, 1985.

Baseball and Billions, Andrew Zimbalist, Basic Books, New York, 1992.

The Baseball Business, James Edward Miller, The University of North Carolina Press, Chapel Hill, 1990.

The Baseball Encyclopedia, Macmillan, New York, 1990.

The Business of Professional Sports, Paul D. Staudohar and James A. Mangan, editors, University of Illinois Press, Chicago, 1991.

Cages to Jump Shots, Robert W. Peterson, Oxford University Press, New York, 1990.

Coming Apart at the Seams, Jack Sands and Peter Gammons, Macmillan, New York, 1993.

Dodgers! The First 100 Years, Stanley Cohen, Carol Publishing Group, New York, 1990.

Dollar Sign on the Muscle, Kevin Kerrane, Simon and Schuster, New York, 1984.

Encyclopedia of Major League Baseball Teams, Donald Dewey and Nicholas Acocella, Harper Collins, New York, 1993.

Everybody's Hockey Book, Stan Fischler, Charles Scribner's Sons, New York, 1983.

Hardball, Bowie Kuhn, Times Books, New York, 1987.

Hit the Sign and Win a Free Suit of Clothes from Harry Finklestein, Bert Randolph Sugar, Contemporary Books, Chicago, 1978.

The Hustler's Handbook, Bill Veeck with Ed Linn, G. P. Putnam's Sons, New York, 1965.

In Its Own Image, Benjamin G. Rader, The Free Press, New York, 1984.

Lost Ballparks, Lawrence S. Ritter, Viking Penguin, New York, 1992.

Once a Bum, Always a Dodger, Don Drysdale with Bob Verdi, St. Martin's Press, New York, 1990.

One Step from Glory, Skip Rozin, Simon and Schuster, New York, 1979.
Pay Dirt, James Quirk and Rodney D. Fort, Princeton University Press, Princeton, N.J., 1992.
Playing Hardball, David Whitford, Doubleday, New York, 1993.
Playing the Field, Charles C. Euchner, Johns Hopkins University Press, Baltimore, MD, 1993.
Professional Baseball Franchises from the Abbeville Athletics to the Zanesville Indians, Peter Filichia, Facts on File, New York, 1993.
The Selling of the Green, Harvey Araton and Filip Bondy, Harper Collins, New York, 1992.
Sports in America, James A. Michener, Random House, New York, 1976.
Stolen Season, David Lamb, Warner Books, New York, 1991.
Under the Influence, Peter Hernon and Terry Ganey, Simon and Schuster, New York, 1991.
Veeck as in Wreck, Bill Veeck with Ed Linn, G. P. Putnam's Sons, New York, 1962.
Voices of the Game, Curt Smith, Fireside Books, New York, 1992.
A Whole Different Ball Game, Marvin Miller, Fireside Books, New York, 1991.

Index